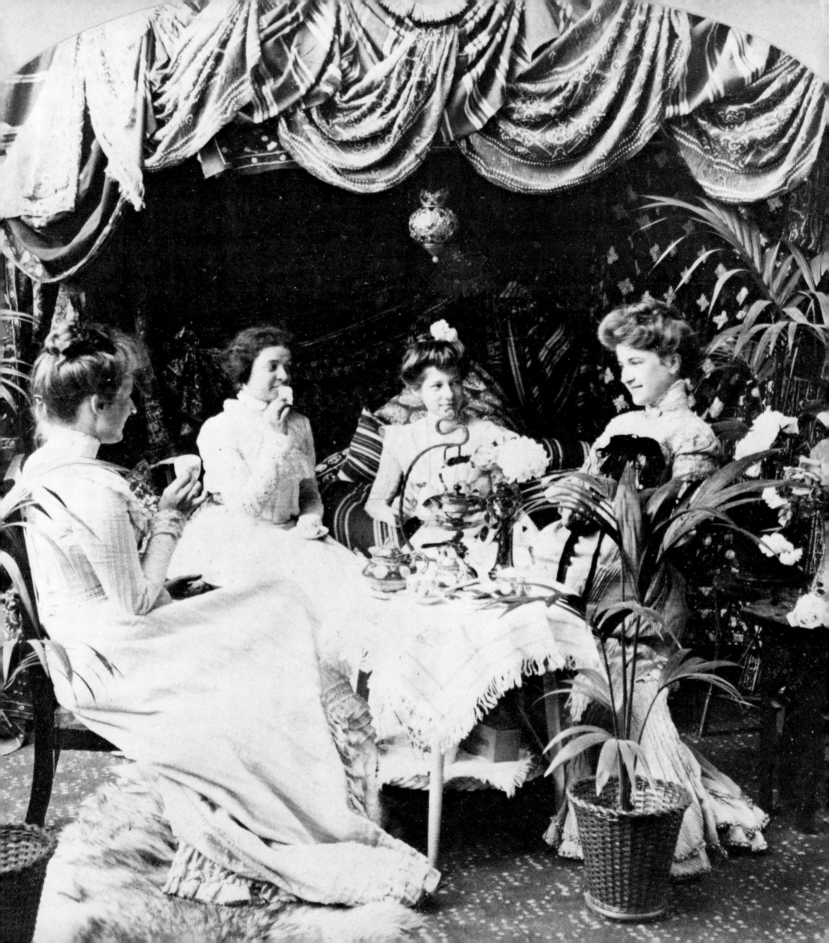

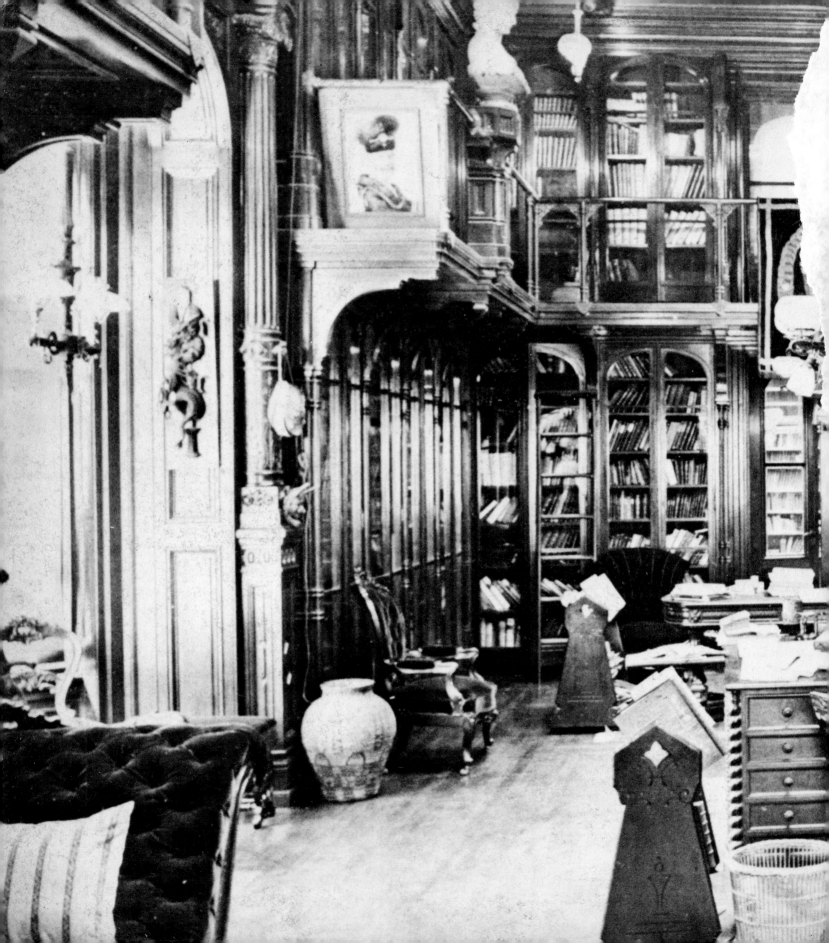

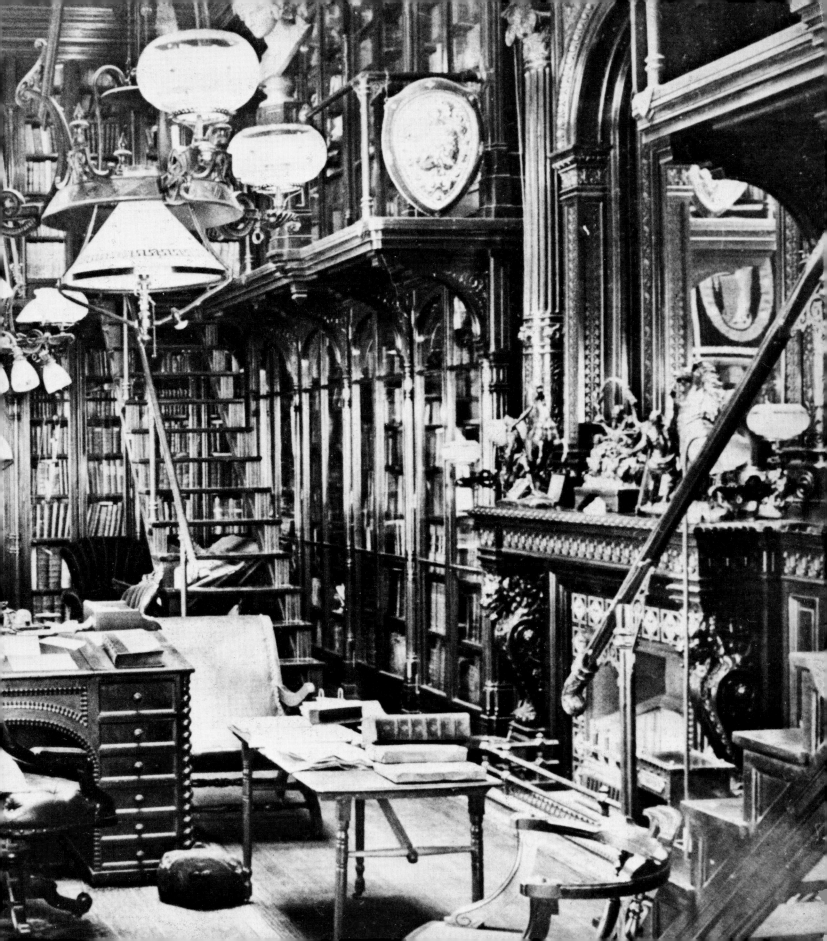

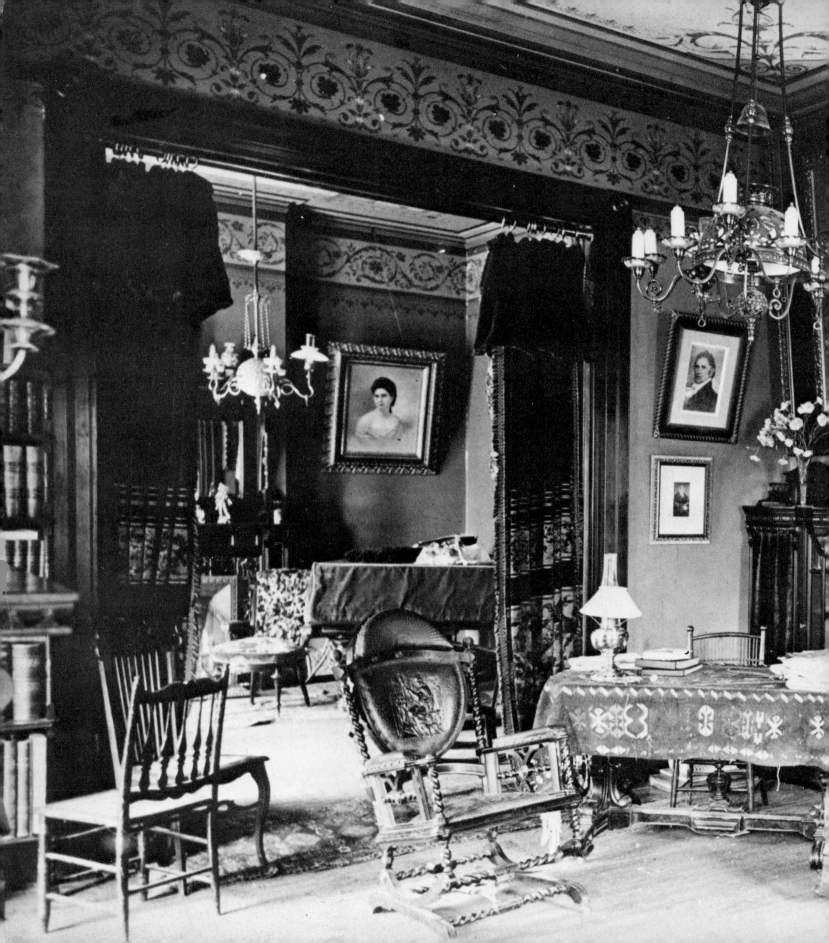

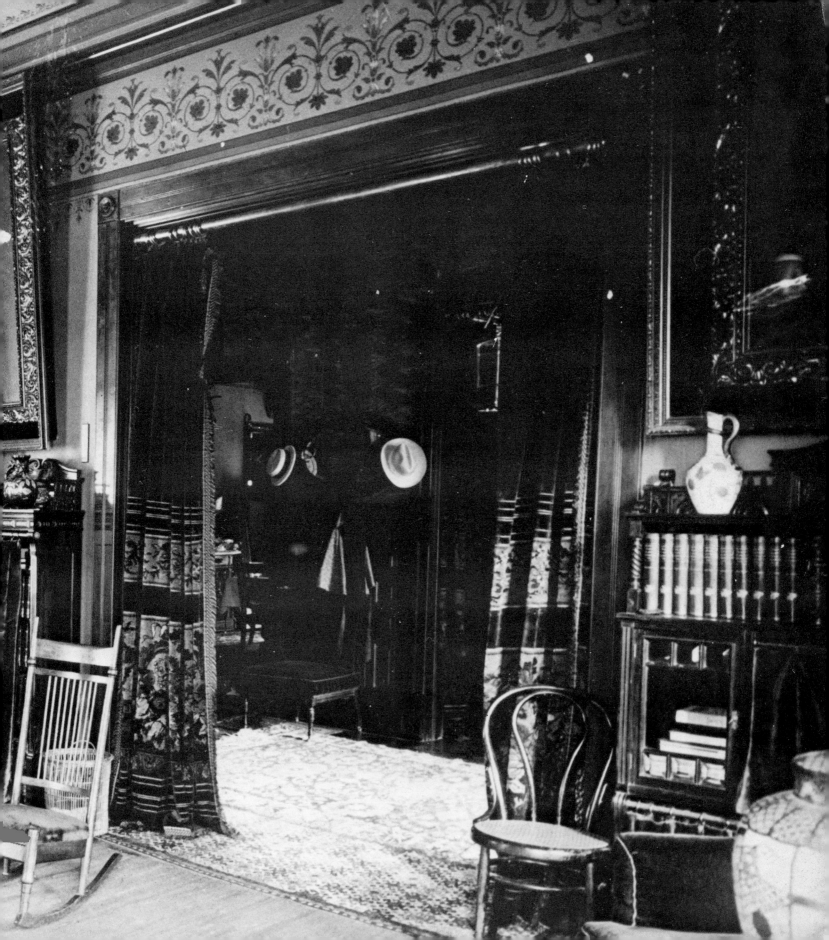

# the
# TASTEFUL

# INTERLUDE

American Interiors Through the Camera's Eye, 1860-1917

William Seale

American Decorative Arts Series
General Editor, Graham Hood

Praeger Publishers    New York

To Lucinda

ACKNOWLEDGMENTS In addition to the individuals and institutions listed in the picture credits, I want to express my gratitude to Alice Reno Malone and Antoinette J. Lee, who took part in the research for the book, joining me in exploring census records, manuscript collections, and newspapers for information on the era, the regions, and the rooms. Dr. Lee further assisted by finding photographs in Philadelphia collections.

I am grateful to Graham Hood for envisioning the manuscript as part of his series, to Brenda Gilchrist, Harriet Bee, and Ellyn Childs for editing the book, and to Ulrich Ruchti for designing it.

Without specifying the parts they played in making this book possible—it would take a second volume to do so—I want to thank sincerely William J. Murtagh, Rodris Roth, Anne C. Golovin, Walter E. Langsam, James M. Goode, Henry-Russell Hitchcock, Adolf K. Placzek, Lonn Taylor, Maricca Chechames, Britt A. Storey, Minnette Bickel, David Chase, Ellen Beasley, J. B. Harter, Margaret N. Keyes, Mrs. Francis S. Chamberlin, Ted B. Powers, Michael Warner, Mrs. Edward K. Webb, Mrs. Paul M. Rhymer, Agnes C. Conrad, Irene Lichens, Hazel Mills, Harriet C. Meloy, Mrs. Jack Gallalee, Dayton Canaday, Helena Wright, Thomas W. Parker, Sinclair H. Hitchings, Terence McGough, A. Robert Cole, Bonnie Wilson, Doug Kent, Dorothy Potter, Nancy Dean, and Mrs. Allen Morris.

Published in the United States of America in 1975 by Praeger Publishers, Inc.
111 Fourth Avenue, New York, N.Y. 10003

© 1975 by Praeger Publishers, Inc.

Library of Congress Cataloging in Publication Data
Seale, William.
    The tasteful interlude.
    (American decorative arts series)
    1. Interior decoration—United States—History.
2. Furniture, American—History. 3. Art industries and trade, America—History. 4. United States—Social life and customs—1865–1918. I. Title.
NK2003.5.S42        747'.213        74-1724
ISBN 0-275-43840-6

Book design by Ulrich Ruchti

Printed in the United States of America

# Introduction

History is never recaptured as fully as one might wish. Assembled from fragments of a complete picture which is lost, depictions of the past are branded with the character of the age which creates them. They say what satisfies their makers. Most people prefer to believe otherwise, insisting that ours is the scientific generation which will at last transcend the destructiveness of hands and the forgetfulness of minds, and sweep up all the bits and scraps of vanished time. But even given the parts, we never know for sure whether the re-creation is truth or merely its shadow.

The historian's dilemma is illustrated in these photographs of interiors. As complete room settings, most of them are quite foreign to us; we identify only with their parts—a familiar type of chair or table or vase. Household things are common fragments of history; their individual meanings and purposes are redefined rapidly, and their contexts are subject to alteration. Some objects survive many years because they are adaptable. Others grow obsolete and are discarded. The thousands of household things that appear in these pictures are seen as they were in actual daily use in the past. It is probable that the rooms did not remain as we see them for very long, for small revisions take place endlessly in any house. Were it not for the cameras of some six dozen photographers, these few scenes would have passed away quietly.

The photographs were taken in private houses in various places across the United States between about 1860 and 1917. While the book is about interior decoration and American taste, not photography, interior photographs are so rare for most of this period that a collection of several hundred—most of them documented —is in itself a curiosity. These trophies of a long search, the works of photographers dead and mostly forgotten, show how American rooms looked and how they were lived in, in large part by middle-class people.

The rooms are a series of moments isolated in time. Lacking color and the third dimension, the photographs are themselves historical fragments. But in nearly every other way they are moments intact, rooms captured exactly as they were while the shutters clicked, and together they provide a compelling tour inside the American home during the fifty years between the Civil War and World War I.

For nearly three full generations after the triumph of the Union in the Civil War, Americans hurried ahead in what is remembered today as merely a prelude to the nation's ascension to world power in World War I. In spite of terrible panics and depressions, the accomplishments of that half century were sufficiently splendid to keep optimism uniformly high; even the wave of gloom that followed the political scandals of the 1870's carried with it the urgency of the Gilded Age to push forward. With little interference from the outside world, the Americans we curiously label Victorians passed from one era of progress into another. Men returned from the Civil War often disillusioned but hungry to create, and their sons, in turn, took up the moralistic challenge to perfect all that was around them.

In an international context, even the finest American interiors were usually insignificant in the years covered here. Even the most famous American designers of the period, like Leon Marcotte and the Herter Brothers at mid-century and Stanford White and Ogden Codman, Jr., at the century's end, were not—in spite of their European connections and affectations—very important beyond New York and other major cities in the East. Even their high-style work was usually a considerable distance behind the best decorating in Paris and London.

The term high style is usually tossed about so generously that it needs some explanation here. In the strictest sense, the term applies to objects and rooms created in the most sophisticated vocabulary of fashionable acceptance at a given time. The date is very important, and ideally, the standard of judgment must be international. High style does not apply to prophetic personal work; it refers to design concepts with identifiable characteristics, such as the so-called French Antique, Anglo-Japanese, Arts and Crafts, or any number of other styles dealt with in this book. High-style room ensembles are usually so far in advance of the popular market that their parts—furniture, fabrics, colors, architectural elements—are not mass-produced but come from comparatively restricted shops and craftsmen. On the other hand, the clearest illustrations of a style are generally those rooms based upon worn-out stereotypes; somehow they get to be called high style. The term should be used with reservation, and, when it is taken on to describe American interiors, it must nearly always be qualified.

By definition, high-style decoration is absolutely not the norm; even so, we expect many more examples of it than we find in the United States before 1917. Among those rich and luxurious American rooms pictured in the series *Artistic Houses,* published in 1882–83, only a few were current high style, and they represented some of the finest houses in the United States. Provincialism and isolation account for some of this tardy taste in the houses of people who insisted on having only the very best. In America today, many houses cost enormous sums of money; many are stylish, and it is possible for many to come closer to high style than would have been the case a hundred years ago.

The meaning of the term changed considerably with the advent of mass manufacture. Present-day magazines

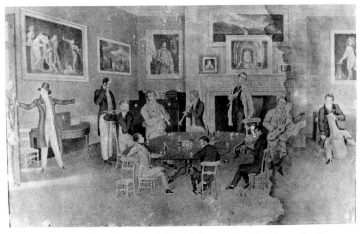

*Dining room, ca. 1825–30. The manufactured Grecian sideboard and Fancy chairs are harbingers of mass production.*

dictate to a vast public the virtues of furnishings that come from factories. Picture articles show us how the products of advertisers can be used in rooms. The resulting packaged taste, though sometimes silly and unrealistic, must be thoroughly understood before any attempt can be made to evaluate interior design in the twentieth century. Popular printed directives on interior design began during the rise of mass production of furniture in the second half of the nineteenth century. By spreading the news, publications helped demolish class lines, which had discriminated against the commonness of the products of big furniture factories.

By the time mass manufacture triumphed in the field of middle-class household furnishings, the leading upper-class interiors in America were still executed, at least in part, by craftsmen. They were rarely conceived of in what could truly be called high-style design, but they were, nevertheless, the works of restricted shops, and represented certain creative decisions on the part of the owner. Toward the end of the nineteenth century, the select cabinetmaking shops became less influential as nearly everyone began to use the new mass-produced furnishings. Now and then, mass manufacture was hot on the heels of high style; it became possible to purchase, at first-class stores, furniture that rivaled that in the cabinet shops. Certainly there was a technical difference in quality; but the point is, the manufactured version was actually available on the market well before its models had ceased to be called high style. So there came to be a sort of popular high style, if you will, not really fine enough to rank with the best, yet sufficiently convincing by the late 1880's to begin providing formidable competition for the expensive specialty shops. One after another, the shops of craftsmen began to close, and the American interior underwent a universal democratization. Even on the highest levels, the creative decision of other times was replaced by a selectivity which applied not only to costly new furniture but, ironically, to antiques as well, giving rise to the "period" room.

In its own era, a new style usually appears first in fragments. Before the age of mass manufacture, people rarely understood a whole style concept at one time, and even after various style clichés became well known through manufactures, most rooms still reflected a piece-meal vision. A so-called French parlor in 1860 was never the worse off for including Gothic chairs and perhaps a twenty-year-old classical center table. Even with the advent of matched sets, the buyer was vulnerable to being hypnotized by the many kinds of things for sale in a showroom and might select six different styles and classes of furniture. Because a house was built or occupied at a certain known time does not necessarily mean that the accepted tastes of the intelligentsia, nor the current high style, determined the decoration of its rooms. People can make unpredictable decisions. The architectural worthiness of buildings can never be taken as proof that their furnishings originally approached similar excellence.

American houses have always been conceived as private places for living; only rarely have houses been mere stages for artistic indulgence. This is painfully obvious, perhaps, but also basic and important to remember. Even the legendary mansions built during the years covered here shared none of the public functions of their

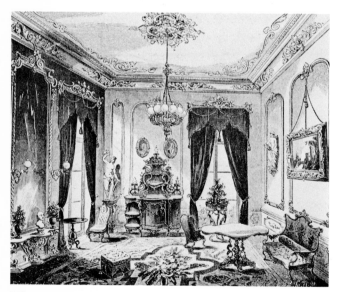

*French Antique parlor, 1854.*

European counterparts. Ceremonial or public spaces were taken for granted as integral features of aristocratic houses still being built in Europe on a grand scale in the second half of the nineteenth century. Comparable houses were nonexistent in America. The very finest houses of the American rich, by the 1890's, drew their closest foreign comparison in the lavish urban residences of the powerful bourgeoisie of Paris and London. This realistic social parallel was understood perfectly in its own day. The several attempts to produce palaces in the United States resulted in spectacular follies which must not be mistaken, over the widening gulf of time, for expressions of established, or even highly significant, ways of American life.

The absence of official function and aristocratic tradition in the United States does not alone account for the belatedness of style in American rooms. There is another, more basic, consideration: the distinctive quality in American houses is their remarkable look of privacy and homeyness, and that has been imposed upon them all, from cottage to mansion, since the beginning of the fifty year period covered here. Over and above temporal style, the ambience of livability lends a special character to American rooms, whether in the chic printed slipcovers and convenient coffee tables of the 1930's or in the equally conscious domestic affectations of one hundred years ago. Such an ideal of comfort comes from a way of thinking not unique to America but one that rose to its full authority in the Western world from about 1750 until a century later. It epitomizes the love of home, family, and marriage that we associate so much with Victorians. But long before that epoch, the deep and sentimental mystique of family life found rich and per-petual fields of expression in America, and was mani-fested in house decoration as soon as the colonial culture arrived at sufficient stability to consider the subject self-consciously. In architecture, this is seen in the domes-tic scale of such big houses as Mount Vernon, and indeed the White House, either of which might, in another climate of opinion, have been a palace.

In America, the appearance of comfort and tranquility, achieved either through clutter or sparseness, is still the prime ingredient in the decoration of domestic rooms. The ideal of comfort is the seed of American leadership in twentieth-century domestic architectural design. That seed began to germinate in the years covered here, and the spirit of comfort hovers over nearly every interior in this book. Sometimes the contrast between the magnificent and the homey is dramatic. Yet in a nation where there were no palaces and where the aristocracy was not really an aristocracy but an upper bourgeoisie, the dominant ideal was quite naturally middle-class. Here a vast majority of the people aspired to little more than a modest home of their own, the unblemished stamp of decency, and worthy reward for their work. These factors must be brought to bear, even more than popular styles, in considering the way typical rooms must have been. High-style interior decoration is usually the least matter of all.

Climactic events in history always make changes in house design and decoration. Between the wars that begin and end this book, there were several tumultuous events of another nature, especially the panic of 1873 and the one that followed it twenty years later. That first panic was the death blow of the Gilded Age in the East, while the second soured a lingering Gilded Age flavor in the Far West. The geographical lag of about two decades more or less characterized American household decoration in the nineteenth and early twentieth centuries. It is vital to bear this in mind when observing these interiors, even though there are exceptions. In rare instances entire room ensembles were transported cross-country to remote places. Leland Stanford had his Sacramento, California, house redecorated in 1868–69; his interiors were equal in every detail to those being commissioned by rich merchants in Chicago and New York who were his eastern equivalents. A Boston parlor might likewise be executed in a style reigning in London; but this was very rare. People far from the centers of new styles more often ordered only a single chair, picture, table, or statue in what was considered the modern taste

from a catalogue, and it arrived packed in straw inside a crate, fresh from the showroom floor. Style typically traveled that way. Contrasts in these pictures are formed consequently not only between different houses but between the different objects within single rooms. And so wide a selection of household furnishings was never available to the general public before the years 1860–1917.

In the three decades before the Civil War, American furniture production was transformed from a craftsman's trade into a vast manufacturing business. While there remained artistic cabinetmakers in the major cities, the new age was created by entrepreneurs who did not pretend to be designers. Central to their economic existence was the fact that the machine multiplied the efficiency of manpower in cheaply producing the things people wanted to buy. As far as designs were concerned, the manufacturer needed to look no farther than the obvious. Revivalism understandably appealed to his business intuition, and satisfied the appetite of the age. The machine had only to prove to people it could do the same work a man could do by hand.

At a steady pace, the market filled with machine-made cabinet and upholstered furniture; and a more general public found within its eager grasp costly-looking household objects at prices far lower than the cabinetmakers'. This completely changed the appearance of the American middle-class interior. To tempt a fast-spreading field of consumers, the manufacturers pitched their products in the most acceptable and pretentious design vocabulary they could find, the so-called French style current in England.

Except for a brief flirtation with Paris from the Revolutionary War until the early 1820's, and the presence of French craftsmen in a few of the larger cities throughout the nineteenth century, American taste compared most closely with that of England. The British were, meanwhile, taking their cue from the French. This was particularly true of that modified classical furniture of the Bourbon Restoration, the reigns of Louis XVIII and Charles X, which ended with the latter's abdication in 1830. Delicate in scale and color, subtle in curve and in the display of classical decoration, this furniture was in high style, a refined and creative adaptation of the archeological court style of the recent Napoleonic Empire. Refashioned by the British, the Restoration mode became much clumsier and rather squat, if often equally diminutive. The English commonly called this furniture Grecian, as opposed to the earlier historical Antique style. In the late 1820's, Grecian furniture was simplified —to the great advantage of those who produced it—by being stripped of the carved or cast classical detailing. To distinguish the new from the Grecian, it was often called either Grecian Plain style or, more typically, Modern, a term universally applied, in the nineteenth century, to obscure or hybrid revival treatments.

Those same names were used in the United States. American taste for the Grecian was established in the East by the mid-1820's, and in the next decade an equivalent of the Grecian Plain style or Modern, developed in this country with a character all its own. It was buxom and heavy, a style with many variations but one we know today as Pillar and Scroll, or less accurately, with its more classical predecessor, as American Empire.

Cabinetmakers found Grecian furniture cheap to build; the boxy basic form could be executed in soft wood with little more effort than that required to assemble a blanket chest. The column or scroll ornaments were not beyond the abilities of an apprentice. Onto the basic structure was glued a thin veneer of expensive imported mahogany, whipping wildly beautiful flames of reddish woodgrain over the bulky and architectural Grecian shape. The furniture had that double dose of innocence and brazen assurance that was its legacy from the best Early American cabinetwork. The Grecian style was a natural for the new mechanical saws, and well before the 1850's it was manufactured in large quantities from Boston to New York, Cincinnati to New Orleans, and aped in solid cherry and other native woods by many a country cabinetmaker.

Ten or so years before the war with Mexico, soon after the administration of Andrew Jackson and the great panic that followed it, other styles of furniture and decoration joined the Grecian in public esteem. They were all, in a manner of speaking, Anglo-French. What is significant is that suddenly two distinct trends in nineteenth-century American furniture design appeared —the new historical revival and what we shall call the creative revival. The design of the historical was based upon actual antiques of the same or similar function, while the creative variety, firmly in the tradition of some eighteenth-century design, took from history a rather literary inspiration for original work.

The creative revivals, like Grecian and Gothic, preceded the historical rivivals, especially the Elizabethan or Flemish, and the Louis Quatorze. J. C. Loudon's *Encyclopedia of Cottage, Farm, and Villa Architecture and Furniture,* published in England in 1833, distinguishes between the two types of revivals in this way: "There is no one who would not be desirous of possessing a chair both of the Grecian and the Elizabethan kind; but the Elizabethan chair would be valued merely as a curious piece of antiquity; while the other would be prized for its expression, for its suitableness as a seat, for its simplicity, and for the great effect produced in it by a very few lines. This effect of the Grecian chair being independent of all historical associations, since it is, in fact, merely an imaginary composition, results wholly

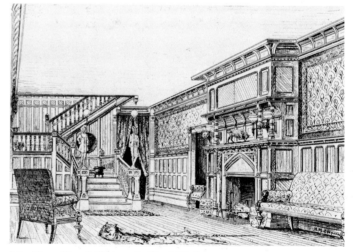

*Medievalized living hall, 1876.*

14

from the beauty of the design. . . . the present taste for Elizabethan furniture is more that of an antiquary, or of a collector of curiosities, than of a man of cultivated mind."

The same was often said of other historical revivals. In America, the Elizabethan style was the most widely known in the inexpensive spool, or Swiss, furniture found in every part of the nation. It was paralleled by another revival, a creative one that began in France as a historical revival called François Premier, and crossed the Channel as Renaissance. Heavy and carved, the Renaissance mode was only a little less creative and architectural than the Gothic and Grecian, but soon after its appearance, it was eclipsed by the styles Louis Quatorze and Quinze of the court of Louis-Philippe. Resembling the eighteenth-century furniture of a century before, these historical French styles were richer and more sensual than the Grecian—and certainly the setting that went along with them was less reserved. As the machine was improving almost daily, styles were now presented to it that broadened its horizon, styles indeed more worthy of the machine's talents than the somber Grecian.

By way of England, which took some of the spirit of its adaptation from the Dutch, the Louis revivals of the Orleans monarch and Napoleon III, who followed him, came to America, with the inevitable increase in size and prudish reinterpretation of carved embellishments. That a more sumptuous sort of furniture was wanting is no surprise, and in the machine's possession it grew lush by the 1850's. With the Louis revivals, and especially Louis Quinze, the manufacturers expressed themselves for the first time in every aspect of American decorative arts. What is more, they created universal admiration for a fancy French sort of room that, in many variations, is still considered appropriate to status in the United States.

Being acceptably Grecian had often meant to a room nothing more than the inclusion of a sideboard with columns and gilded brass drawer pulls, or a little worktable with a harp-like base, or a long sofa with scroll feet; it would be filled in elsewhere as best as could be managed, with no special attention paid to uniformity of style. Fully appointed Grecian rooms were somewhat vague in their total conception, and seem to have been scarce. The new French Antique, however, was an entirely different matter, ideally involving a whole room setting, all the parts of which could be bought in a store. There were statues in real and imitation marble; Brussels and Wilton pile carpets, veritable bouquets of dazzling analine colors supposedly Aubusson in inspiration; gilt-on-brass picture pins, curtain pins, cornices, and bell levers; wallcoverings of ever-cheaper wood-pulp papers in many colors with borders; damasks and brocades and muslins with fringe and galloon, and borders and tassels that looked like minarets; prints, porcelains, and, of course, the increasingly rich and curvilinear French chairs, tables, sofas, and French-plate mirrors set in gilded frames. Even clustered French furniture arrangements were now made possible in dark English-type American rooms through the innovation of gas lighting. Gaslight could be made to glow from mock bronze gasoliers with matching wall brackets, all gilded and covered with cherubs and vines and whatever other kingly splendor democratic pocketbooks might permit.

In the French Antique style, American manufacture found its first really significant design vocabulary. This was a historical revival, if not actually very authentic, nor intended to be more than a clear suggestion of a prototype. There were many price levels, from the inexpensive

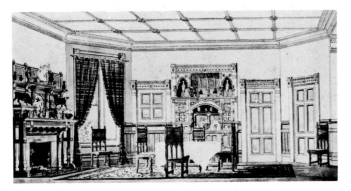

*New Gothic dining room, 1876.*

cottage versions, small and sometimes painted, to the fewer costly mansion and hotel pieces created in fine woods by cabinetmaker John Henry Belter of New York and his urban contemporaries. A public only beginning to be enraptured with the availability of household furnishings in quantity was bewitched by the idea of objects made by machines. The French Louis styles had irresistible magnetism, and universally called to mind a cliché of a manufactured Louis Quinze saloon with carpet, center table, sofa, side chairs, mirrors, curtains, and prints. Much of the desirability of such rooms was less the virtue of style itself than the special way in which they advertised a man's success in life. That there might be thousands of rooms that looked quite the same was no disadvantage but properly American and democratic and, in the context of the times, more unique than variation. In this parlor ideal there was not the faintest spark of antiquarianism; the French Antique room was a frankly modern room, even though the furniture was considered historical. Like nothing else before it, the French Antique, regardless of how few or how many times these settings were actually executed in complete detail, took on a recognizable character in the popular American vision. It was the first whole room ensemble to reach maturity in the American mind. Even Elizabethan, Renaissance, and Gothic rooms, which had their own thematic identities, were in other respects predominantly French Antique.

After the close of the Civil War, the Louis Seize revival became the desired drawing-room motif for new mansions; but the popular market, still pleased with the cabriole leg and heavy carving, preferred the Renaissance and the Louis Quinze—which was often called Louis Quatorze anyway—for cabinet pieces and tables. This was true throughout the late 1860's. Bearing nearly as remote a resemblance to the original as the other two Louis revivals, the Louis Seize brought a marked preference for straight lines and restraint. Expensive cabinetmakers took its basic and simple form and began to experiment. Manufacturers noticed the way these men used ebonized surfaces, burl, and various contrasting

textures and ornaments; and those subtle devices began to find rough parody in mass production. French models became more difficult to discern in the new furniture. Manufacturers never troubled themselves with historical investigation, and the cabinetmakers they were trying to copy were playing with abstractions.

While this was taking place, people made an about face and began to frown upon houses filled with matched furniture. Once available from craftsmen only at great expense, the matched set, or suite, for the parlor, dining room, or bedroom made its impact on the popular market well before the Civil War, and was the particular contribution of mass manufacture. At the outset, the public was delighted with the novelty of complete sets. Those thousands of people who shifted and relocated in postwar America found the matched set a sort of symbol for their new lives. But it did not take long for bare-boned manufactured rooms to become boring. At their best, the rooms lacked the homey originality of those of days gone by; once houses had been, by their very nature, individual, with clusters of transient objects —bandboxes, pictures, papers, bonnets, sea shells, shawls, artificial flowers, and other odds and ends. Where was that variety of contrast which had come from mixing classes and styles of things? Houses had once told a great deal about the people who lived in them.

Recollections of past rooms began to abound on the printed page. Magazines and popular newspapers of the 1870's ran humorous and nostalgic features about country and prewar life. In the last year of the decade, Mark Twain wrote a long description of a house of about thirty years before and dovetailed it into the unfinished manuscript of *Huckleberry Finn*. He has his hero pay a visit to Colonel Grangerford's plantation somewhere along the lower Mississippi River: "It was a mighty nice family, and a mighty nice house," Huck Finn begins. "I hadn't seen no house out in the country before that was so nice and had so much style. . . . There warn't no bed in the parlor, nor a sign of a bed, but heaps of parlors in towns has beds in them. . . . There was a clock on the middle of the mantel-piece, with a picture of a town painted on the bottom half of the glass front, and a round place . . . for the sun, and you could see the pendulum swing behind it." On each side of the clock was a "big outlandish parrot . . . made out of something like chalk, and painted up gaudy. By one of the parrots was a cat made out of crockery, and a crockery dog by the other; and when you pressed down on them they squeaked. . . . There was a couple of big wild-turkey-wing fans spread out behind those things. On a table in the middle of the room was a kind of lovely crockery basket that had apples and oranges and peaches and grapes piled up in it, which was much redder and yellower and prettier than real ones is. . . . This table had a cover made out of beautiful oil-cloth, with a red and blue spread-eagle painted on it, and a painted border all around. It come all the way from Philadelphia, they said. There was some books, too, piled up perfectly exact, on each corner of the table. One was a big family Bible. . . . One was *Pilgrim's Progress.* . . . Another was *Friendship's Offering,* full of beautiful stuff and poetry. . . . Another was Henry Clay's Speeches, and another was Dr. Gunn's *Family Medicine.* . . . There was a hymn book and a lot of other books. And there was nice split-bottom chairs." Colonel Grangerford's walls were decorated with framed pictures, "mainly Washingtons and Lafayettes and battles, and Highland Marys and one called 'Signing the Declaration.' There was some that they called crayons, which one of the daughters which was dead made her own self when she was only fifteen years old." At the windows were roller shades, "beautiful . . . white, with pictures painted on them of castles with vines all down the walls, and cattle coming down to drink." The floors were carpeted, and there was a "little old piano, too, that had tin pans in it, I reckon, and nothing was ever so lovely as to hear the young ladies sing 'The Last Link is Broken.' "

Here was remembered a rural mixture of the manufactured and the homemade, as it was just prior to real mass production. Mark Twain would never have drawn a parallel between the stylish, so-called art clutter of his own new house of the 1870's in Hartford, Connecticut, and the old-fashioned parlor of Colonel Grangerford. He viewed the Colonel's house with a tender kind of amusement; about his own he was dead serious. While his attitude was that of an era ready to applaud the superiority of everything new in architecture and decoration, similarities between the modern interiors he admired and those of his childhood are not hard to find. What had come into its own by the 1870's was the personalized room. Justified on all its levels in the name of art, it represented a strenuous effort to revitalize rooms by arbitrarily giving them again the aura of human warmth and individuality they had lost.

The practice of consciously personalizing rooms did not begin entirely as a negative reaction to manufactured furniture and goods. More accurately, it was a means of improving the appearance of standardized room settings by giving them an individual stamp. Manufactured furniture increased to gigantic quantity; the public bought more sets than ever. With the advice of magazines and books, and their own intuition, homeowners supplemented the basics with essays in personal selection. Now there was a deliberate attempt to avoid any similarity to those stuffy and predictable French Antique rooms, which had enslaved fashion in chains of tastelessness for nearly twenty years.

Meanwhile, high-style furniture, and a surprisingly large amount of manufactured furniture, began to drift into the realm of the creative revivals and away from all but token adherence to historical precedence. The change, already evident in the Louis Seize revival, soon took hold in a new and revised Renaissance revival. English reformers introduced a kind of medievalism which demanded the geometric forms the manufacturers liked, and it was in great evidence on the American market by the mid-1870's. Sometimes known as Eastlake, from Charles L. Eastlake's book of the late 1860's *Hints on Household Taste in Furniture, Upholstery, and Other Details,* the American version of this furniture seldom bore much resemblance to plates in the celebrated English publication. American Eastlake was instead only a part of the broader creative revival movement, which dominated furniture design from about 1870 until the early 1890's. Eastlake, like many other authors, wrote his book as a common-sense guide to buying furniture for the general public. He echoed many other thinkers when he urged people to avoid cheap sets and gimmicks sold by manfacturers, saying that they would be far better off patronizing that thinning breed, the rural cabinetmaker, by giving him simple and honest vernacular designs to copy. Vernacular to Eastlake meant the furniture of early England, then already of some interest to designers in Great Britain. "There seems to be a great want of popular information," bemoaned Eastlake; and for everyman he offered a solution.

If the term Eastlake style is in the long run meaningless, it is not unfair to credit the author with popularizing, to an extent, some current high-style standards of selection that included a dressed-up sort of medieval revivalism and an interest in returning to furniture made by craftsmen. Had his American book sales multiplied tenfold, *Hints on Household Taste* could not by virtue of numbers alone be considered a major influence in American households. Eastlake's ideas, like those of nearly everyone else, were popularized by manufacturers whose material interpretations of his views are what reached most people. American Eastlake furniture was given his name because the name developed advertising appeal much as Louis Quatorze and Elizabethan were used to describe furniture that in truth represented neither. Most of the kinds of furnishings today lumped under the single name Eastlake represent one or more of the creative revivals, and the most abstract of these seems actually to have stemmed from the Louis Seize revival of the 1860's. In its day, some of our Eastlake was more correctly understood by the name of Renaissance, Norman, Gothic, or New Grecian, all springing from specific and identifiable revivals that were popular earlier in the nineteenth century. If the inspiration was French, the furniture was generally known as Louis Quatorze, Louis Quinze, or Louis Seize, depending upon whether it was fancy-carved, plain, curvilinear, or straight in line.

With historical sources in all the revivals ever more obscure because we have lazily tended to give them general titles like Victorian and Eastlake, determining creative revival roots today can be extremely difficult. People in the nineteenth century were satisfied with the smallest suggestion of a literal device; for example, a cameo of Cleopatra made a sofa sufficiently Egyptian, while a grotesque bust could mean Renaissance, a quatrefoil Gothic, and vague suggestions of urns and incised classical borders comprised New Grecian. Often motifs were mixed; in that case the dominant one usually established the name. It was readily explained that these revivals were not meant to be slavish imitations of antiques—which, ironically, no revival yet had actually been—but new designs in the spirit of ages past. The creative trend eventually included what was known as Art furniture, a type based less upon historical than upon exotic themes, as the Japanese, Moorish, and Turkish. Though very similar to one another, and often considered quite the same in the nineteenth century, there is a difference between creative revival and Art furniture: Art furniture rejected historical sources in favor of cultural ones, while the creative revivals sought to capture the flavor of history. In the latter case, which was by far the dominant one, even the American colonial vernacular was dredged up as a theme.

The basic setting of the American home of the second half of the nineteenth century was, therefore, furniture which came from two different kinds of revivalism of very long standing, creative and historical. Creative revival furniture was ultimately simple in its appearance, with a boldness that makes it seem to us more traditionally American than English, a fact Americans sometimes noted with pride a century ago. In the creative revival's best mass-produced form, restraint remained foremost and was even dramatized by incised and white-touched or gilded lines, a sensitive distribution of surface textures and colors, and whimsical contrasts between geometric verticals and horizontals, bulbs and curves. It varied in the quality of its design less than today's manufactured furniture, although that judgment may be rose-colored by time.

The public did realize that manufactures made it possible for them to have the most modern rooms but, as the pictures on these pages demonstrate, people hardly ever understood what modern really meant. Seldom did the average man realize a single concept of style in toto while it was new, and when style was eventually shown to him through manufactures, he rarely accepted it all. Therefore, even if simplicity did finally become a factor in furniture design and room decoration of the better sort, the average interior was quite another matter. To the American of the 1870's there was a distinct difference between style and taste. Style pertained to design themes in purchased household objects, such as a Renaissance bedroom set, a Louis Quatorze parlor table, or a Gothic wardrobe. Taste regarded that personal way an interior was finally put together, from arranging and supplementing the furniture to hanging the pictures, curtaining the windows, and selecting colors. The word taste simply meant judgment: a house was expected to be not only an essay on the intellectual judgment of its principal inhabitants but a lesson in judgment for the young. What was more, household taste was supposed to symbolize, at first glance, the decent conduct of a family's private life.

A chief influence here was that, generally speaking, the man was no longer the builder of the house or the one who furnished it. Household art, by the 1870's, was

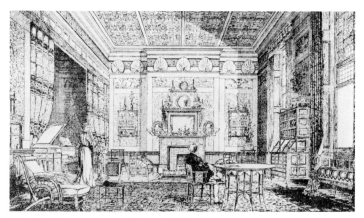

*Anglo-Japanese parlor, 1878.*

in the hands of women; the architect's client was now female, and the wise owners of furniture stores—and auctioneers—capitalized on that fact. To the American room, women brought criteria that they applied to matters of personal dress. Now they were put to the task of adorning rooms. The parlor set or dining-room grouping, all carefully chosen at the furniture warehouse or by catalogue, was only the beginning. Around those basic stanchions of style were gathered great quantities of objects which would have horrified the more idealistic male writers and the fewer female ones. That, of course, did not matter in the slightest to the average housewife, who was unaware of their writings on taste and their scorn. Those swarms of things she somehow pulled together denoted much about her personally, and, without them, the room looked neglected to her and most people's eyes; and what could be worse than the neglected hearthside? Even the authors agreed with that.

The resulting rooms were combinations of many trends. In the 1870's and 1880's objects were normally clustered in art units—a practice perhaps inspired by the way the earlier gaslight lit in circles. By the 1890's, it was believed desirable to blend objects into the room's architecture so that there were flowing banks of things instead of individual tableaux. In addition to the changing philosophy of placement, there was a consistent yearning to recapture the lost sense of contrast of the sort Mark Twain commemorated in describing the Grangerfords' parlor. Nearly always, it was believed desirable to retain the conversational French furniture arrangements that had characterized the Louis revivals of around the time of the Civil War. Unceasingly, popular magazines suggested stylish conceits which were sure to enhance the effect of good taste. Most significant of all, however, the finished interiors were visual proof in sheer force of numbers that the giant increase in manufactured household things did not repel the public at all but was being welcomed eagerly.

On its least sophisticated level, but often its most successful, the resulting personal room sometimes achieved a happy originality that its costly contemporaries did not share. The plain and fancy, the cheap and expensive, could find in such rooms equal purpose toward the effect of the whole. These pictures include many personalized rooms, with their mixtures of furniture, their gay festoons of printed materials and crisp, embroidered mull curtains, their sea shells, pillows, curios, shawls, potted plants, and other ornaments that could be obtained by one's own good effort and were kept lively and vital by daily primping. Beside a new upright piano might rest a guitar and a folio of music, the three united by ribbons climaxed by great satin bows, all for the purpose of proclaiming the musical talent of a member of the household. Soon the piano might be further decorated with a plaster bust of Bach, tastefully arranged with harps and musical notes made of paper flowers and hair. On the mantel might stand an irregular line of porcelain vases and jugs, with a flock of Japanese paper fans on the wall above, just within a rainbow of hand-painted china plates.

In spite of the demand for an abundance of objects, and the cost, the popular dream of a beautiful room could be realized for very little money. The principal ingredient was the personal look. No stylish house could be without it, and the effort to have it was made in both the plainest cabins of the Dakota farmers and the big-city houses of Manhattan.

The panic of 1873 was not the most widespread financial crisis the American nation had in the nineteenth century, yet it blew an awakening chill over the glib citizenry and had a moralizing effect on the decorative arts. The panic hurried the universal popularity of the personal room, for hard times always heighten man's interest in human things. Personal rooms came to be seen as being inherently American, and as the decade advanced this was further stressed by the introduction of colonial motifs. The colonial revival was in turn given national attention by the Centennial celebration of 1876 and the many events that accompanied it. Subdued as it initially was, like all historical sources in the furniture of the times, the colonial revival is nevertheless often the most immediately recognizable to us today because the subsequent popularity of eighteenth-century American antiques has made us more keenly aware of its sources.

To say that the homey colonial replaced the urbane styles in an age of post-panic piety is wrong, if a tempting generalization. The colonial revival in the United States paralleled, and slightly followed, a thriving English movement known as the Queen Anne. This Queen Anne style was the most conspicuous as it applied to house architecture, and its effect upon interiors was considerable. Inspired originally by the appeal of a distant and simpler age in English life, Queen Anne buildings were deliberately quaint and irregular piles, usually in red brick. Americans used red brick too, but also developed a popular version of the Queen Anne with wood-shingle walls and dark green painted trim, evoking the weathered texture and romantic appeal of old farmhouses along the New England coast. In either brick or shingle, Queen Anne had that quaint look which people turning from the brazen glamour of the Gilded Age seemed to like almost immediately. American Queen Anne, in the late 1870's, began to take on very subtle colonial motifs, and by the 1890's, the colonial revival style could be seen all over the country. At first it was sometimes hard to tell what

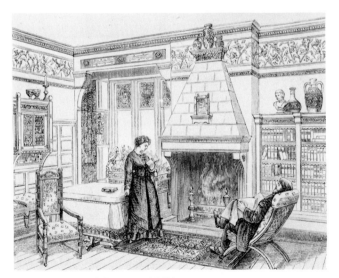

*Queen Anne library, 1878.*

was meant to be Queen Anne, what was Free Classic, and what was actually meant to be colonial. In the instance of the latter, wooden detailing of the Georgian vernacular was applied to Queen Anne forms already established. A colonial room of, say, 1885 tended to be picturesque and irregular, with curving walls and nooks. The plans were open and rooms flowed together in a way never possible before central heating. Colonial revival houses were not at all what comes to mind today in imagining the colonial. When the Queen Anne dimmed in the 1890's, the colonial revival house was rearranged into proper rectangular shapes which gave it a more identifiable character. The principal designers were in the East, so they selected regional motifs close at hand—overdoor pediments, wooden balustrades, and mantels with pilasters. Quite naturally, the formal colonial revival then assumed everywhere a vaguely New England look.

Mixed with colonial revival furniture in rooms of the 1880's were now sometimes real antiques, although the age still preferred the new, by far, over anything old. Spinning wheels, and other colonial affectations, began to appear in personal interiors and an actual look of the past began to encroach upon the mere suggestion of it. A self-proclaimed junk shop in Virginia merely reflected a beginning movement when, in 1883, it advertised a

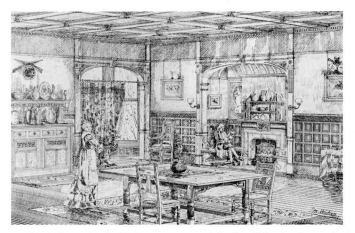

*Colonial revival dining room with fireside inglenook, 1884.*

specialty in "Virginia relics." If real colonial antiques were few in the Far West, there were, nevertheless, substitutes available in the furniture stores or in the catalogues from Milwaukee, Chicago, and St. Louis. And there were already collectors of Western artifacts, long before the Wild West was tamed. The objective was seldom anywhere to have a setting wholly antique or colonial; old things—and, in the East, family things—were initially only a part of the personal effect. By the late 1880's and, more so, by the mid-1890's, dark woodwork was being replaced by a glossy off-white known as colonial ivory. While the colonial revival in interior decoration became a national style, it was always taken the most seriously by upper middle-class suburban families and the minor rich; and this colonial, as the years went by, became entwined with the genealogical interests of its prime supporters. Colonial homes, to use the language of the era, were being numerously built by "well-fixed" families—another term which almost describes the symbolic appeal of the revival style—in every part of the United States by the time of World War I.

Acceptance of the colonial helped bring Americans slowly back toward new historical revivals, which were thriving abroad, and away from the earlier kind of personal room with its matched sets or its samplings of the many creative revivals. The tasteful interlude did not end; the pictures here show that the personal room was still being taken seriously in some places, only with less effort perhaps, well into the twentieth century; and it had reappeared in a new, uncluttered, form late in the 1890's, constituting, often in the hands of professionals, a nervous sort of selectivity called Good Taste that still haunts the upper middle-class American house today.

Mass communication made its first significant effects upon American household decoration in the last quarter of the nineteenth century. There had been popularizers earlier. Andrew Jackson Downing's books about house and garden had sold widely in the 1840's and 1850's; the *American Family Encyclopedia of Useful Knowledge,* published in 1845 by T. Webster and Mrs. Parkes, was reprinted in many editions, offering among other things, advice on furnishing and interior decoration. What became far more important were the many magazines of a more general nature that printed articles on domestic taste. The great increase in the quantity of printed matter that occurred during and after the Civil War made the distribution of the earlier books seem insignificant by comparison, and the printed production of the 1860's seemed humble by the decade of the 1890's. By the end of the century, scores of books could be bought on nearly every subject in interior decoration and architecture. The major companies producing paints, wallpaper, furniture, oil, gas, and electric lamps, and the like all had catalogues and carried on extensive, nationwide mail-order businesses. Feeding those companies and the editors of magazines with ideas was that growing practitioner, the interior decorator.

The practice of architecture in the United States began to approach professional standing only shortly before the Civil War. Interior decorating as a field was about forty years behind that, for although there were advertised decorators in New York, Boston, Philadelphia, Baltimore, and New Orleans at mid-century, interiors were usually created by the contractor or architect, the house painter, or the owner himself. Decorators prospered through the enormous rush of public and commercial building in the Gilded Age and the late 1870's. They proved their worth so well to the businessmen that, by

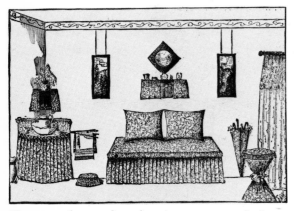

*Homemade parlor furniture covered in pink and green cretonne, 1888.*

the mid-1880's, they were not uncommon on big projects, and they were being hired by the rich nearly everywhere to "do" houses as they had once been hired to execute the interiors of office buildings, railroad-train cars, steamboat saloons, and the many parts of hotels. Sometimes they collaborated with architects, though it was seldom in harmony, for architects have ever considered decorators trespassers in their buildings. Most of the early interior decorators seem to have been connected with furniture companies or outlets; this has remained an effective means of hawking a store's wares, and, even in private practice, decorators today are important in the spread of new furniture styles.

Through popular publications of the late nineteenth and early twentieth centuries like *The Ladies' Home Journal* and *Century Magazine,* and trade magazines like *Architectural Record* and *Good Furniture,* Americans were exposed to the work of professional decorators. The average person's ideas about interiors were sometimes more absolute than his ideas about architecture, simply because of what he had read in magazines. Those illustrated publications kept his taste in a constant state of flux, and his house often showed it. The confusing mixtures in some of the rooms in this book probably demonstrate less intellectual conviction than massed collages of fleeting preferences. At the turn of the century, the manufacture of furniture had reached such an unprecedented peak that the consumer's span of possibility was nearly infinite. Even the exotic taste that threads through the whole of the nineteenth century, and was evident on an inexpensive level in what was called fancy furniture in rattan, wicker, and iron, found its way into furniture catalogues.

The new historical revivals that began in the 1890's were like those of forty and fifty years before, usually foreign and predominantly French. There were now, however, also Spanish, Dutch, and several periods of English. At their grandest, the new revivals were carried out magnificently in mansions; most cities of even moderate size in the United States had an example or two of these big houses, usually somewhat simplified versions of the popular Renaissance classicism, or hulking red brick masses in even less likely revival forms and hybrids. They were fitted out with doors containing iron grilles, or beveled and leaded jewel glass. Marble floors and balustrades, broad, open, and welcoming living halls, from which large spaces swept one into another, were characteristics of thousands of these American houses. Interior decorators filled them with imitations of Louis Quinze furniture and ornaments which were not liberally conceived like the old French Antique, but serious and realistic. There were also copies of Chippendale models. Beyond the unsmiling demeanor of the formal rooms, the bedrooms were furnished in light brass or the more stylish Louis Seize copies, painted white and piled with cushions. Scattered here and there, if it did not enjoy predominance, was always the colonial, its constantly changing interpretation attesting to its continuing popularity as a source of revival inspiration. At the windows cut-velvet curtain panels framed flat expanses of lace, behind which some of the glass was stained and the rest clear, pouring light onto reproduction American oriental carpets and thick portieres with cut-steel borders and silk fringes. These rooms were meant to look stark, assured, and tasteful. In common with the middle-class revivals of the 1850's, everything for the interior of this type was also manufactured, if only in greater quantity, and the demand for such high-class and first-rate appointments could be filled in Kansas City and Seattle almost as quickly as in New York.

By World War I, the revivals had made their impact upon countless smaller houses in the form of odd pieces and sets. There were the so-called reproduction Spanish, Italian, English, and French pieces suitable for modest houses and apartments, but they in no way equaled the popularity of the colonial. The creative revivals slowly waned, after a nearly thirty-year triumph, and while they did not die, were finally replaced in the mainstream by a single common denominator which was not a revival at all. This was in the Arts and Crafts furniture which crossed class lines more freely than any that had gone before it.

Arts and Crafts furniture was accepted in England long before it made its American appearance, although certainly the creative revivals had paved the way for it. In some respects, it was a negative and anti-manufacture movement, the result of an intellectual yearning to return to the simple and handmade. The crafts philosophy developed ostensibly from the fear that the mechanized age was taking joy and personal fulfillment from human life. Revivalism had expressed in its ensembles a theatrical fancy for romantic history, but revivalists were not particularly concerned with the inner nature of the subject, which was the principal interest of the Arts and Crafts movement. With its emphasis upon hand-crafted objects, the Arts and Crafts room was neither an enforced composition nor a period ensemble; instead, it was an amalgamation of units brought together not necessarily in relation to one another, but as a setting blending the individual work of many craftsmen, both professional

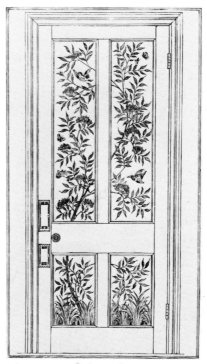

*A common door becomes fine art, 1883.*

23

and nonprofessional. Personal taste, while theoretically the principal ingredient, here paradoxically became inseparable from style, producing rooms far more stilted than ever before.

In Britain, the idea of returning to honest hand craftsmanship was, by the 1870's and 1880's, a part of the philosophy of the Aesthetics, whose rejection of the mechanized world gave impetus to an optimistic quest and a positive viewpoint on how to live well in an industrialized society. It must be remembered that in addition to the Art furniture which came from the Aesthetic movement and so clearly paralleled creative revivalism, there was in England a yeoman-cottage or vernacular style which was the immediate inspiration of the Arts and Crafts styles in the United States. Arts and Crafts furniture thus often had more in common with the creative revivals than it did with the more ethnic moods and abstractions of Art furniture. A certain element of society had praised the look of humble hand-crafted houses and furniture since the late eighteenth century. The interest had been manifested in rustic lodges, garden shelters, and all manner of organic furniture made from planks, the branches of trees, and shells. But a full century had passed since the pastoral days when the rich built imitation peasant cottages; gone also were the days of the picturesque villas of the 1840's through the 1880's. In a

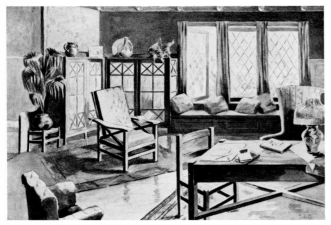

*Arts and Crafts library, 1910.*

raw industrialized society, the romantic associations and warmth of the yeomanlike hearth now offered the middle class as well a kind of sensible and cozy contrast to a world moving very fast.

The creators of the Arts and Crafts movement were serious artists and considered themselves commonsense innovators of the art of good living. They said their message was not for a small and exclusive class of people, but for all. Whereas the housewife of the 1870's had believed her fancy domestic efforts comprised a personal statement of private life and good taste, the adherents of the Arts and Crafts believed that through simple forms of art that same house could be beautiful in a universal sense. Shunning their contemporaries—the builders of classical mansions with Louis Seize salons—the reformers proclaimed that they had found the design vocabulary of democracy. The movement involved craftsmanship in pottery, glass, metal, wood, and textiles; in theory, it did not demand any certain design motifs but rather offered a special way of looking at commonplace things as art and at the world through art.

The Arts and Crafts movement was not an American movement in the 1880's, for it did not become really established here until several years after the panic of 1893 had made its terrible mark on history. This financial crash came, ironically, within a week of the opening of the Columbian Exposition in Chicago. The dramatic way in which the fair glorified Renaissance classicism in public architecture, and inadvertently helped popularize the new historical revivals in interior decoration, too often overshadows a national panic in which every town, city, and farm in the United States suffered. That panic's effects were more far-reaching than those of the panic two decades before.

The sudden flight of prosperity helped bring success to the Arts and Crafts movement. People sought solace in the noble, the plain and the true. This was manifested at once in American interiors in the heavy wooden and upholstered furniture which looked honest, rather in the spirit of the Arts and Crafts philosophy, but far from Arts and Crafts in its appearance. It was seldom very plain, whether in the form of huge sideboards with French beveled mirrors, or as puffed and swollen black or green leather chairs, or as high-backed beds, their cross-grain oak glistening under many coats of varnish. Manufacturers advertised its hand-crafted, wooden look to smooth over the fact that it was, indeed, machine-made, though the deliberate bulk and practicality of this furniture did lend to it an air of honesty. Although it lacked the subtlety of the creative revivals before it, this massive mode followed closely in their footsteps, borrowing motifs from the colonial, Flemish or Elizabethan, and French revivals. Public building commissions admired it as Anglo-Saxon, while private citizens revered its sturdy practicality. By 1895 it had taken over the market.

Through the massive mode, American taste was prepared for the more characteristic expression of the Arts and Crafts yet to come. Launched at the turn of the century, this was called by its chief exponent, Gustav Stickley, Craftsman furniture, the name that became the trademark of his manufactory and the title of his popular magazine. Unlike the massive mode, this Arts and Crafts type could not be linked visibly with revivalism to an American's eye, even though some of it was considerably like English work by C. F. A. Voysey and others, whose peasant cottage style did have revival overtones in the 1880's and 1890's. The English influence on Gustav Stickley is a matter of fact; on his contemporaries it can only be suspected. In any event, although Stickley himself became head of a big business and distributed thousands of Craftsman objects, many companies besides his helped spread Arts and Crafts furniture over America. Vast quantities of chairs, tables, benches, bookcases, and the like were purchased on the popular market from such manufactories as Charles P. Limbert of Grand Rapids and the more expensive and inventive L. and J. G. Stickley, brothers of Gustav, of Fayetteville, New York. In addition to two more competing brothers in Grand Rapids, Stickley had literally hundreds of competitors in mass manufacture.

The American interior was not entirely dominated by this horizontal furniture of boards. After the return of good times, toward the end of the 1890's, the rich began again to patronize the historical revivals, and the general public to purchase a wide variety of furniture in the massive mode. Oak was the prevalent material, and it could be obtained weathered, dark-stained, waxed, and natural or, most popularly, in an ochre color known as Golden Oak, a term which, even in its own day, was a blanket title for most examples of the massive mode. There was also a revival of eighteenth-century Queen Anne, which became a middle-class compromise of sorts between the informality of Arts and Crafts and the formal living associated with the historical revivals, including the colonial and a revival of Grecian furniture known by manufacturers as American Empire. Queen Anne, considered more or less colonial, was available ebonized, but was more often seen in varnished black walnut, oak, or mahogany. In much of it, panels of woven cane connected the frame; loose cushions with springs were made to fit. As Queen Anne was enjoying its day, still another style came into vogue for the parlors of people in search of the elegant. This was called Quaint, or Fancy French, or Fancy Shape, and reflected English adaptations of the current French Art Nouveau. Sometimes lacquered in white or robin's-egg blue for bedrooms, this style was now and then seen gilded, or with floral decorations applied

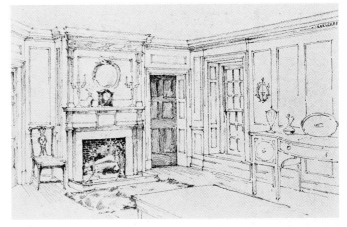

*Colonial revival interior of the early twentieth century.*

in color. Available in sets as small as three pieces, the Quaint style had variations including themes of Chippendale and Queen Anne, and combinations of spindles and balls. Some versions had hand-painted panels showing scenes of French court life in the eighteenth century; usually such French affectations made the furniture merit the name of a Louis, still a winning appellation in the marketplace.

This book begins and ends with revivals: at one extreme, revivalism embodied the wish to resurrect, if not actual history, certainly a mood of historical romance; at the opposite extreme, revivalism was the point of departure for original design. In the first instance, a revival room was meant to be an illustrative setting, no matter how inaccurate it may seem to us in retrospect. In the second, the individual object alone was the issue. Like its eighteenth-century model, a Louis Seize revival chair of, say, 1870 could stand alone by virtue of the completeness of its design. This had not been so with a Louis Quinze revival chair of twenty years before, which required its companions in the set to complete the rich effect.

In the Arts and Crafts movement, popular furniture design for the first time in American history began to venture completely away from revivalism. There had long been bentwood furniture, horn furniture, and fantastic design experiments in iron. These were never intended to be furnishings to fill whole houses, but were invented as practical and economic accessories, primarily for public uses, and only as accents in private dwellings.

The Arts and Crafts movement of the late 1890's provided the middle class with a radical new type of furnishing, and through middle-class support it became the most pronounced vocabulary of American interior design. As its popularity increased, the revival styles became more historically correct than they had ever been. On the eve of World War I, leading manufacturing companies like the Imperial Furniture Company of Grand Rapids, Michigan, and the Barnard F. Simons Company of Rochester, New York, sold historical reproductions that they claimed defied the best knowledge of antique collectors. Quite as good manufactured lines existed in

Golden Oak on an Arts and Crafts theme. Costly hand craftsmen like John Helmsky of New York made convincing copies of museum originals of every sort from the Louis Treize to late Georgian, and from Flemish to Spanish baroque. Elsewhere in the United States, architects and designers like Frank Lloyd Wright, Will H. Bradley, Charles S. and Henry M. Greene, George Maher, and Harvey Ellis made further creative explorations in furniture design, following the lead of the Arts and Crafts movement.

Creative design and historical reproduction could now be considered separate forces in American decorative arts. Sixty years after World War I, the same two currents, sometimes quite at odds, determine the principal character of American rooms.

The birth and history of photography parallel the growth of the manufactures that influenced every room in this book. Brought to America late in 1839, the infant invention of the camera was, by the close of the 1850's, known to professionals and hobbyists everywhere in the United States. Most cities had daguerrean parlors which operated on sunny days, taking portraits for moderate prices. During the decade of the 1850's the stereograph, so named by that pioneer camera buff Oliver Wendell Holmes, became very popular, and the earliest interior scenes here are taken from those double images which could appear three-dimensional through a viewer. The stereograph was the first significant means of photographing interiors, although even those pictures were taken with great difficulty for lack of sufficient light.

Gas lighting was inadequate illumination for photographing rooms, so the photographer had to depend upon light from open windows. Otherwise he needed to take time exposures which could last for hours and, for that reason, could never include people. During a time exposure, the photographer moved in and out of the picture constantly adjusting window curtains and reflectors to attract maximum light; if he did not remain too long in one place his image was lost. Most of the pictures here, which were taken prior to the turn of the century, were probably time exposures of anywhere from a matter of seconds to several hours. Artificial lighting did exist in complicated forms; there were burning magnesium wire and the faster magnesium tapers for use when there were movable subjects. One experimenter recommended that chalk dust be powdered over dark carpets and furniture to help brighten rooms for photographs. Patience and planning on the part of the photographer were essential before the advent of the electric bulb.

Probably few of the scenes in this book were the works of professionals. Amateur photographic societies were popular everywhere. Before the Civil War amateur groups, including enthusiastic ladies, could be seen enjoying holiday sunshine in parks and meadows, carrying pairs of wooden boxes, one the camera, the other a dark tent and chemicals. With just such equipment, and by the late 1880's, with George Eastman's Kodak, many of the rooms here were recorded for posterity. Professional work can usually be identified. Some superb examples of early photography have been rejected for this book in favor of pictures of lesser quality that better describe this interlude of fifty years. Setting has been given more weight than the presence of individual objects.

Pictures of interiors become plentiful after about 1910. The vast majority in this collection were made prior to that date and come from a firsthand survey made of hundreds of archives, libraries, and historical soci-

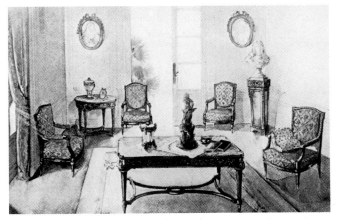

*Louis Seize parlor, ca. 1904.*

eties in the United States, as well as many inviting attics where old albums and scrapbooks lay. Most of the interiors are identified as to the location, owner, and date; some exemplary ones are anonymous.

The fifty years covered were crucial ones. A book about the following half century of American rooms would show fewer changes. So mighty and so fast were the alterations in every aspect of American life from the Civil War to World War I that those years in retrospect appear to run together as a single era. This is not entirely wrong; the five decades between the wars can be thought of as a hinge of American history for, during this time, the threads of all that had been before were woven into the cords of the new and future world.

City life became a reality in the first decade of this period. The postwar generation moved to town, clinging to an American ideal of a good, pure, wholesome, and Godly agrarian way. Farm backgrounds were sentimentally commemorated in personal rooms, behind windows that curtained away city stench and realities. People clung tenaciously to an image of the past while the explosive changes of the late nineteenth and early twentieth centuries took hold. They saw their ideal materialize in rows of bungalows on lots in thousands of suburbs. Looking up from backyard vegetable patches, they saw the ideal epitomized in 1893 at the Columbian Exposition, in the beauty of the White City on Lake Michigan. Though reformers at heart, these middle-class Americans worried little about the cold realities of city slums that thrived and grew downtown, away from their farms or apartments or the houses at the end of the streetcar lines. To the people who lived in the houses pictured here, slums were temporary ways of life; they were places one had been, would leave soon, or where one might unfortunately be headed if one did not live right. Likewise, the Vanderbilt mansions at Newport and on Fifth Avenue and the most palatial houses of Chicago, St. Louis, Pittsburgh, Buffalo, and San Francisco were not seen as realistic standards of living to the average American. He accepted these extremes without much questioning. The enchanted garden of the American good life lay precisely in between.

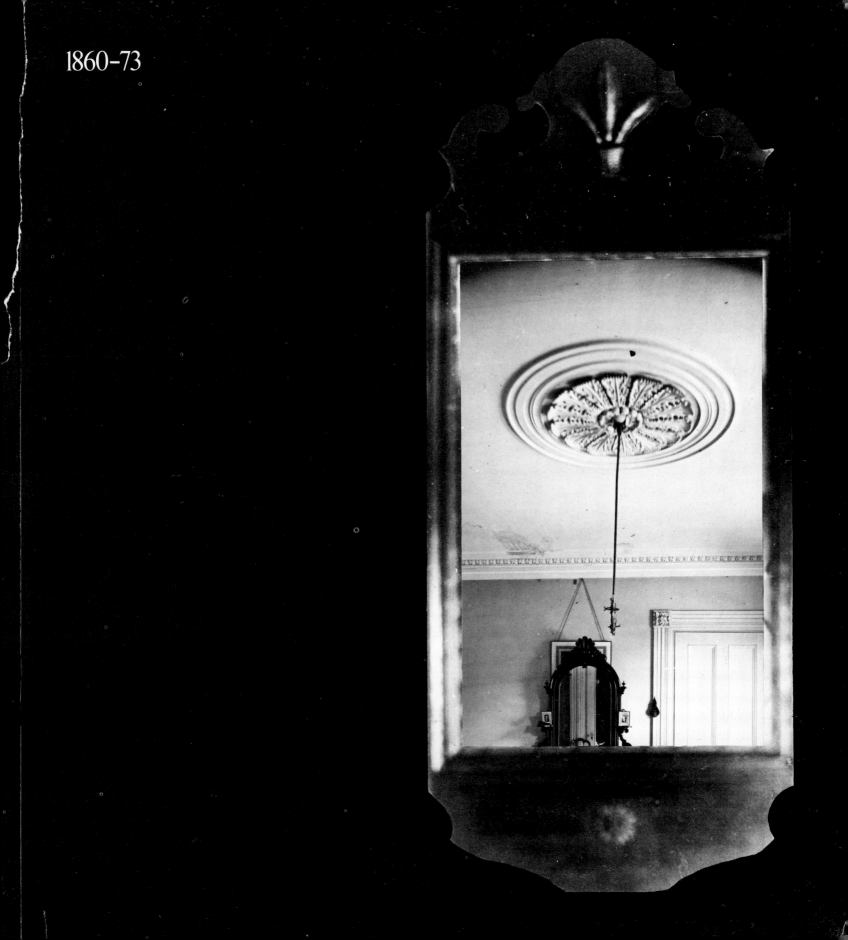

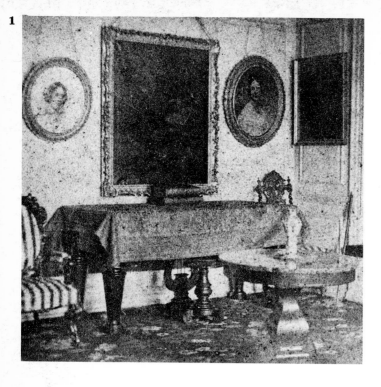

### 1. Reception Room, House of John Hancock, Boston, Massachusetts, ca. 1860

This was one of New England's most important colonial mansions; yet only the family Bibles and the patriot's walking stick are as old as the eighteenth-century paneled walls. The French Antique and Elizabethan chairs, upholstered *en suite,* the Grecian center table and piano, all of about 1840–50—together with portraits of about the same era—make the room seem a century later than it really is. One might suppose that the attic was full of eighteenth-century furnishings, all set aside without regret in favor of the refinements of more modern taste. The house was demolished for site development in 1863. All cries of objection were drowned out by a grander issue, the Civil War.

### Drawing Room, House of Mary Hampton, Columbia, South Carolina, ca. 1860

**2.** When she sat for this stereograph on the eve of the Civil War, the widow of the first of three legendary Wade Hamptons had occupied her large house on Blanding Street for thirty-six years. The house had been made acceptably Grecian shortly before General Hampton's death in 1834, and around 1847 their daughter Mrs. John Smith Preston added a great wing to the rear, reorienting the house to face a four-acre tangle-wild garden. A staff of some twenty-two slaves maintained the establishment. This drawing room, although situated in the new wing, and designed more or less in the prevailing style of the 1840's, reflects the taste of Mrs. Hampton in her young married years. Her painted fancy settee and armchair are a kind manufactured in many localities, including Columbia, in the 1820's, and the covered table might well have been made there as well. While the woodwork, black baseboards, and deep wooden wainscoting express the spirit of the older part of the house, the carpeting, downy French Antique chair, and wallpaper belong to the new age of mass manufacture, which Mary Hampton seems to be fending off with her little flower arrangements, handmade letter basket, and garlanded deer antlers.

2

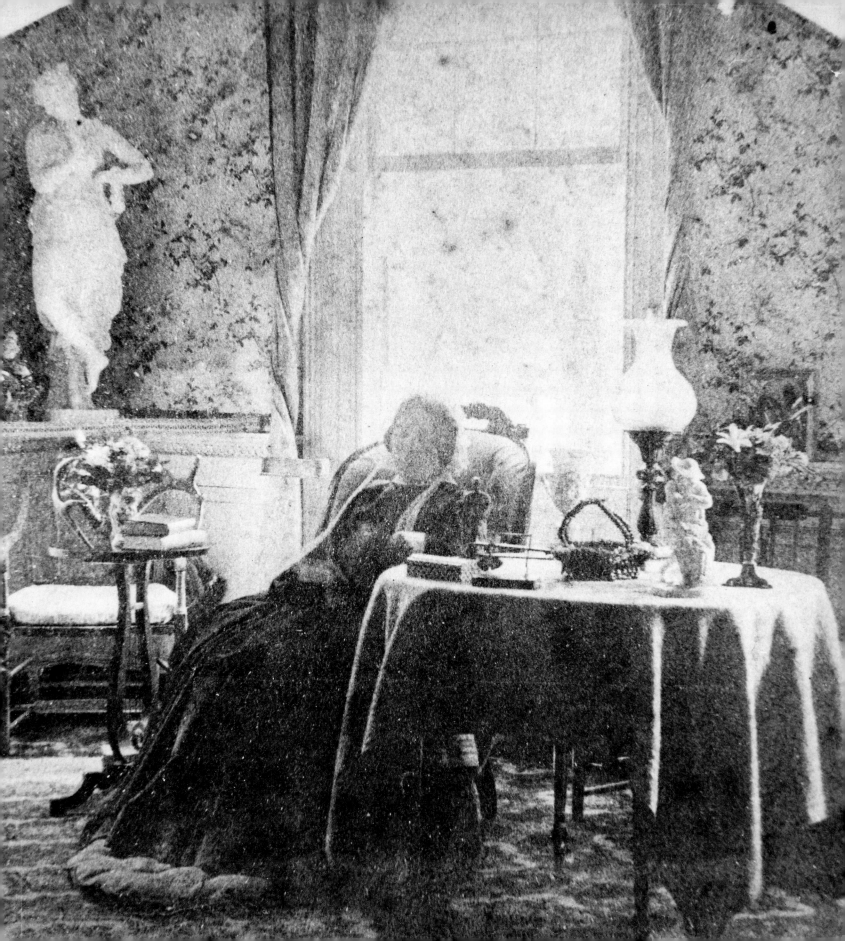

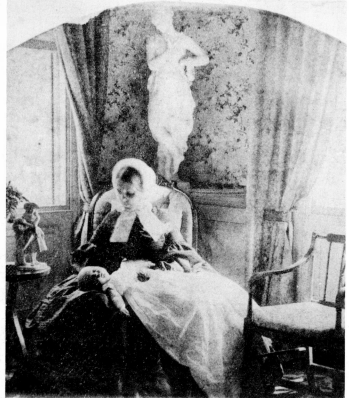

3

**3.** Mrs. Hampton's young guest Sallie Baxter Hampton is posed with her sleeping baby in a family christening gown which Hamptons still use today. The chair, lyre table, and flower arrangement have been shifted to be included in the picture. Likewise, some importance must have been attached to the commonplace copy of the Antonio Canova marble on the corner shelf. Sallie was a New York girl; her friend and confidante William Makepeace Thackeray had bemoaned her marriage to the rich Southerner, whom she had met at Saratoga Springs. This peaceful scene belies the anguish Sallie expressed in her letters over the impending crisis of war. While neither Sallie nor Mary Hampton was to live long enough to know it, the Civil War would draw a final curtain on the plantation world they knew. The contents of the Blanding Street mansion were dispersed at a public auction in 1867.

**4. Evening Prayer in an Anonymous Library, ca. 1860–65**

"The center table," wrote Andrew J. Downing in 1850, "is the emblem of the family circle." It was an old idea he urged people not to abandon. This room reflects urban middle-class taste of about 1840–50 with the old man seated in a Grecian chair adapted from the klismos found illustrated on ancient vases. The classical astral lamp was a predictable fixture on center tables of better quality. Fabric is shirred behind the glass of the Grecian bookcase, a practice followed in nearly every instance to protect bindings from the light. The walls are papered in panels that simulate painted stucco. On the right, the lady's Elizabethan chair seems to be the one exception in this otherwise Grecian room.

4

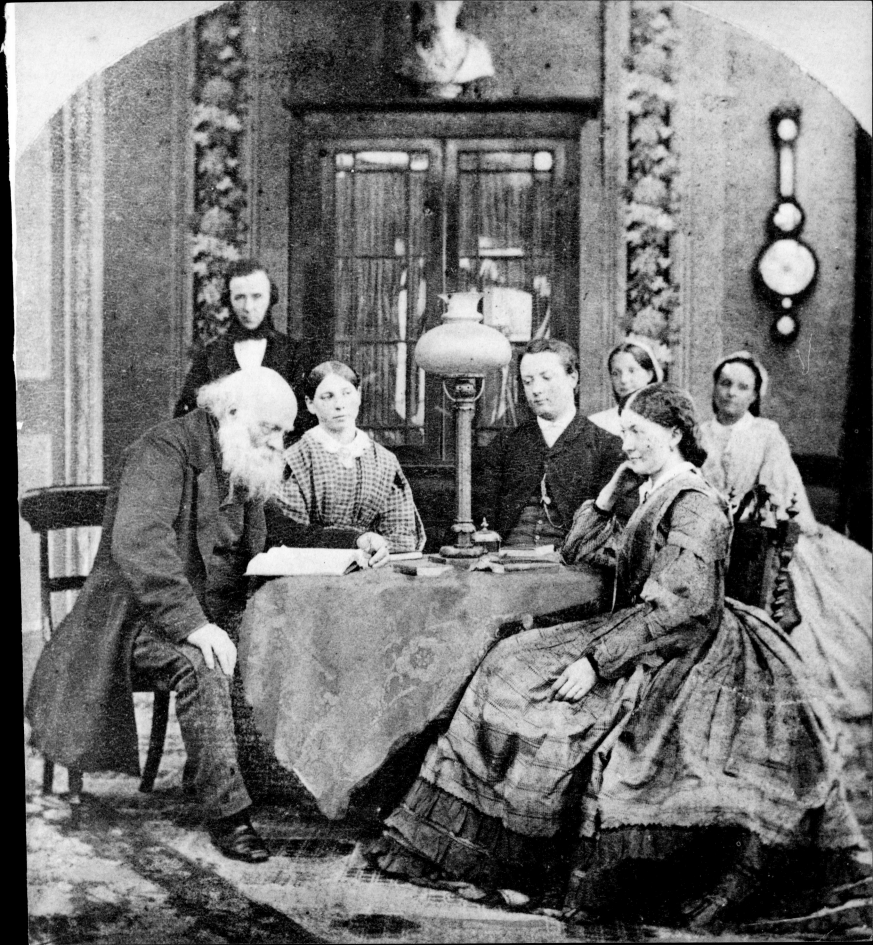

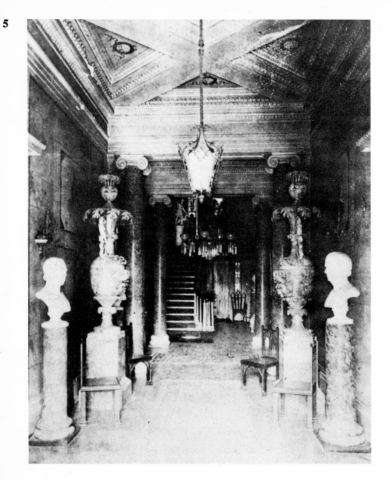

**5. Hallway, Phil-Ellena, House of George W. Carpenter, Germantown, Pennsylvania, ca. 1860–65**

With the assistance of Nathan Smedley, a master builder, and possibly the architect William Johnson, Mr. Carpenter built his mansion, Phil-Ellena, in about 1840–42. It was the great pride of his life, and in 1883 he wrote a book describing its magnificence. The house reputedly cost $150,000; it had the look of some English pump rooms in planned cities of the Regency era. The entrance hall ran the depth of the central block. It was cold and monumental in a way considered ideal for Grecian interiors. The gasoliers were of a kind manufactured in Philadelphia at mid-century. There were rich plaster ornaments, frescoes, and marbled columns. Marble busts, giant vases, and Gothic revival side chairs were set along the central passageway leading to the stairs. Off another hall that crossed the entrance hall were parlors, library, and dining room, while farther back the stairs rose to an art gallery and bedrooms. The roof was crowned by a lantern designed after the Monument of Lysicrates that was accessible from the rest of the house. Phil-Ellena, destroyed in 1900, was pre-Civil War American domestic building at its grandest.

**6. Parlor, Woodlawn, Richmond, Kentucky, ca. 1860–65**

Built in 1822, Woodlawn was considered, until its demolition early in the twentieth century, one of the choice examples of so-called Kentucky Federal architecture. The parlor shows the accumulations of forty years, and is a virtual index of early furniture manufacture in America. There is a fancy chair from the 1820's, a Grecian mantel glass perhaps of the same decade, and a library table and scenic wallpaper which must have been contemporary with the house. During the 1830's and 1840's, the family probably acquired the Grecian Plain style sofa, which is covered in horsehair, the stool covered in damask, and the rocker in morocco. The doors are grained, and all the woodwork is white, except for the mantel, which, following a very common custom, is painted black and varnished. An oil lamp of about 1860 is seen on the right. In its overall impression, this parlor illustrates the Grecian taste of about 1840.

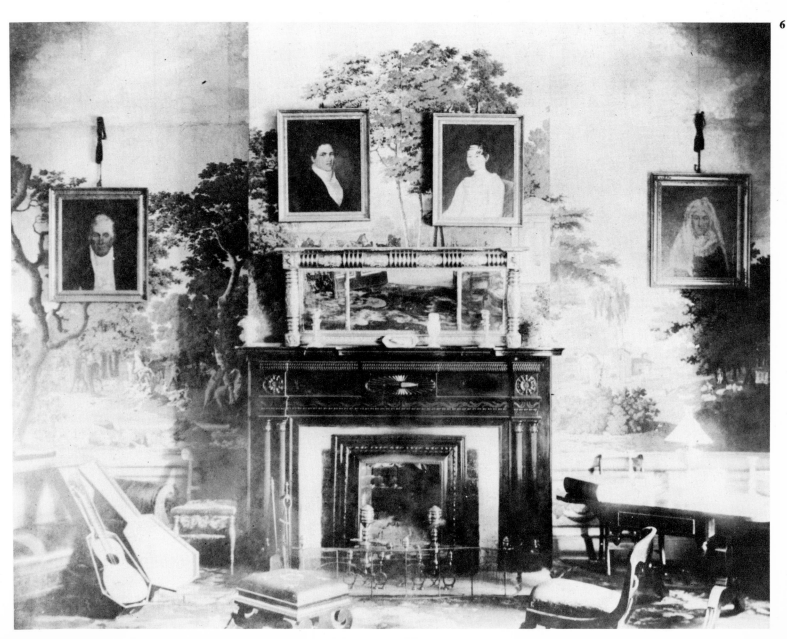

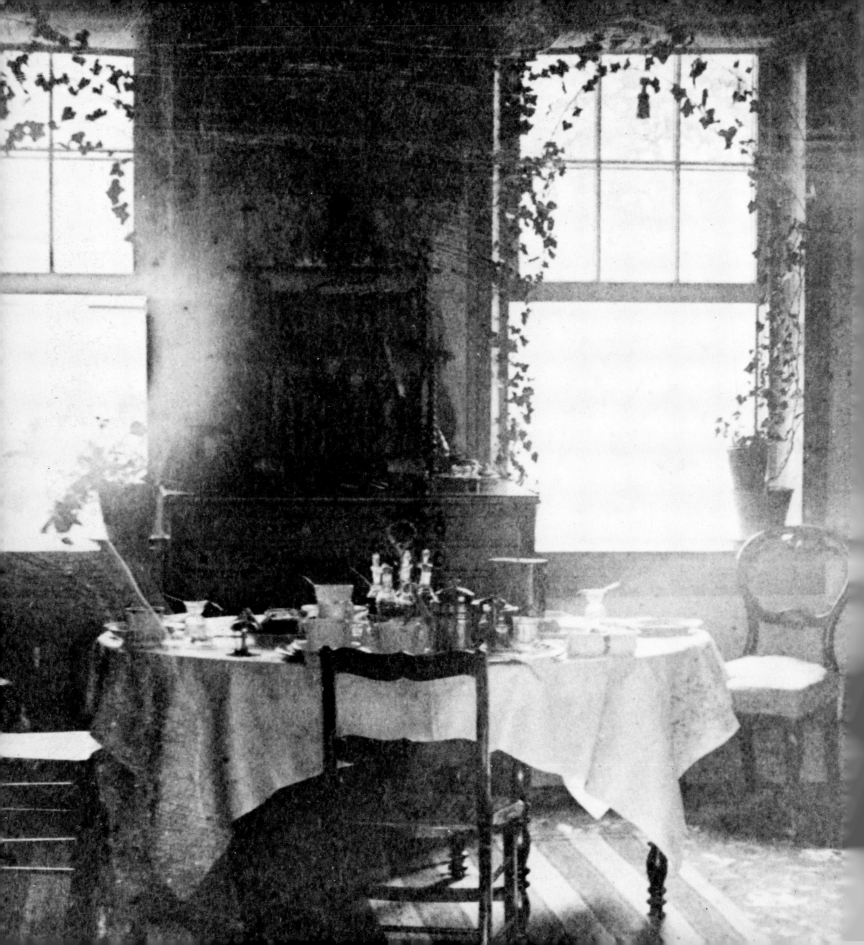

## 6

**House of Titian Ramsay Peale, 256 G Street, Washington, D.C., 1862**

A son of the famous naturalist and painter Charles Willson Peale, Titian Peale was principal examiner of the United States Patent Office and was an early and important amateur photographer. Perhaps he made some of the following views inside his three-story red-brick row house as an experiment, to occupy an idle summer afternoon during the Civil War. As was apparently the case in many similar middle-class row houses, there were two rooms to a floor, with bedrooms at the ground level, parlor and dining room on the second, and bedrooms above that. The kitchen was either in the basement or in an outbuilding.

7. Overlooking the vine-hung back porches of houses in the next block, the dining room seems to be set for breakfast, with big coffee cups, an egg boiler, egg cups, jellies, and bread. An oilcloth is spread over the carpet beneath the table to catch crumbs.

8. In another season, the dining room has become a library, with an Elizabethan secretary-bookcase whose doors are curtained, a trough beneath the window for prints, and books on the sideboard. A table cover not unlike Mary Hampton's *(2)* is on the dining table, which has a center lamp fed by a hose from the gasolier. Brussels carpeting covers the floor of this room and the adjoining parlor that faces the street.

9. The parlor, separated by double doors from the dining room, is the most ornamental room in the house. Titian Peale, after having doubtless set the camera himself, poses among works of art by members of his family.

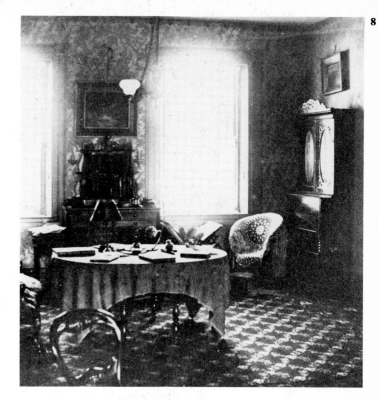

8

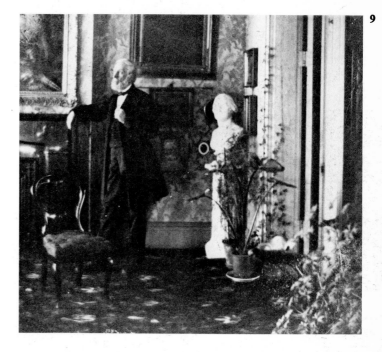

9

7

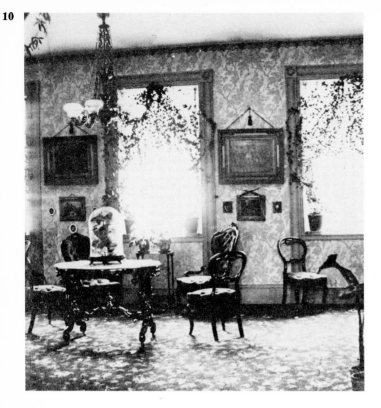

10

**10.** From where Peale was standing, he probably got this view of the parlor with its patterned wallpaper and what is likely to be fawn-colored woodwork. The gasolier is a mate to the one in the dining room, only it has six jets instead of four; these were sometimes called a parlor pair, made for just such rooms as these. Potted vines have been trained to drape over the street windows. The pictures are clustered and seem to panel the walls, their hanging devices made fully noticeable to add drama and geometric interest to the arrangement. While this room, in contrast to the Grecian parlor at Woodlawn *(6)*, is the beau ideal middle-class parlor in the French Antique style, the center table is Renaissance revival and the smaller table a common version of an Elizabethan revival piece.

**11.** The tufted side chairs in the parlor are apparently covered in figured damask. A parlor grand piano of a kind that sold for $100–200 from 1848 until about 1855, was the universal symbol of middle-class refinement in America for forty years. This one, beneath a huge oil painting almost certainly of the kind executed by the gross in Europe for the United States market, is further dignified by the presence of one of Rembrandt Peale's portraits of Washington. Small arrangements of real and artificial flowers show the era's aesthetic love of imitating reality and throwing true and false together for contrast.

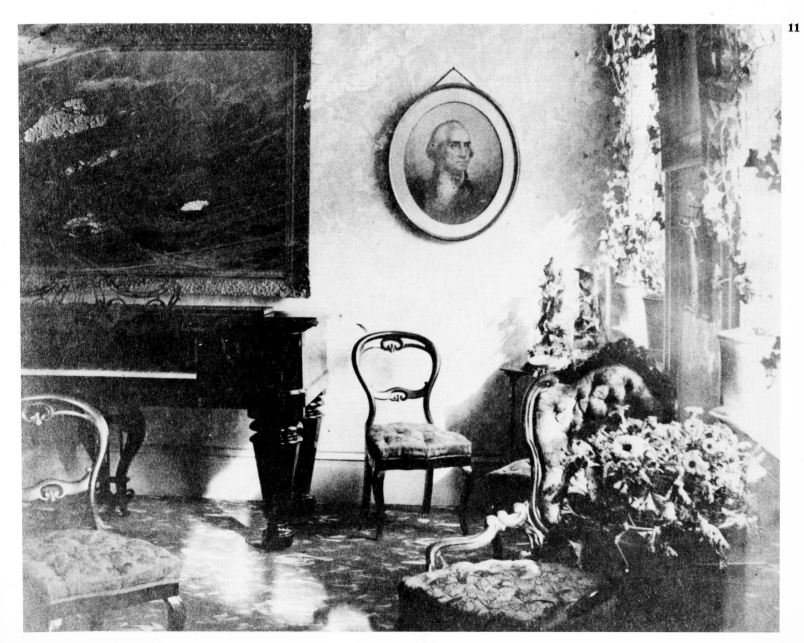

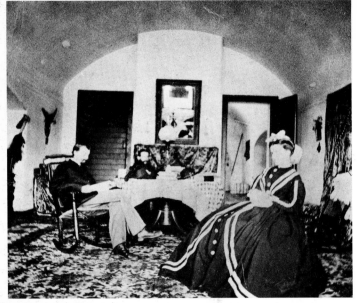

12

### 12. Casemate Interior, Fort Monroe, Virginia, 1863

Fort Monroe, at the tip of the Virginia peninsula, was a bastion of Union strength and a crossroads of Union movements during the Civil War. Upriver, on the James, lay Richmond, the capital of the Confederacy. It has always been the lot of military families to improvise in decorating their quarters, and this room, partitioned off in one of the raw-brick vaults beneath the walls of the fort, is beautified largely with fabric, such as might have been folded away quickly in a trunk. Ill-fitting curtains, a makeshift lambrequin on the mantel, and what appears to be a draped box in the left-hand corner, are mixed with a fine oil lamp, a few little pictures, a stuffed bird, and furniture and carpeting probably provided by the army.

### 13. Bedroom, House of Dr. Henry K. Oliver, 10 Joy Street, Boston, Massachusetts, 1866

In Dr. Oliver's house of about 1830, a mahogany bedroom set in the Renaissance revival style of the middle 1850's has been placed in the second room of what was usually called a double parlor. With housing so scarce in postwar Boston, and so many veterans in town looking for work, perhaps the Olivers had rented some of their bedrooms on the upper floors. At any rate, it is summertime and the bed was probably moved from the confining and hot left-hand corner to take better advantage of evening breezes, even though it covers what must be a hall door and lies dangerously beneath the gasolier. Straw matting has been tacked down over the floors, probably on a bed of newspapers or greens, and might well have been replaced or covered up by carpeting in the autumn.

13

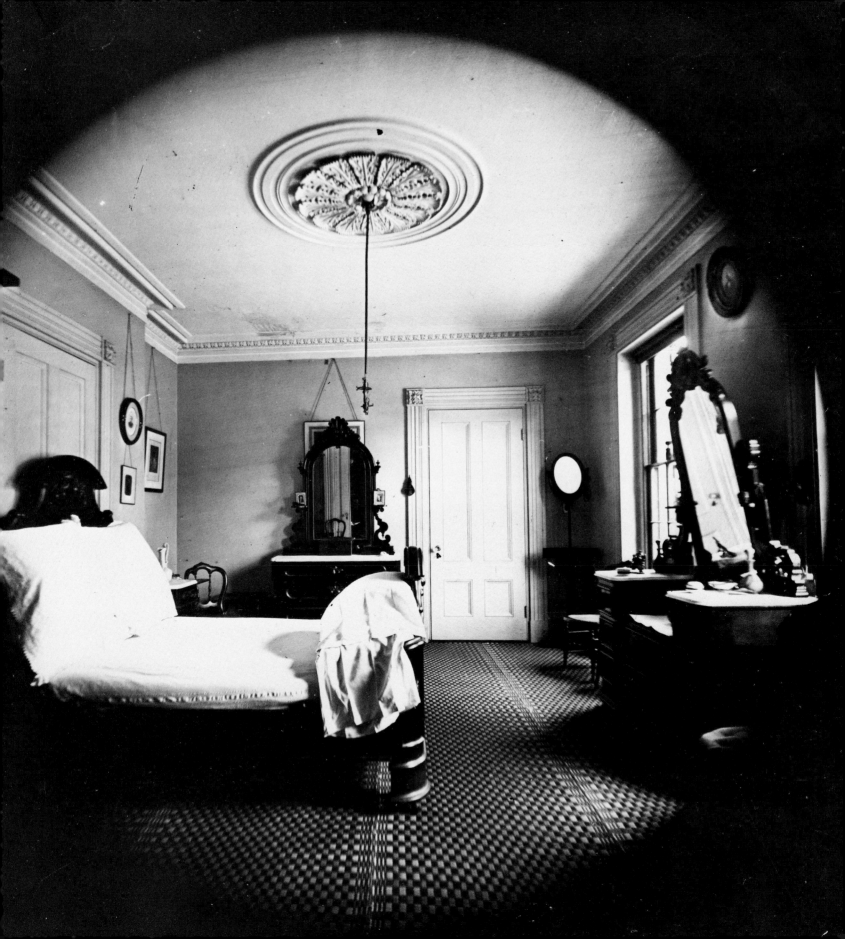

## 14. Drawing Room, House of James and Eliza Brown, 21 University Place, New York, New York, ca. 1868

Brown, a prominent Manhattan banker, had commissioned Leon Marcotte to remodel this room in 1846. Marcotte specialized in making both fine furniture and interior architectural elements, and had shops in New York and, until 1862, in Paris, by virtue of his partnership there with his father-in-law, a well-known French decorator named Emmanuel Ringuet LePrince. For the Browns, Marcotte probably executed the rich profile ornament and other embellishments, as well as some

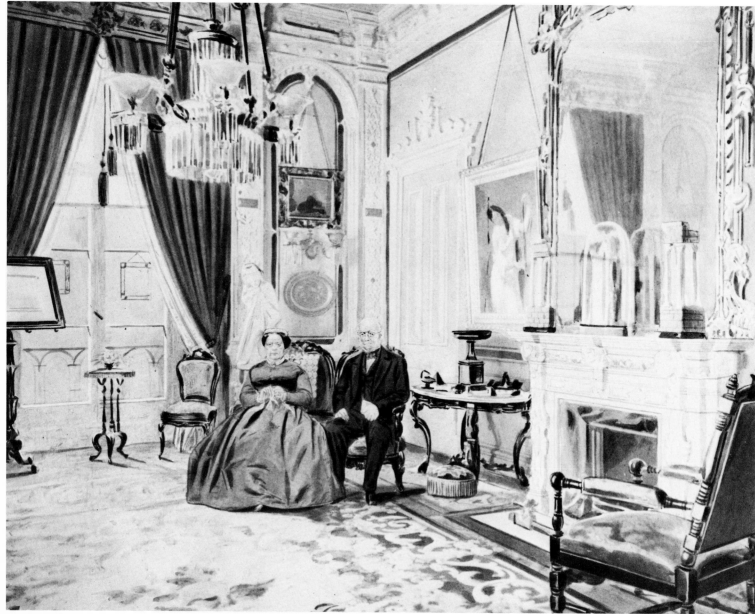

14

furniture. Through remodeling, the Grecian interior was converted to the François Premier taste. There are Renaissance tables, an Elizabethan easy chair, and other modes, but the room is predominantly French Antique. Eastman Johnson's later portrait of the Browns—now in the Metropolitan Museum of Art— shows the room had stone-colored trim, blue-green walls with darker borders, carpeting in russet, blue, and gold, and crimson hangings which look as though they were silk taffeta. Brown's wealth greatly increased during the Civil War, and when he built his new house on Park Avenue in 1869, he had some of Marcotte's ornaments torn from the old parlor and installed in the new. This photograph, though heavily retouched long ago to preserve a fading image, records the Brown's last days in their house on University Place.

### Elm Park, House of Le Grand Lockwood, Norwalk, Connecticut, ca. 1868–70

Elm Park was one of the most opulent private houses in the United States when it was completed in 1868. Begun during the Civil War from designs made by Detlef Lienau, who had studied architecture in Paris, it was extravagantly finished inside by Marcotte and furnished, in part, by the Herter brothers of New York. Le Grand Lockwood was one of many aggressive businessmen who made enormous fortunes, directly or indirectly, from the government's wartime needs. This house, still standing, has sixty rooms and fourteen bathrooms, as well as a great rotunda and immense halls. Monumental scale was used to effect a series of visual surprises among lavishly comfortable and friendly rooms. Lockwood died in 1872, and his widow, caught by the national panic, lost the house because she could not meet the final payment of the debt.

**15.** The Renaissance library, with adjacent conservatory and veranda, was executed by Marcotte largely in black walnut. As a high-style product of an interior decorator, this Venetian room is carefully calculated to achieve the desired effect: it is all new and it is all Renaissance in style, from the easy and side chairs, which seem to be covered either in plush or terry, to the great canopied sofa. The architectural woodwork and cabinets are seen against walls covered in imitation morocco. Fanciful lambrequins shape the light through the etched-glass doors to the conservatory, and the sofa and windows are similarly draped and laden with trimmings. While the

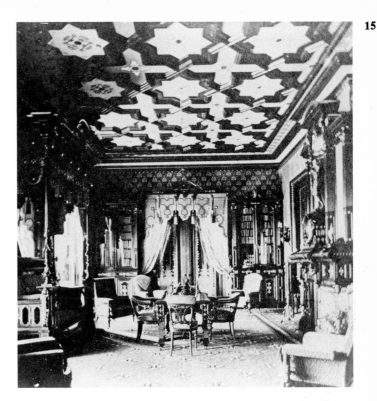

15

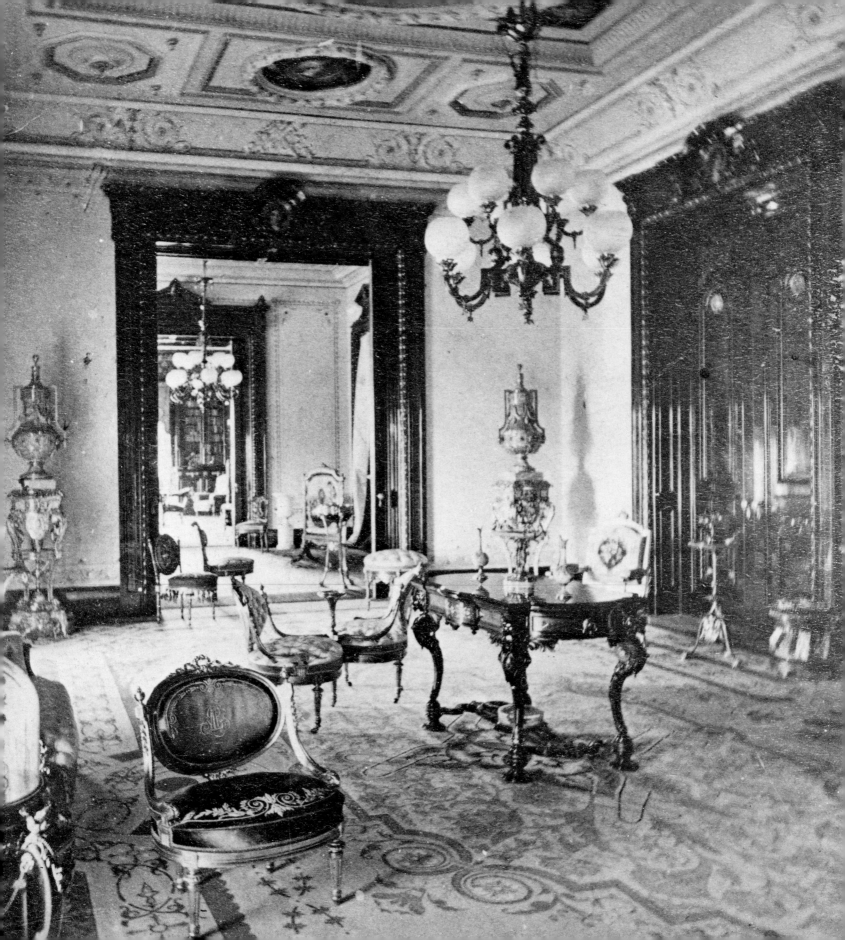

effect is very rich, a close look reveals that the room is actually restrained and anything but cluttered.

**16, 17.** In New York, both Marcotte and Christian Herter advertised their close connections with Paris, although in Paris neither were very important shops. This parlor is an Americanized version of the Louis Seize revival style current in the France of Napoleon III. The ceiling mural is called *Venus at Play with Her Cupids* and was ordered by Lockwood from the exclusive Paris shop of Pierre V. Galland, who specialized in that sort of interior decoration for public buildings and for the mansions of *nouveaux riches* businessmen. The carpeting here appears to be all one piece, rather than the customary strips, and its design echoes the patterned ceiling. As a foil for this detailing, the walls are left plain—not even paneled with pictures, according to the custom of the day. Central heating made possible the omission of a fireplace, although an elaborate French one was soon added. Sparse and airy, with its gay floral curtains, few objects of art, and one "old" item, the round girandole mirror of 1830 or so, this parlor shows the American Louis Seize revival in its first departure from actual historical models.

**18.** All the furniture in the music room was, presumably, by the Herter brothers; and their splendid woodwork is inlaid with cherubs performing music. Curiously, there is not a musical instrument in the room, and the Louis Seize revival furniture drifts even farther from historical reality in the center ottoman and delicate little side chairs. Between the two doors to the rotunda is a marble fireplace with divided flues that frame an etched-glass sheet, making it appear that there is no chimney. A major ingredient in the interiors of years to come was this sort of gadgetry, and a certain sense of humor which reminded the viewer that the room was not to be taken entirely seriously.

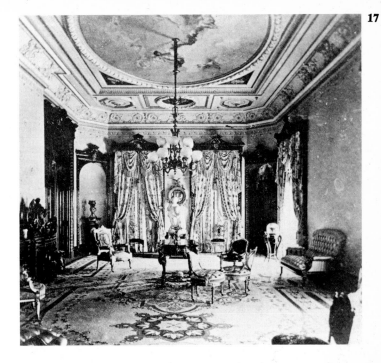

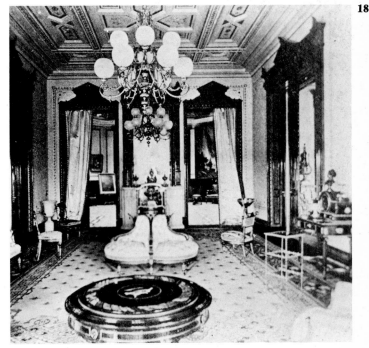

## 19. Sawtell's Ranch House, Fremont County, Idaho Territory, 1872

Contemporary with Lockwood's mansion but of a type which, in many variations, was far more familiar to most Americans, was this rough interior in the Idaho Territory. It was in a house built of logs, with stone chimneys and slab floors. Sand strewn over the floor and whitewash on the walls, joists, and ceilings kept the room fresh and improved its odor. Transient personal objects here outnumber everything else. Homemade tables, stools, shelves, and even a whittled Windsor chair to the left serve the Spartan shelter, while the heroic arrangement of rifles, pistols, gun belts, and spurs on the fireplace wall, though doubtless utilitarian, bears the unmistakable touch of the age.

## House of Leland Stanford, Sacramento, California, 1869–71

Leland Stanford, a young and obscure New York lawyer, moved West well before the Civil War and, after making a fortune as a Sacramento retail merchant, entered banking and finally the railroad business and Republican

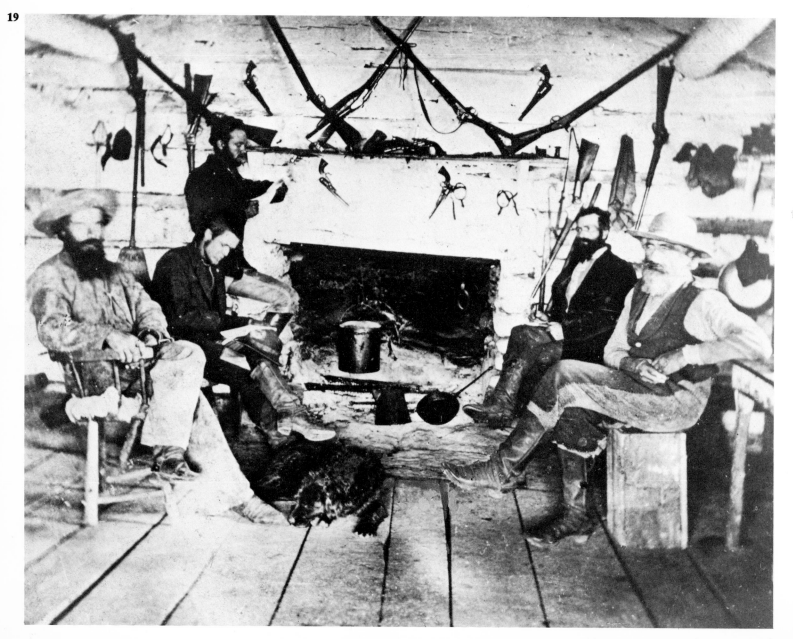

19

politics. In 1868, his big Italianate house in Sacramento was ruined by a flood, and he and Mrs. Stanford completely redecorated its interiors, ordering furniture, curtains, and accessories from stores in the East, more than likely under the direction of a single outfitter, or commission merchant. Probably the furniture and ornaments were sent West by railroad late in 1869, for Stanford himself had driven the golden spike earlier that year, uniting the Central and Pacific lines and thus creating the first transcontinental railroad. Stanford could have afforded almost any kind of interiors; yet these, in marked contrast to Lockwood's modern rooms *(15–18)*, could have been assembled, more or less as they appear here, in the mid-1850's. While these rooms are not quite out of style, they are far from high style. On a smaller scale, they could have been found behind many brownstone fronts in St. Louis, New York, Chicago, and Pittsburgh.

**20.** In the sitting and music rooms, Brussels carpeting covers the floor, and a gilded picture molding—probably ochre-laquered silver leaf—is apparently the only break in the stark white walls and woodwork. A damask lambrequin, trimmed in fringes, tassels, and

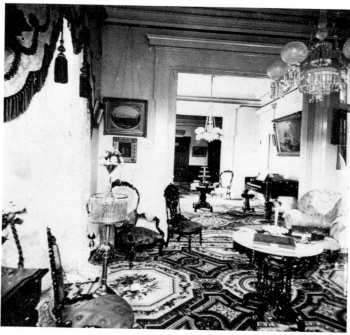

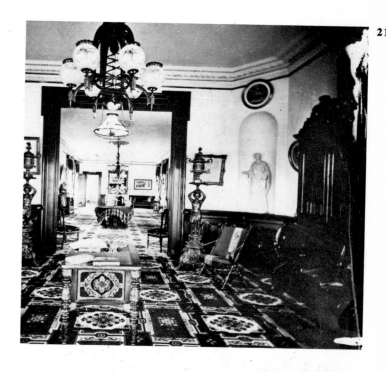

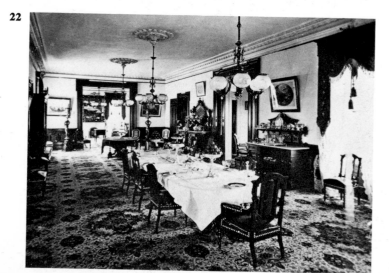

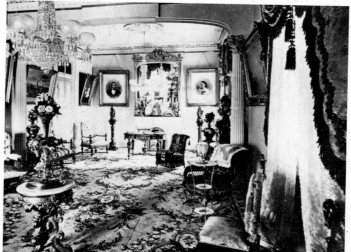

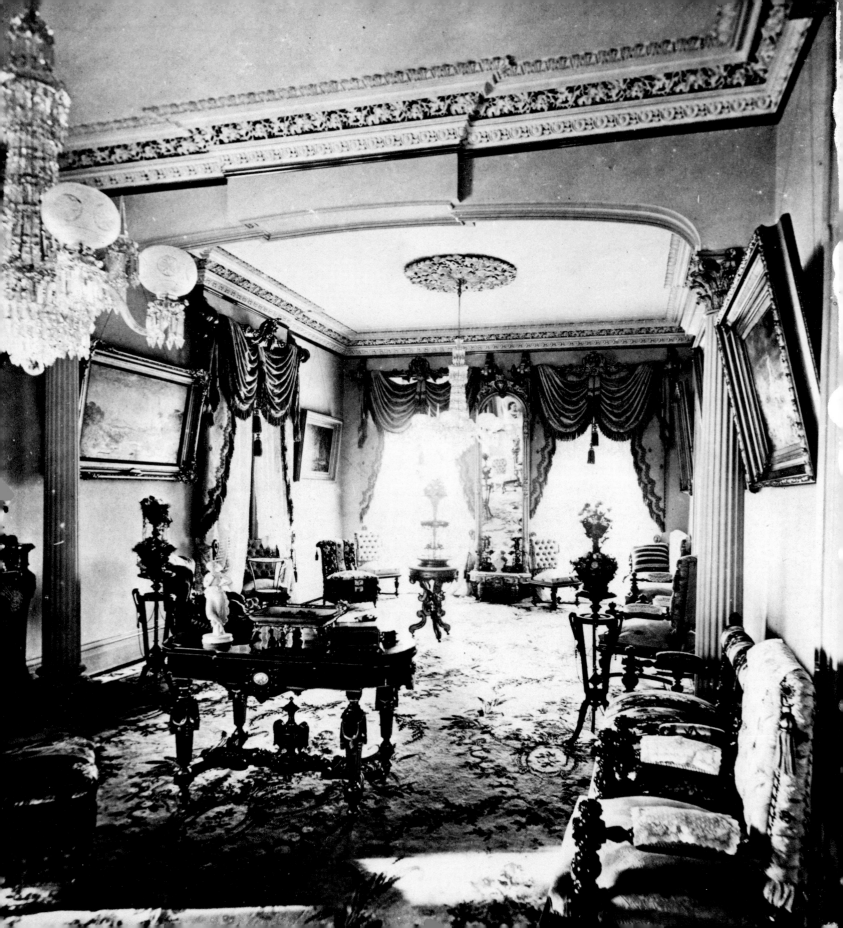

gimp, makes a valance over lace curtains. French Antique chairs and an easy chair, or so-called comfortable, in that same style are mixed with Renaissance center tables and an Elizabethan side chair. The antimacassars are probably the work of Mrs. Stanford herself; if so they are the only personal touches in any of these rooms, besides the flower arrangements.

**21.** The view from the library mantel into the dining room shows a comfortable wainscoted chamber decorated with white walls, damask lambrequins, and marble statues set into niches in the corners. Over the statues are round photographs of classical sculptures. The gasolier hanging above the Flemish center desk has a separate reading lamp on a movable arm, which lowers and, by means of an India-rubber hose, gives gaslight up close.

**22.** The dining room, which opens at the side into the music room, is furnished in the Renaissance style with leather seats on the chairs. Prints, enlarged photographs, and what appear to be quantities of silverplate— very popular at the time—are the main decorations. The room, with the table set for dessert, is famous for a certain banquet. Leland Stanford, Jr., born to parents who had been childless for many years, was brought to this table at a stag party for his father's friends; the infant, on a bed of rosebuds, was concealed beneath the silver meat cover until just the right moment. "Gentlemen," said Stanford, lifting the cover, "I present my son!"

**23, 24.** While their architectural features are Italianate, the parlors are primarily French Antique. The basic parlor set is Elizabethan, but it is deeply tufted in a pale fabric and mixed with a Louis Quinze center table, and a bigger table in the Louis Seize style is situated near the fireplace. There is at least one French Antique chair, and the carpet would have been considered French, as were the pier mirrors. Such a lined-up furniture arrangement belongs more to the Grecian mode than to its French Antique successor, which could fill the whole floor, taking full advantage of the gaslight overhead. Brocade lambrequins are enriched with swags cast, or thrown, over gilded wooden poles; the lace curtains are crisp and spotless and tied back low, almost at the level of the baseboards. Presumably the flowers are real, for the Stanfords were great gardeners, importing camellias and

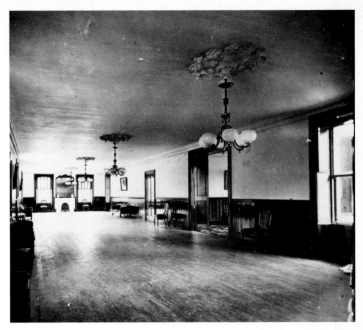

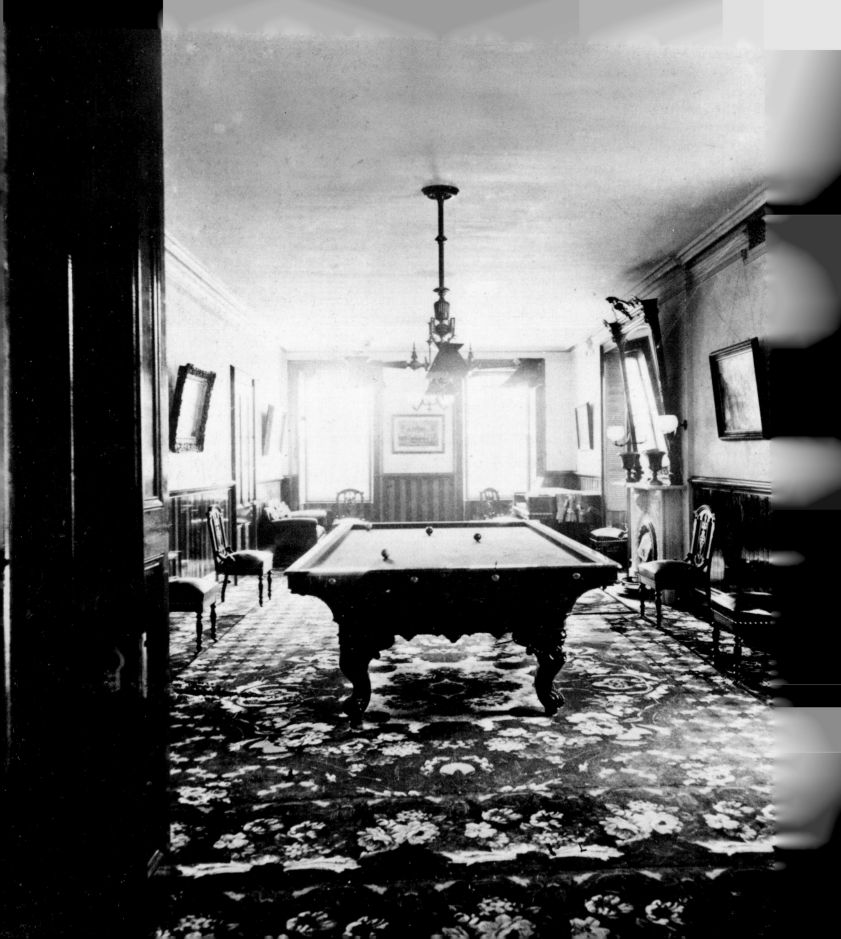

many other flowering plants to Sacramento in the 1860's and 1870's before they moved on to San Francisco to a far more magnificent house.

**25, 26.** An exercise room and a billiard room were frequently found in mansions of these years. Such interior spaces supported the popular idea that a house should be a place of family amusement and entertainment. The idea rapidly became part of a philosophy of American house-building, and by the 1890's, "finished attics" were quite common even in small houses. Stanford's billiard table seems to have been manufactured using some of the components of a French Antique parlor piano. The chairs are like those in the dining room, and the gasolier was a kind made especially for use in this sort of room, hospitals, and in saloons. Exercise rooms could be used as play-rooms or ballrooms. Nearly always plain, they were frequently ceiled with cheap, pine railroad-car siding.

### 27, 28. Parlor, House of Benjamin Silliman, 34 Hillhouse Avenue, New Haven, Connecticut, 1870

This Yale professor was an outspoken critic of the decorative arts, saying, "The solemn affectation of Greek and Roman forms" was "ridiculous" and that classical furnishings were "ponderous and frigid monstrosities." His own parlor, according to these pictures, contained little that was not classical. Though behind the times, the room does show changing trends. Mixed with the scenic wallpaper, the family portraits, the prints, and the Grecian chairs, tables, and rocker from various periods, are quantities of little things—shells, teapots, photographs, statuettes—which show an increasing interest in the addition of personal touches. The careful arrangement of pictures on the face of the mural is also expressive of such personalizing, although it seems to have been quite common to hang pictures on scenic wallpaper. In this instance, some of the personalizing may have been the work of the professor's daughters. It was, by and large, a household of females, with three Irish servants; and Professor Silliman led an active public life elsewhere.

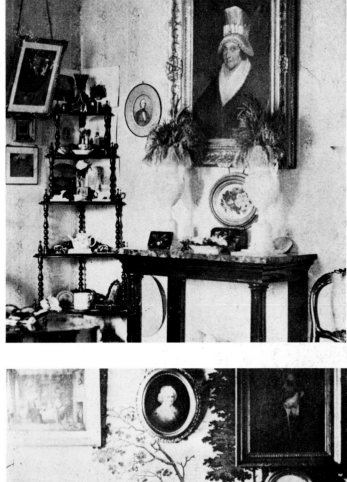

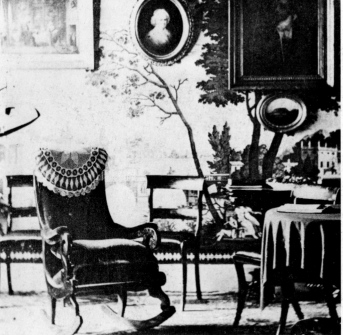

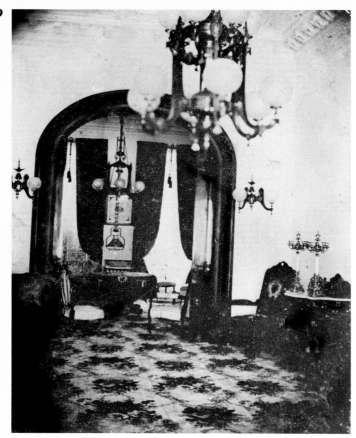

### 29. Double Parlor, House of Marcus Mead, 149 Madison Avenue, New York, New York, 1870

In summer attire, the Mead parlors are a mixture of French Antique and Elizabethan furniture, with what appears to be a center, or dining, table of about 1830 in the rear. The gasoliers are rather new, and the one in the second parlor has a reading light, similar to Leland Stanford's *(21)*, pulled down over the table. Notwithstanding the predominantly Elizabethan furniture, this room, for its architecture alone, would probably have been considered Renaissance. The contrast between vast white walls, dark-grained woodwork, and dark furniture, all set firmly on the lavish floral carpets, doubtless in reds, blues, beige, and violet, imparts some of that sense of sumptuousness a middle-class parlor could achieve.

### 30. Parlor, House of Nathaniel Wheeler, Bridgeport, Connecticut, ca. 1870

Wheeler bought his house in 1866 from the widow of its builder, Henry Harral, and soon did some redecorating. Two New York City painters—usually then called decorators—changed this from a Gothic parlor into one in the New Grecian style, with brightly painted ceilings and borders. The object of the New Grecian style, one of the foremost of the creative revivals, was to build upon the already familiar interior and furniture designs of the earlier Grecian movement and create something totally new. Bright colors were employed in making polychromatic, necklace-like borders on the walls; ebonized woodwork and furniture was used as a foil to many kinds of Grecian colors and textures. This set of French Antique furniture in the Louis Seize style is covered in satin, either pale blue or pink, an attempt to conceal most of the historical qualities the set might have, so it would not interfere with the New Grecian theme. The two major tables are New Grecian and contemporary with the photograph, as is the New Grecian pier mirror and credenza, the latter being one of those mammoth inventions of the time meant to replace the fireplace as the focal point of the centrally heated room. A heat register from the furnace is worked into the design of this credenza. Wheeler's parlor is an excellent example of the drift from the historical to the creative revivals that began in the late 1860's.

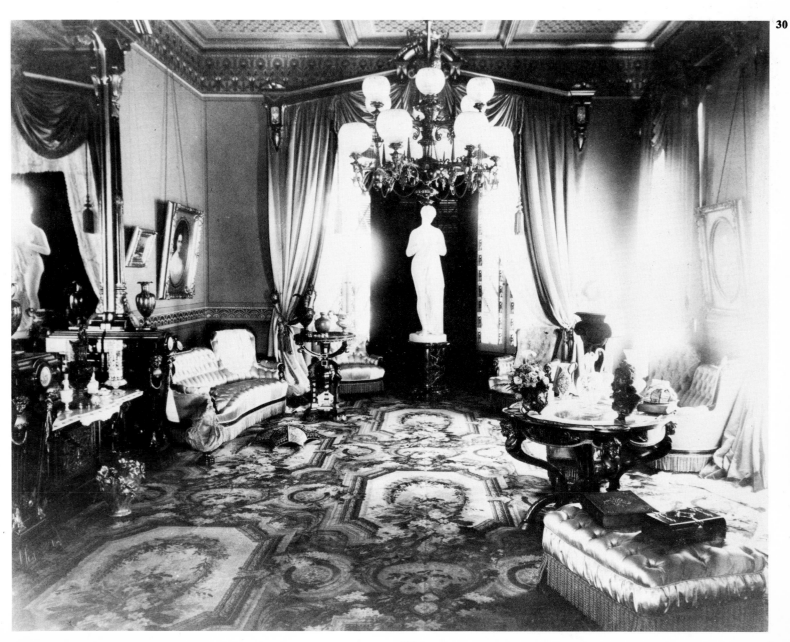

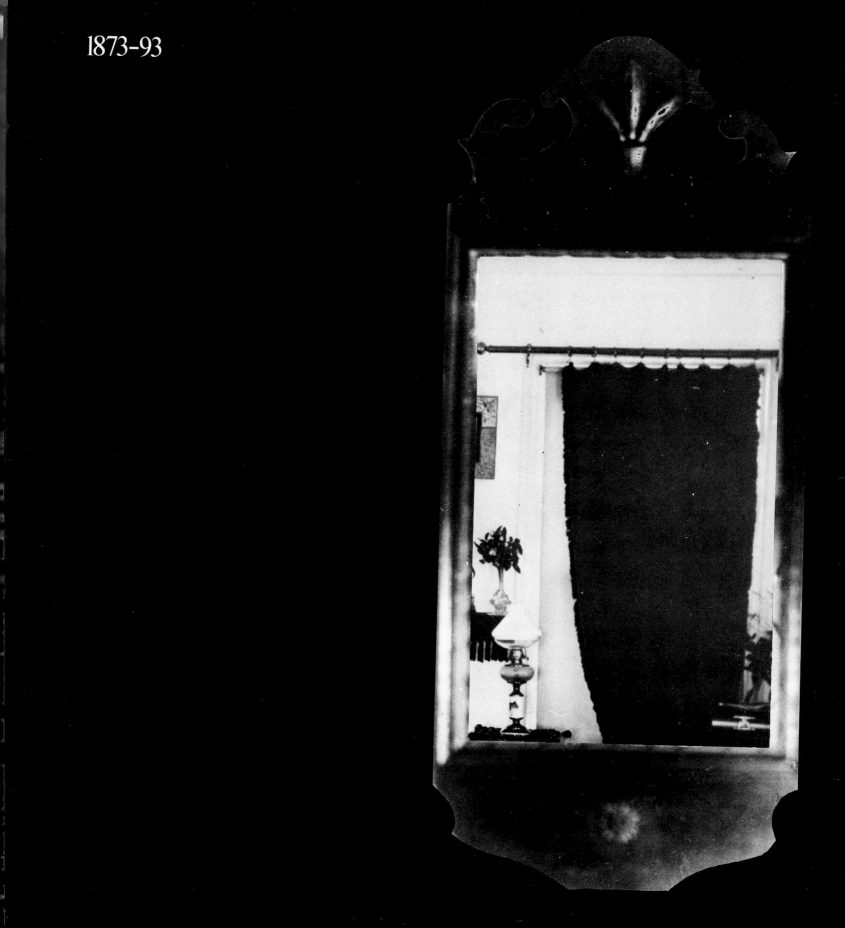

1873-93

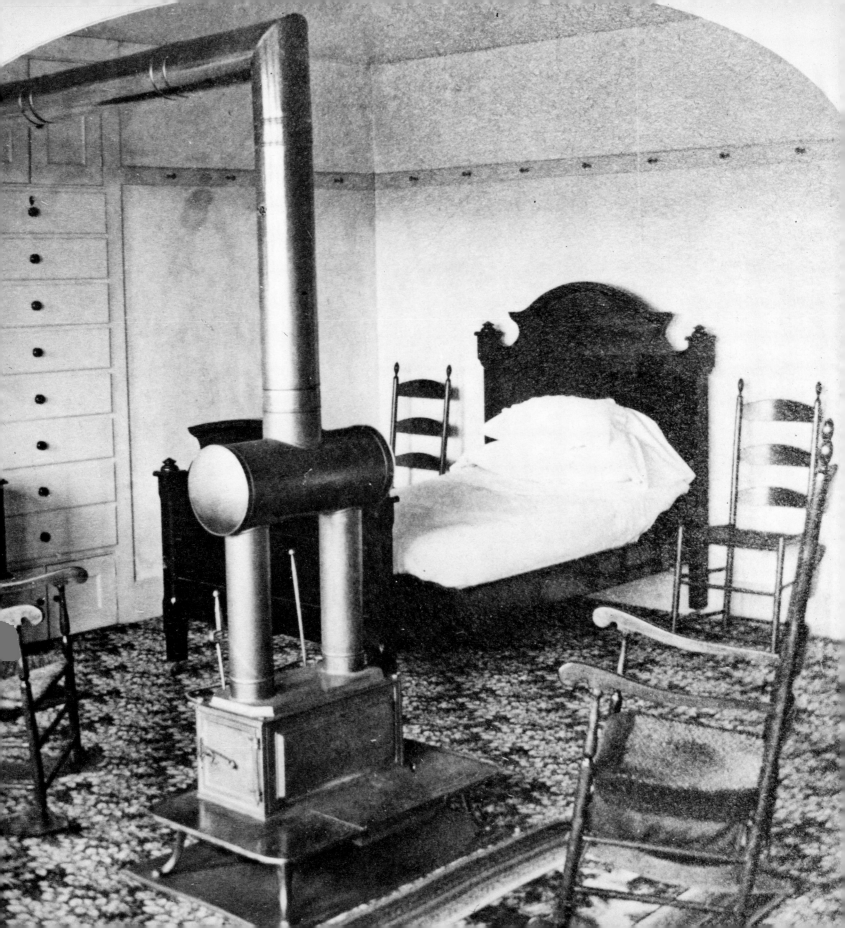

### 31. Shaker Retiring Room, Enfield, New Hampshire, ca. 1870–76

The force of the new in decorative arts was being felt everywhere; the message was heralded by the masses of manufactured styles which appeared nearly everywhere. Furniture historians are interested in the Shaker sect because it brought together and perpetuated many kinds of vernacular designs. In the face of the rise of manufactures, the Shakers clung to the old, making only subtle and practical modifications reflecting contemporary interests in comfort and convenience. But after the Civil War, divisions grew within the Shaker communities, and rooms such as the one pictured here reveal the new shade of worldliness that possessed some of the believers. The floor is covered with a floral carpet, and the hearth rug is cut from a fancy French Brussels pattern. Though the bed is plain, it is unmistakably designed in the Renaissance vocabulary of mass furniture production. In that bed, the Shakers follow manufactured style quite as closely as they follow vernacular style in the more characteristic Shaker chairs. This kind of contrast, however, was occurring all over the United States.

### 32. Parlor, House of General Joseph Anderson, 113 West Franklin Street, Richmond, Virginia, 1870–75

Disrobed for summer, the Anderson parlor is stripped of its window hangings and carpeting, and straw matting has been tacked down on the floors. Here is a walnut Renaissance parlor set, of medium price, mixed with better furniture of older vintage. The setting is the work of a decorator, with its French Antique and Gothic side chairs, classical bust and mantel garniture, the remainders, undoubtedly, of a time when the whole room more or less matched the big mirror, window cornices, and French-style gasolier. In spite of the mixture, the room is essentially in the French Antique vein, kept consciously up to date by the addition of new manufactured furnishings.

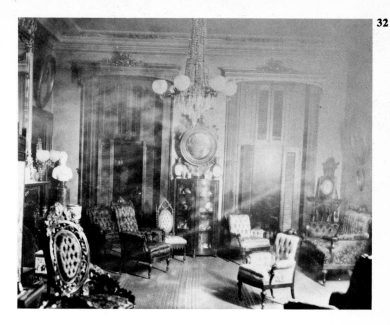

32

31

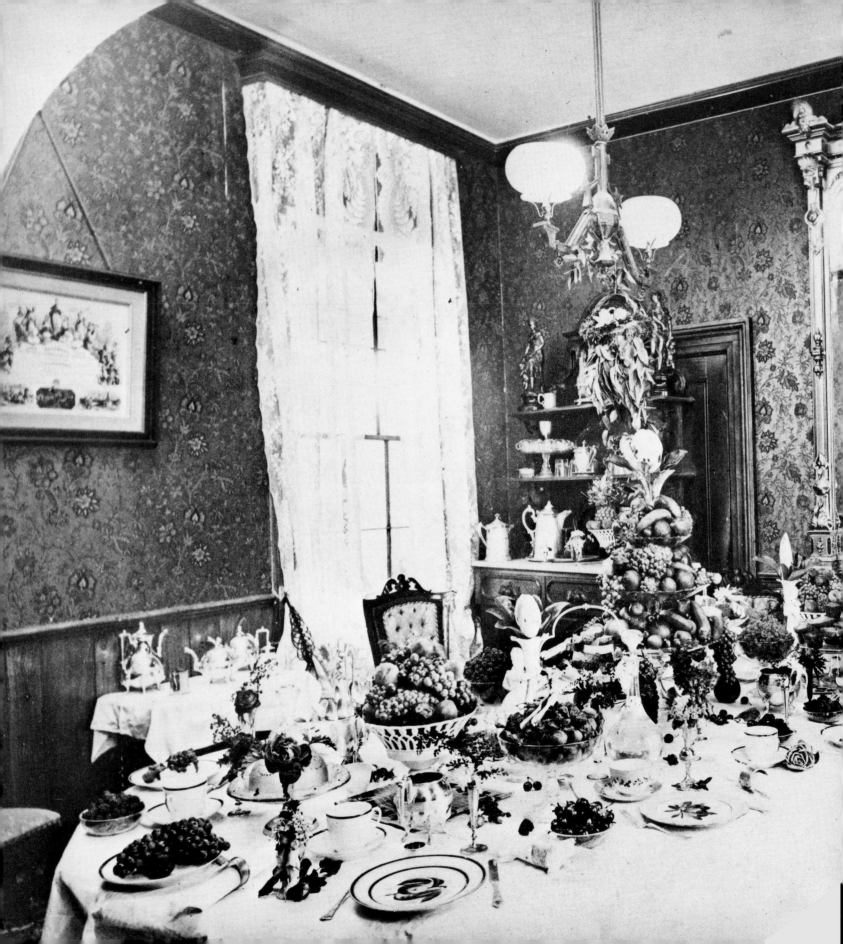

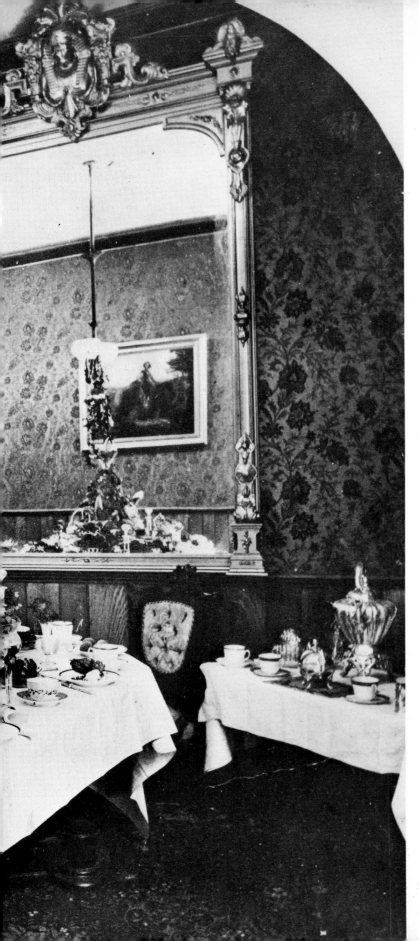

## House of John Thomas Little, Pacific and Buchanan Streets, San Francisco, California, ca. 1875

A native of Castine, Maine, John Little arrived in California at the peak of the Gold Rush, having crossed the Isthmus of Panama in the winter of 1849. He soon engaged in the mercantile business, and later in the grain business. He moved into this house in 1866 after returning to San Francisco from seven years in Canada. Here he lived with his wife and eleven children, and enjoyed success as an independent real-estate agent.

**33.** The dining room table, set for dessert for twelve, is covered with a crisp cloth and crowned with an epergne piled with fresh apples, oranges, bananas, grapes, and plums. Glass bowls of strawberries and blueberries, and china fruit baskets filled with plums, grapes, and cherries give varied height to the table setting; loose cherries are scattered in an orderly way among the decanters, cups, plateaus, plates, silver, and vases. Cascading from the lighted gasolier, a bird's-nest of leaves and fruit meets the centerpiece. Table settings, of course, do not last; but they were some of the grandest and commonest expressions of nineteenth-century domestic art, which thrived on the temporary. As many varieties of table furnishings were manufactured as there were sets for parlors.

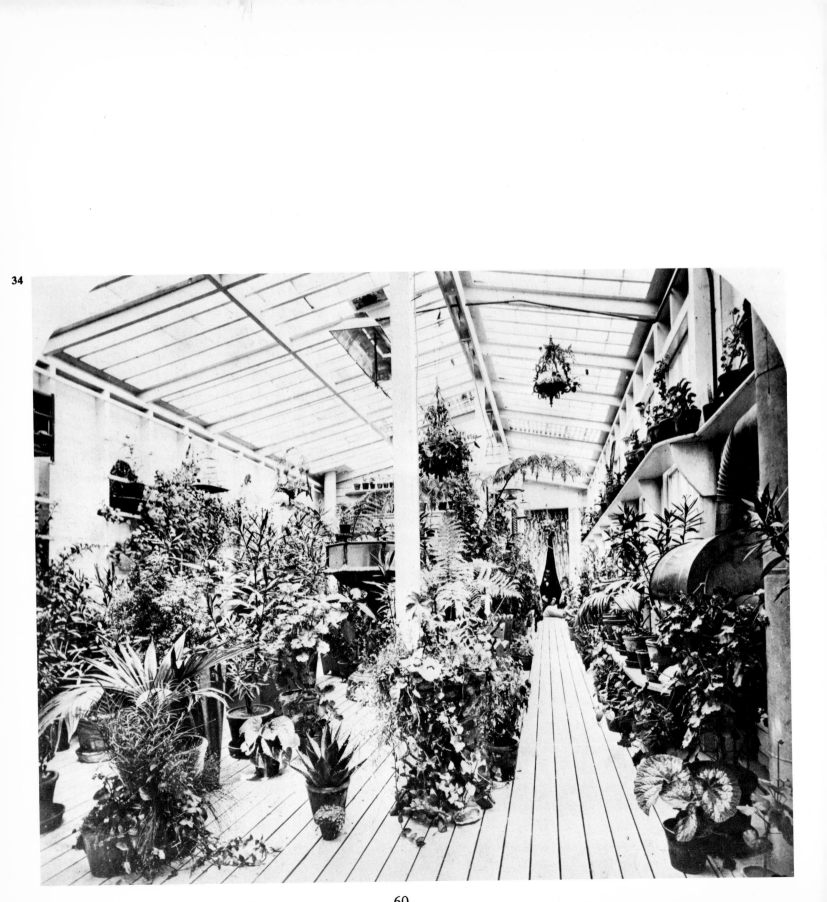

**34.** Another temporary fascination was the conservatory, which could be an adapted window box or, like Mr. Little's, an elaborate contrivance in wood and glass attached to the house and opening from a main parlor or hallway. Finished in cheap lumber and probably whitewashed inside, the Little conservatory has rows of potted plants set upon shelves and on the slatted floor. A fountain in the center of an informal arrangement of larger plants, sits beneath a special conservatory gasolier with reflector. Parlor floral pieces rested, and were renewed, beneath the skylights, and stoves warmed the chilly air.

Ten days or two weeks without water and this whole scene, so lovingly assembled, would vanish. Healthy and well-maintained house plants and flowers, besides being organic and thus aesthetically appealing, were the proud symbols of the vigilant housewife.

**35, 36.** The first photograph shows the Little parlor as it was decorated probably in the late 1860's; the second view shows it in the mid-1870's, when changes were made to accommodate the upright piano. Initially, the Littles had a French parlor, its walls paneled with picture molding and its floors carpeted with Brussels. The furn-

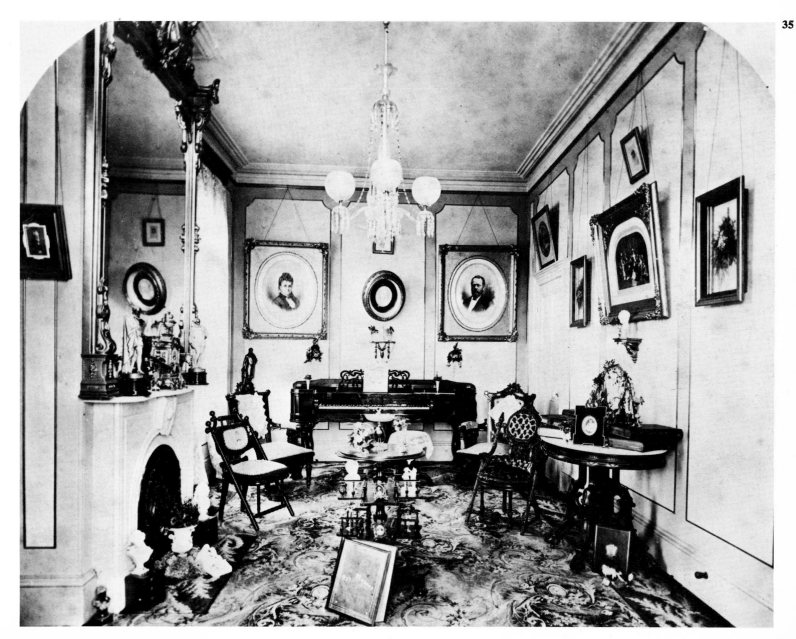

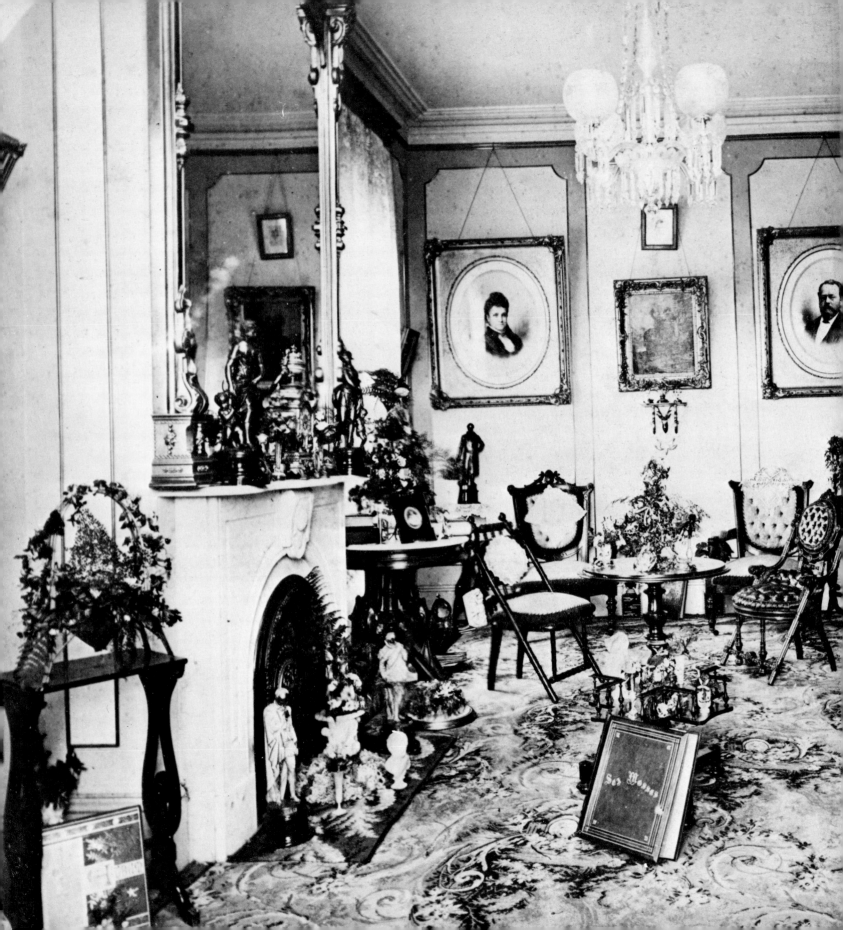

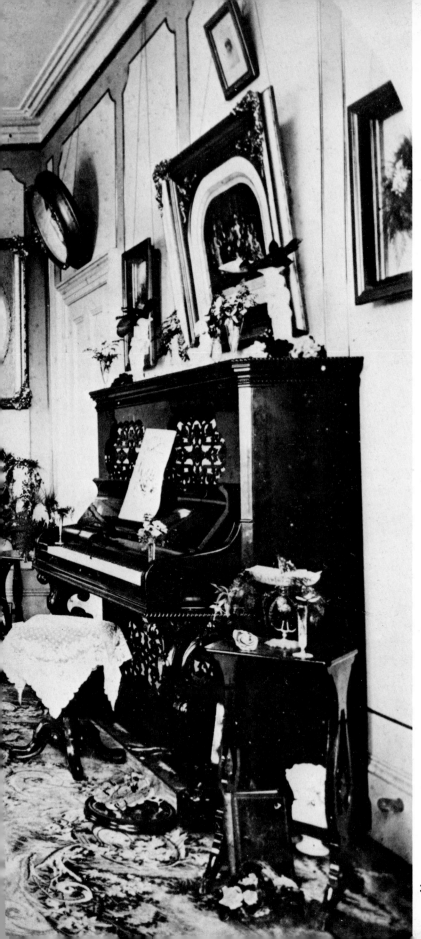

ishings were creative revivals of the late 1860's and early 1870's stemming from several early revivals, like the Grecian table to the right, the two Louis Seize armchairs flanking the square piano, and the two Renaissance chairs forward. Photographs and art pictures adorn the walls. To the rear, between the photographic portraits, is a cameo *bas-relief* probably of a family member. Such cameo profiles could be commissioned by mail from various places in Italy and the United States by sending only a photograph to the studio.

In the new furniture and object arrangement, the cameo has been hung over the doorway. Floral arrangements have been brought in from the conservatory, and the accessories have been regrouped into art units, which are now the dominant features of the parlor. This pair of photographs illustrates how the concept of arrangement in rooms changes as fast as style, and that transient objects are the most telling features of room decoration.

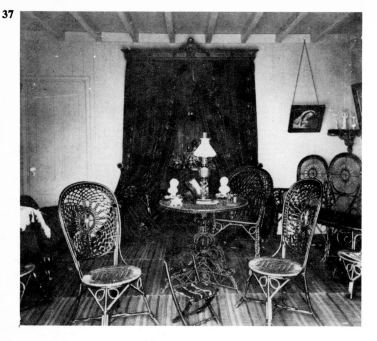

**37**

**38**

### 37. Parlor, Summer Cottage, Oak Bluffs, Martha's Vineyard, Massachusetts, ca. 1875

Rattan furniture became popular in the United States in the 1850's. Not necessarily porch or summer-house furniture, it was considered appropriate to mix with heavy parlor sets for variety of material and mass. This rattan, painted dark and varnished to a high gloss, contrasts with the whitewashed walls and straw matting. A French Antique Récamier sofa is seen to the left, near the doorway into the dining room, with its theatrical hangings. Decorated only for use in the summertime, the room imitates a summerized town parlor.

### 38. Parlor, Summer Cottage, Oak Bluffs, Martha's Vineyard, Massachusetts, ca. 1875

A cottage set, upholstered in tufted horsehair, is outfitted with antimacassars for this summer house. The kerosene lamp on the center table stands beside a stereoscope of the kind that might have been used to view the original of this very picture. Matting, inexpensive prints in whittled, or rustic, frames and a piece of rattan complete the scene, with dark portieres on the dining-room door.

### 39. Parlor and Library, House of Commodore Cornelius Vanderbilt, 10 Washington Place, New York, New York, ca. 1875

Probably photographed several years before the Commodore's death in 1877, these rooms were of great interest to the public, for they were occupied by the most brazen of American self-made men, and one who had weathered the panic of 1873 unscarred. While the oriental porcelains and the embroidered silk cushion foretell the spread of the Anglo-Japanese style, the comfortable parlor and library are anything but palatial. The Turkish overstuffed sofa and chairs and the Louis Seize revival tête-à-tête are the luxurious trademarks of the finest hotel lobbies and riverboat saloons. It was, after all, such luxurious interior decoration that had first set the Commodore's Hudson River steamers apart from those of his competitors. New Grecian woodwork, French Antique gasolier, and flowery wallpaper, mixed carefully with the furniture beneath a ceiling of dark-stained wooden strapwork on a white background, have the uninspired, but adequately fashionable, look of a house brought up to date by an interior decorating company.

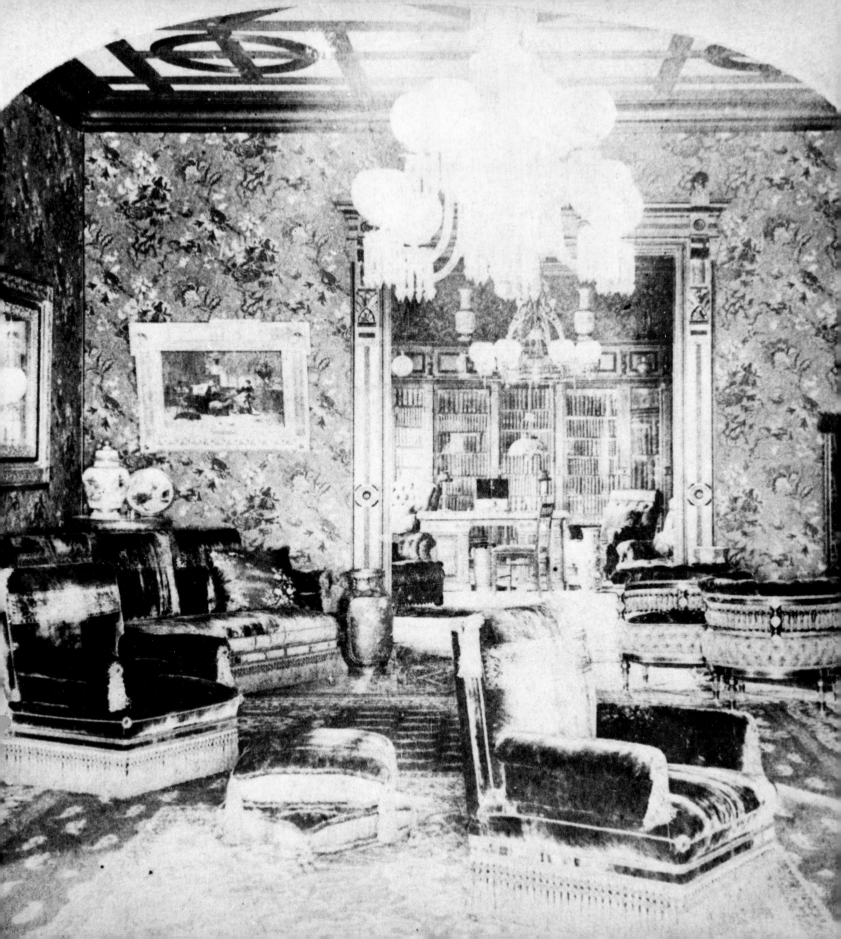

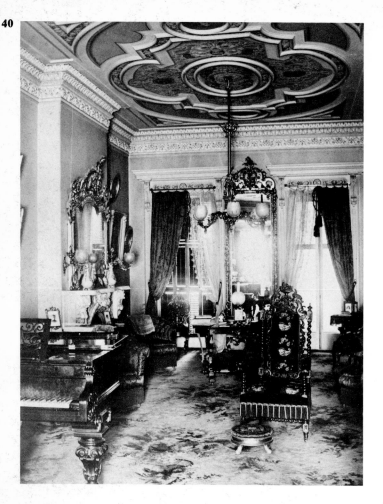

40

## 40. Parlor, House of William Seth E. Pecker, 82 Beacon Street, Boston, Massachusetts, ca. 1878–79

Pecker, his four children, and two Irish servants occupied this house in 1880, and this photograph is believed to have been taken prior to Mrs. Pecker's death, which occurred shortly before that. The Renaissance parlor's elaborate stucco ornament and ceiling painting is matched historically only in the library table, which would also have been considered Renaissance. French Antique mirrors and several chairs in that style are in accord with the Brussels carpeting, which was almost certainly in reds, pinks, green, and yellow on a beige background. The windows are curtained for winter, in the French style, on French rods, convenient in this case for the French doors but widely popular since the late 1840's even for English sash windows. The Elizabethan chair in the foreground is covered in Berlin-work embroidery in a paisley design, and is far more historical as a revival than the Turkish set, obviously the room's newest addition.

## 41. Miner's Shanty, Colorado, ca. 1878

The Colorado silver strikes of the 1870's created boom towns in the region around Cripple Creek. Miners' dreams of riches thrived in wretched living circumstances near the diggings. For all their legendary squalor, the predominantly male-populated towns aspired to a certain level of decency. These two miners with patched trousers seem comfortable in their log shack, which has a dirt floor and, probably, a dirt roof. Using saplings and branches, they have created not only a snug house, but rustic furniture of a kind fashionable in more settled places for summer houses and porches. A fiddle, newspapers, a magazine, and purchased foodstuffs await only a miner's loss of spirit to be transported away in one of those railroad suitcases, leaving the shanty quite bare and raw.

41

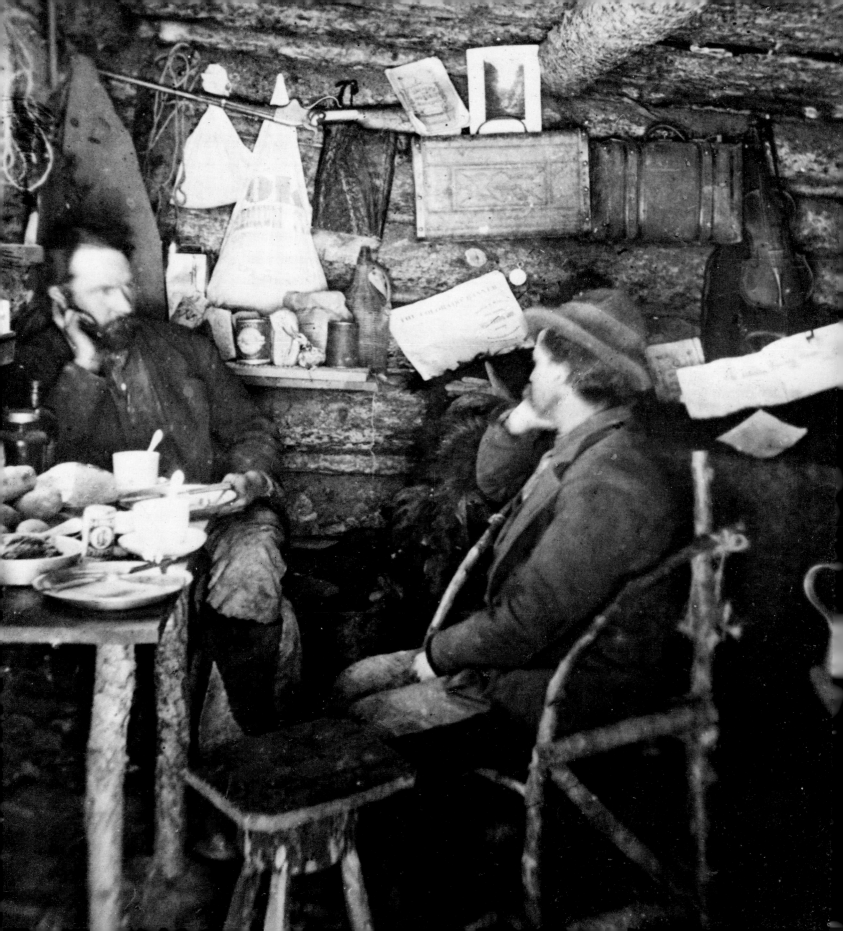

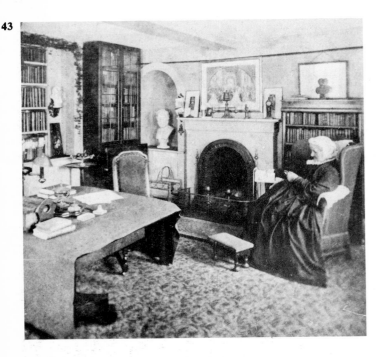

**42.** **Dining Room, House of James M. Beebe, 30 Beacon Street, Boston, Massachusetts, 1875–80**

Built on part of the site of the John Hancock house a few years after its demolition *(1)*, this city mansion had a dining room decorated in what might be called the monumental Renaissance style. The great sideboard has shelves for the display of porcelain and various decorative arrangements of sweets, cheeses, fruits, and flowers set in compotes and bowls. China "candles" conceal gas jets so that the flame flickers as though it is candlelight; real candles are scattered about, their flames shielded by the fringed shades one normally associates with the late nineteenth century. An oil fixture, designed as part of the gasolier, is intended to serve in emergencies. For meals, tablecloths were spread over silence cloths, or silencers, as shown here, but between meals only the linen silencers remained, as did extra little mats under important objects on the sideboard. The room is upholstered *en suite,* with matching portieres and deeply cushioned Renaissance chairs, all almost certainly the work of one of Boston's interior decorating firms of the 1860's.

**43.** **Library, House of Mrs. Bronson Alcott, Concord, Massachusetts, August, 1879**

The wife of the famous educator and reformer moved into this house in Concord in 1857 with her family, about whom the daughter Louisa May wrote the novel *Little Women* in 1868. Prior to the appearance of that best-selling book, the family had known very few fat years, for the controversial Alcott had constantly moved from one endeavor to another, with no financial success. The library looks here much as it did—or should have—in the late 1850's; it is understandable why people such as these with so little security for so long would relish the old and familiar more than the new. A covered Grecian dining table is used for a center table. Mrs. Alcott sits in a slip-covered easy chair which is perhaps late eighteenth century. The bookcase on the left is Grecian of about 1835–40, and the other one is probably from the early 1870's. Although this room might indeed pass for 1860 or so, certain details give it away, particularly the very obvious clutter of papers in letter-pockets and on clips on the wall beside the niche, the pictures scattered on the mantel, and the dropped picture molding.

## 44. Library, House of James Shearer, 701 Center Street, Bay City, Michigan, 1880

The domestic ideal of late nineteenth-century America is epitomized in this comfortable room. It was probably first occupied in about 1875, and passing years saw the addition of the rattan chairs, the new colonial rocker, and possibly the semioctagonal china cabinet seen through the door. Plaster moldings, essentially Greek revival in character, are picked out in colors and stenciled, totally modernizing their appearance. The same house painter, perhaps, grained the doors in imitation of walnut with burl panels, and the bookcases, which seem to have been attached, are probably also grained with paint. Cornelius and Sons of Philadelphia shipped gasoliers of this kind anywhere in the world in the 1870's. Furnishings are otherwise a mixture of the new and the old, like the recent New Grecian mantel garniture and the French Antique settee of about 1860. Over the fireplace, in a French Antique frame hangs a print, *Washington Crossing the Delaware*. Patriotic subjects were always the special joy of printmakers, and they produced such things as this all through the nineteenth century.

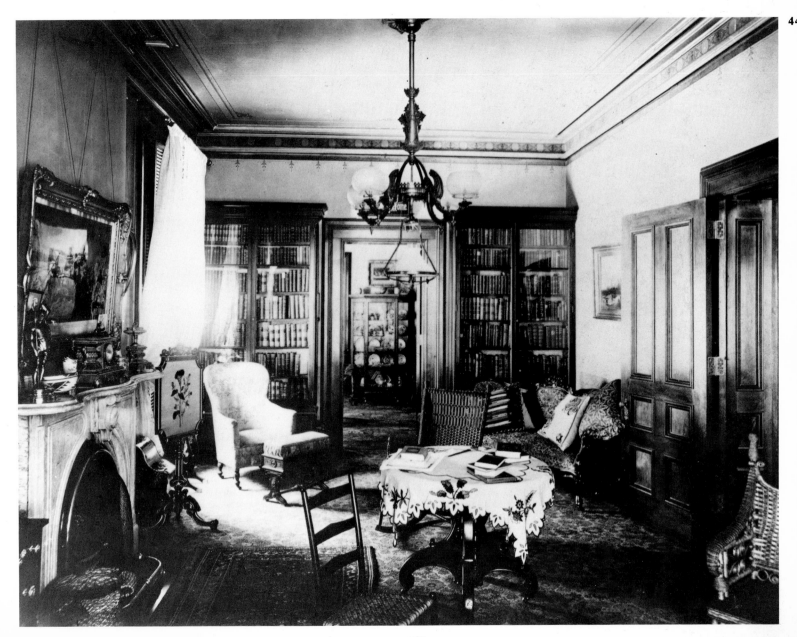

44

69

### 45. Parlor, House of Captain William Corliss, 14 Forest Street, Gloucester, Massachusetts, 1880

This room is rather out of date for 1880, but it is very typical of the American middle-class parlor of a couple who had begun married life prosperously, say, twenty years before. There is a Renaissance parlor set, of which the Renaissance center table is not necessarily a part. It is probable that Captain Corliss's cold and manufactured-looking parlor was used for only the grandest family occasions. Beyond the door, the dining room contained, besides the usual table, chairs, and sideboard, a comforta-

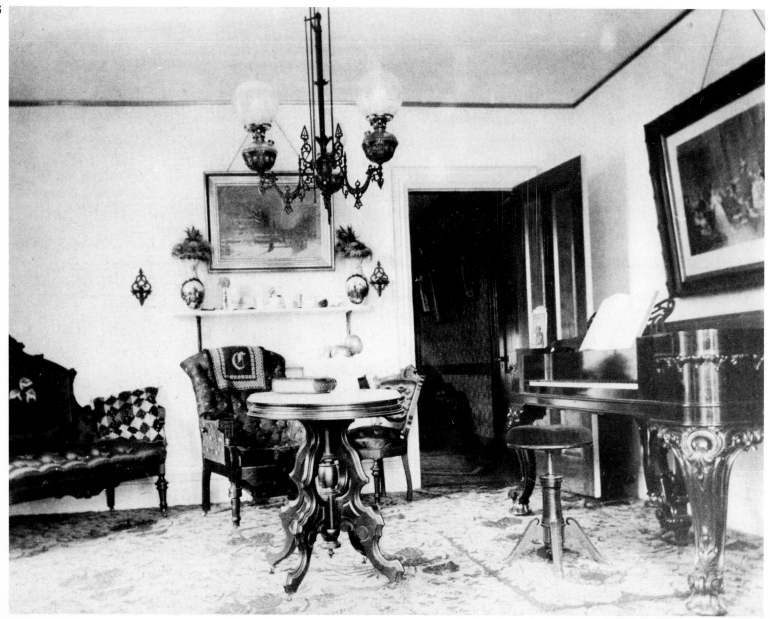

45

ble lounge, suggesting its other role as the Captain's actual sitting room.

## 46. Library, House of the Fox Family, Champlost Hall, Fern Rock, Pennsylvania, 1880

This comfortable room is in a large country house of the late eighteenth century. The wall-to-wall carpet is modern, in the oriental style. The gypsy, or fairy, table to the left has bobbin turning, a variant on the spool style. Screens, widely used by this time, flank the archway into the hall, and wallpaper and painted-out classical crown molding allow the room to be somewhat oriental. But there is not really an effort here to be wholly modern. This is essentially an ensemble of very familiar objects, both French Antique and Elizabethan, and a few big early pieces, such as the eighteenth-century bookpress of the architectural type, and the Queen Anne tea table near the hall door. It is apparently summertime, for the heavy rods and rings indicate that very large window hangings are temporarily absent.

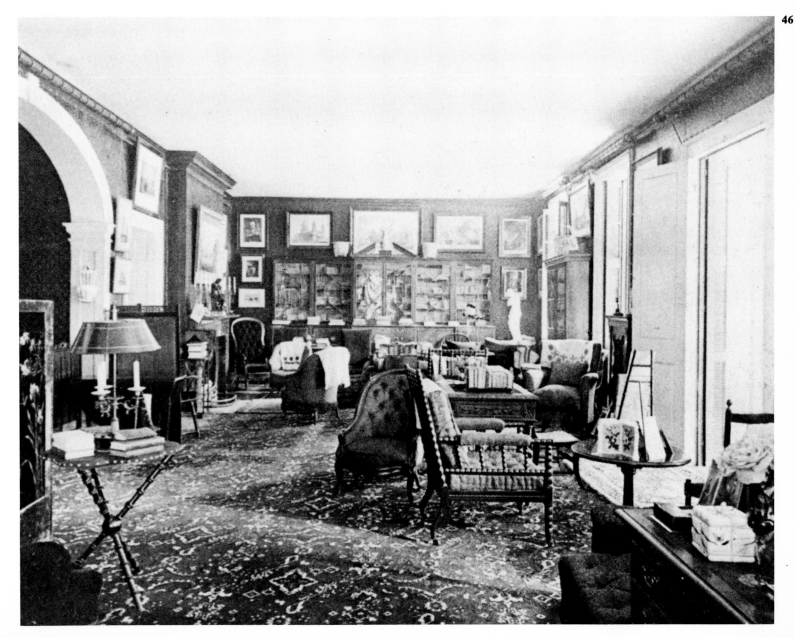

**47. Dining Room, House of General and Mrs. Peyton Wise, Adams and Main Streets, Richmond, Virginia, 1880**

Here the dining room serves as a daytime sitting room, with a Spanish chair of about 1845–50 in tufted leather, rattan rocking chairs, and a cheap 1870's creative revival dining set with sources in the Renaissance revival of mid-century. Mrs. Wise kept house here for her husband, a commission merchant, and his two brothers, one of whom was also a commission merchant and the other a lawyer. The census listed no children in 1880. This interior, es-

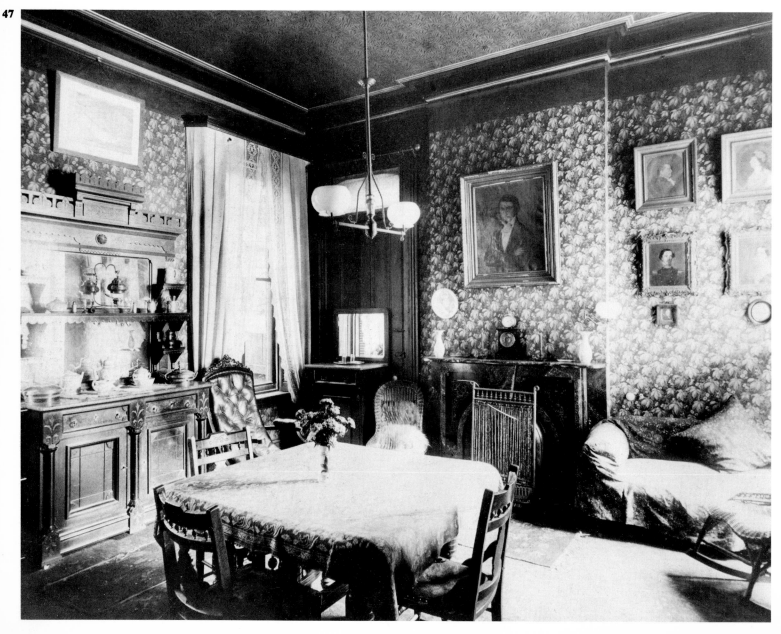

47

sentially modern, with its dining set, wallpaper, and marbled iron mantel, has been filled out with old family portraits and china.

### 48. Parlor, House of Chun Afong, Honolulu, Hawaii, ca. 1880

A native of China, Chun Afong migrated to the Sandwich Islands and became a rich merchant and sugar planter. He married a half-Hawaiian woman, and they and their fifteen children occupied a group of houses, of which this Greek revival cottage was the central feature. The parlor is decorated for an occasion, perhaps a wedding; its Grecian detailing—the triple sash windows, ceiling, and marbled washboards—is covered by greens. A fine new rattan settee, rugs, a Chinese table and vase, and a cut-glass chandelier for kerosene seem to hide among the cascades of flower-filled netting and big floral arrangements. It was probably a double parlor, and the richly foliated screen of rosewood, or teak, framed the opening against a background of white ceiling, dark woodwork, spider-web wallpaper, lace curtains, and embroidered black silk lambrequins.

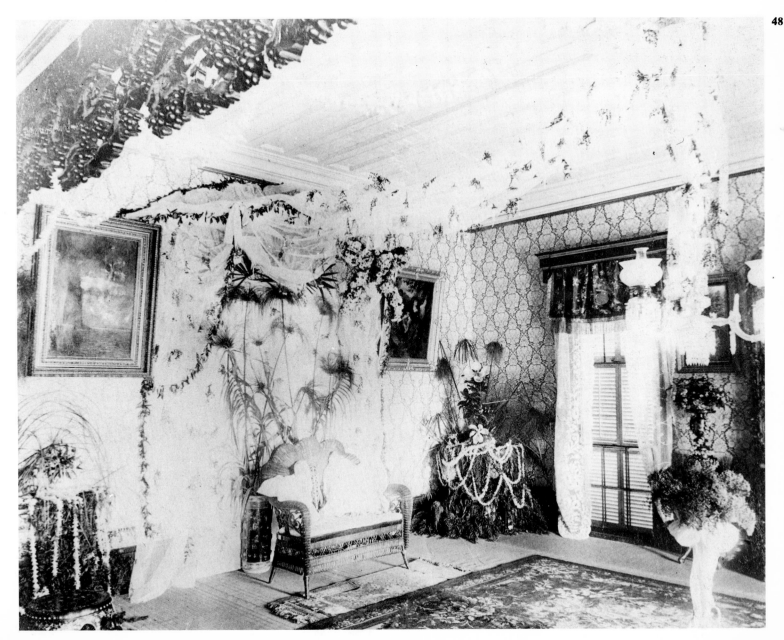

**49. Drawing Room, House of Oliver Ames, Jr., Commonwealth and Massachusetts Avenues, Boston, Massachusetts, ca. 1884**

This luxurious room, quite in the spirit of the English Aesthetic movement of the 1870's and 1880's, is one of the few high-style interiors to appear in this book. Decorators carefully created for Ames a variety of artistic rooms, the best coordinated being this one, with its shiny loaves of silk upholstery which seem only incidentally to be chairs and sofas and its careful scattering of porcelains to accentuate the Japanese flavor. The white and gilt paint on the furniture is extraordinary, for normally colors were very dark and highly polished; light color was far into the realm of high style, even in England. The furniture in the room has its roots in the Louis Seize revival and Grecian styles. It epitomizes the creative revivals, although it was probably called art furniture in its day. Every inch of the drawing room showed the conscious touch of artistic effort, from the jewel-like ceiling to the overmantel shelves and cabinet of porcelains opposite them, to the shimmering glass gasolier and brackets and heavy hangings with their embroidered bands. This was the essence of Aesthetic interior decoration, in the hands of a professional decorator.

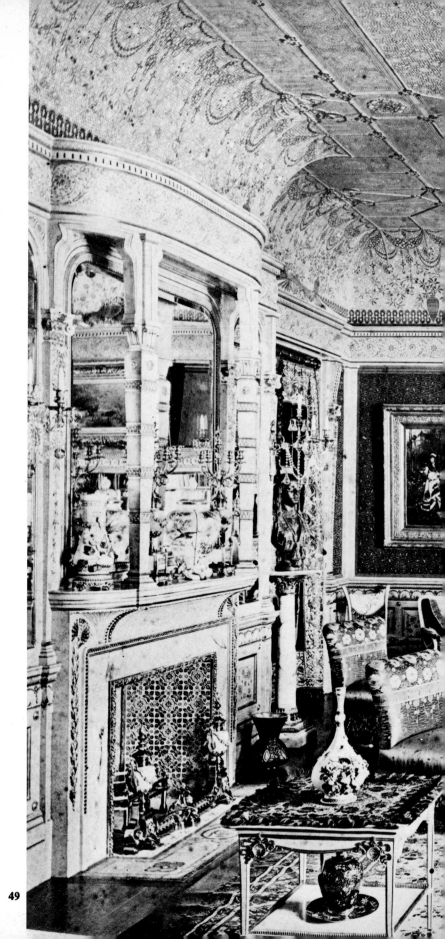

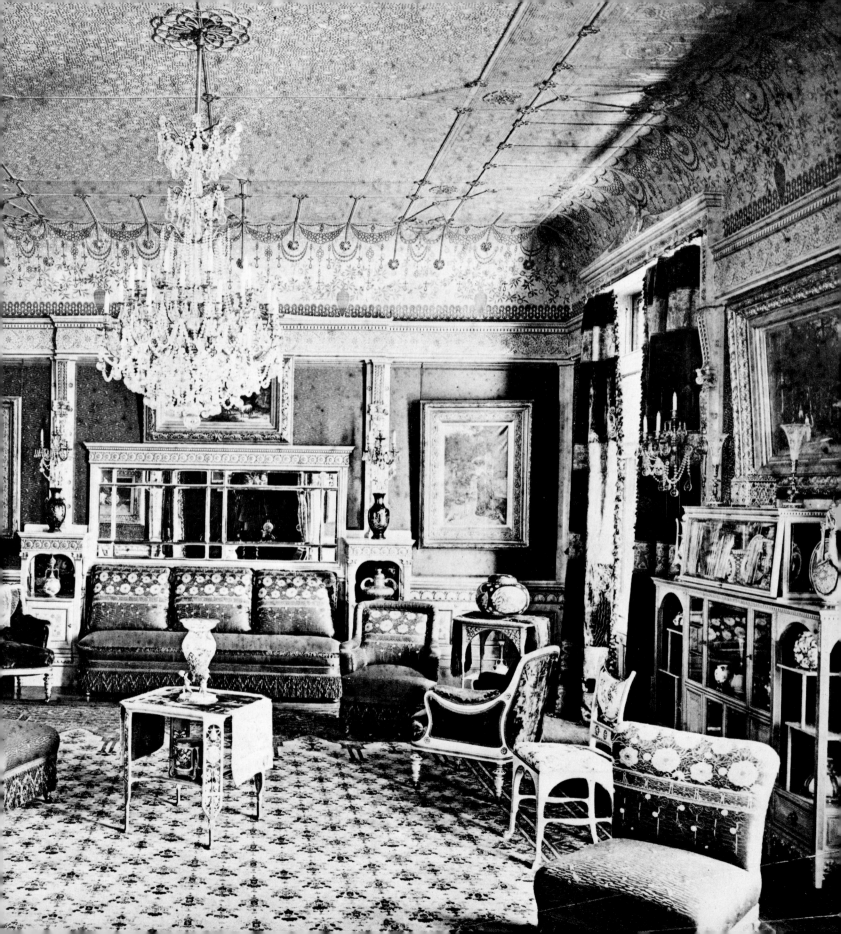

**50. Parlor, Gulf Coast, 1880–85**

Although far humbler than the Ames drawing room *(49)*, this parlor is no less consumed by the Japanese fever. Palmetto fans and Japanese scrolls set the theme in an inexpensive way, while real leaves have been picked and pasted, as borders, on the walls beside the upright piano. Vines and ferns, plates, statuettes, books, and many pictures personalize the room. An old Grecian card table, French Antique side chairs and mirror, and a new easy chair with fringed arms and a reclining back comprise the furnishings. It is summertime, and the mirror has been

covered with gauze, to preserve its gilt frame from fly-specks; this was a very common practice which also applied to glass and gilded chandeliers.

**51. Parlor, Lower Brandon Plantation on the James River, Virginia, 1884**

In a house built in about 1765 by the Harrison family, this parlor, rich in century-old architectural detailing makes every effort to be modern with what is close at hand. Over the Grecian center table of about 1835 is thrown a cheap printed cover; likewise, a Moorish, Egyp-

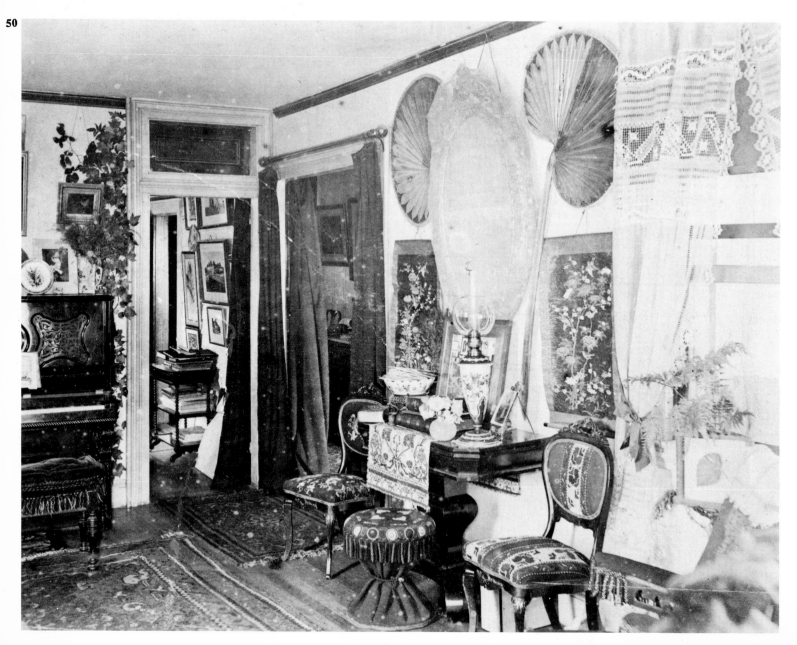

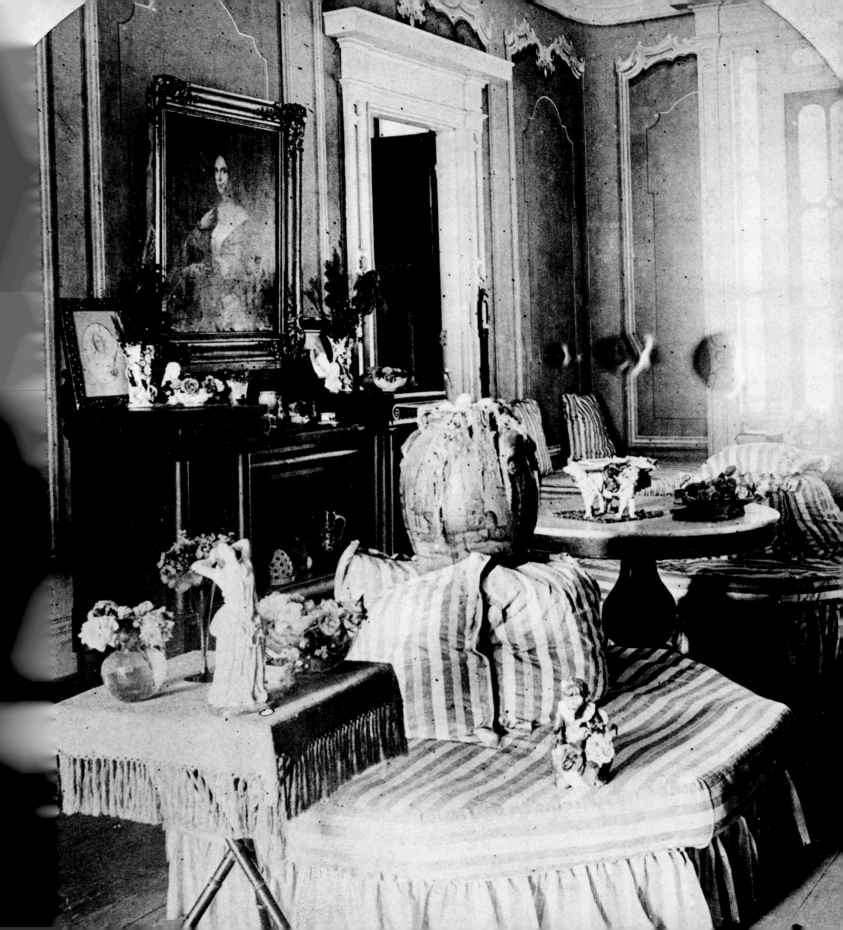

tian, or Arabian stripe covers a small Renaissance cottage table of about 1870 beneath the window. A fancy embroidered shawl has been attached to the wall above the piano, Japanese style, and on a nearby table a painted tea set and copper teapot form a Japanese vignette, all overlooked by family portraits and photographs of ancient and recent date. Crumbling plaster, the need for fresh whitewash or paint, faded curtains, and the wide range of shabby furniture, most of it only old enough to be out of style, reveals much about what had happened to the great plantations by the late nineteenth century. With the modern Japanese touches here must be noted the fine old Chippendale chairs, now brought down from the attic and into the center of the room as acceptable colonial relics.

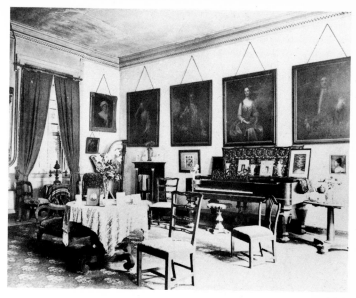

**51**

## 52. Salon, House of Princess Ruth Keelikolani, Honolulu, Hawaii, 1882

The Princess Ruth, reputedly the richest woman in the Pacific islands, owned vast estates in the Sandwich Islands and plotted to have the Hawaiian crown for herself. She was a woman of enormous size; and, like all Hawaiian royalty, she had numerous houses. This salon in one of her houses in Honolulu was newly decorated when the photograph was taken. It is furnished largely in the French Antique style, with Louis Quinze revival and creative revival Louis Seize furniture, as well as some Turkish overstuffed chairs and an English table in the belated Grecian style of the 1870's. The furniture arrangement follows Anglo-French ideas. Dark-stained and polished woodwork, together with some other woodwork painted ivory and trimmed in gilt, stands out boldly against the intense but very orderly Moorish wallpaper, which is outlined with dark borders. Porcelains, books, and lush arrangements of fresh flowers and ferns complete the setting. The Princess never lived in this house, but was so fond of it that she moved into a smaller and more comfortable house across the street and admired it from there.

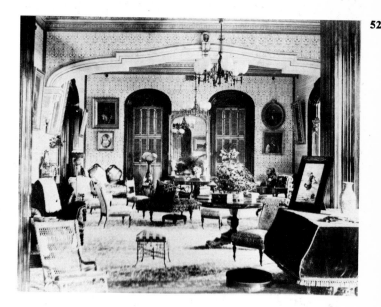

**52**

**53. Salon, Beauvoir, House of Jefferson Davis, Biloxi, Mississippi, 1884**

The former president of the Confederate States of America lived in retirement with his family at Beauvoir, a comfortable Gulf Coast estate bequeathed to him by a female admirer. While he wrote his memoir of the southern nation in an adjacent outbuilding, his lively and ambitious wife held court to a curious public in the galleried house, which had a magnificent view of the Gulf of Mexico. Her enthusiasm effected everything, not the least being the interior decoration of Beauvoir. If her pocketbook was somewhat limited, her affection for things modern was not. She spruced up the frescoed central hall with a pair of downy ottomans, slipcovered in what was probably striped linen. Little gypsy tables held art objects, and there were shiny pots and statuettes in porcelain. The old-fashioned Grecian sideboard, situated in the hall, as they so often were early in the century, seems quite at home, even in the midst of Varina Davis's artistic affectations. Oscar Wilde came to call while in America preaching the Aesthetic gospel, and Mrs. Davis sketched his portrait as he sat in the Beauvoir salon.

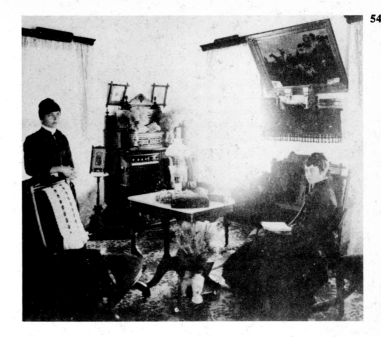

**54. Parlor, House of Mrs. Youmans, Orlando, Florida, ca. 1885–88**

S. J. Morrow posed these twin girls before his camera in Mrs. Youman's house, where they apparently were guests. The room is a fine example of a middle-class parlor with manufactured furniture of the creative revival kind, in this case, a derivitive of the Renaissance and Elizabethan revivals of thirty years before. The walls are white, and in Orlando at this date they might well have been whitewashed, to prevent mildew. Lace curtains hang from behind what appears to be walnut cornices that match the furniture. There is probably a stove in the room, for a mantel is simulated by the shelf between the windows, a practice common enough when there was no fireplace. Curtained in a lambrequin and carefully fitted out with vases, books, and ornaments, and surmounted by a parlor painting hung in the tilted manner which had been popular since the 1840's, this false mantel demonstrates the tremendous force of some customs in room decoration. Where an interior decorator would have used a parlor organ or some form of heavy furniture as the unifying feature, Mrs. Youmans obviously feels strongly the absence of a fireplace mantel.

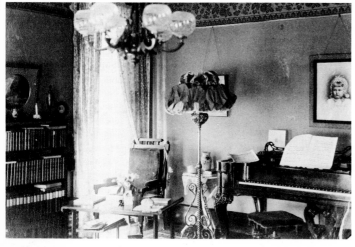

55

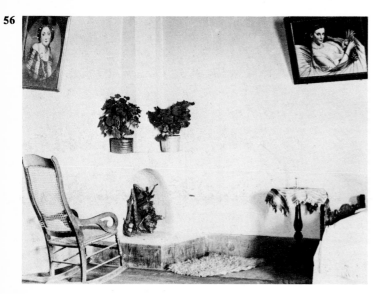

56

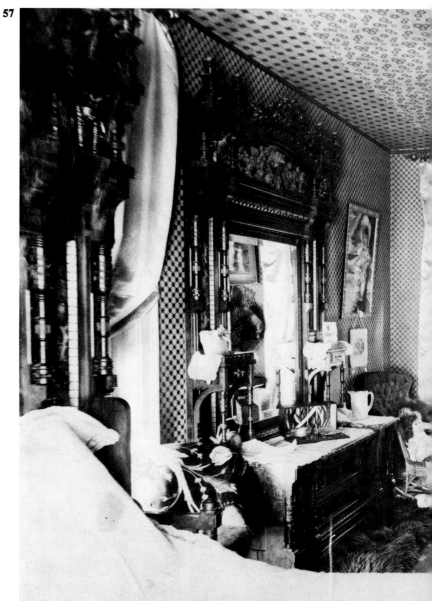

57

## 55. Parlor, House of Mrs. Frederick Shear, Skaneateles, New York, ca. 1885–89

Here is a parlor put together by a lady named Servanoke Shear; her furniture is arranged more or less in the French Antique way. None of the furniture is old, although the Japanese tea table in the foreground and the stylish piano lamp are the only things which would have been considered modern. The easy chair combines various Grecian, Elizabethan, and Renaissance characteristics of the past into a creative revival hybrid which undoubtedly bore one or another of the names of its several

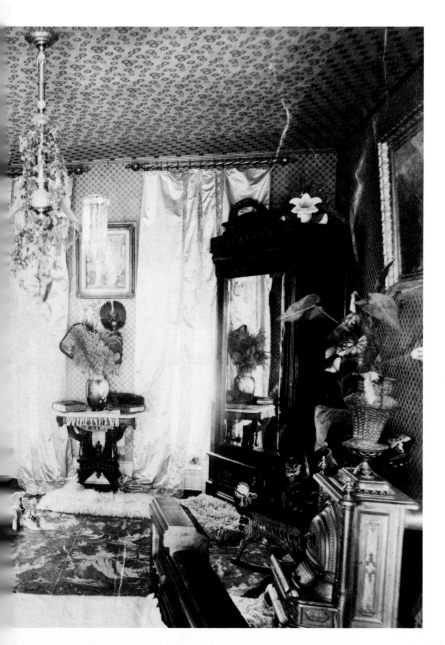

sources. Sets of books fill a simple bookcase and an art-square rug is on the floor. Around the ceiling, high on the wall, is a broad wallpaper border separated from the painted plaster wall by a gilded picture molding from which pictures hang. This youthful family seems not to have been especially interested in interior decoration; but it is well to study this room for that very reason.

## 56. Bedroom, New Mexico Territory, ca. 1885

By the 1880's, styles were making an increasingly fast progression, through manufactures, across the United States, intermingling quickly among regional traditions of many kinds in states with old settlements. This bedroom in the house of a Mexican family of New Mexico is a case in point. For all its heavy plasterwork, its corner fireplace and whitewash, and its little bed more or less in the local vernacular, the old table is an Anglo-American import, the prints on the wall are manufactures, perhaps Mexican, of the 1870's, and the rocking chair, like the cans holding the geraniums, was produced in a factory probably east of the Mississippi in the early 1880's.

## 57. Bedroom, House of H. A. W. and Baby Doe Tabor, Denver, Colorado, 1885

The contrast between the Ames drawing room in Boston (49) and the bedroom of the legendary wife of the silver magnate is sharp, but the bedroom better exemplifies how wealthy Americans interpreted Aesthetic ideas than does the Boston drawing room. Personalized with baby dolls, mementoes, shawls, fur rugs, and photographs of Baby Doe's daughter Lillie, the room has lost the whole meaning of Aesthetic restraint. The furniture is an expensive art set, a creative interpretation of the Renaissance revival, perhaps in cherry wood, inset with sumptuous carved panels and borders in color. Before the century's end, Baby Doe lost her fortune and such luxurious things as these. She lived until the 1930's, old and mad, at the abandoned Matchless Mine, dreaming of good times that never returned.

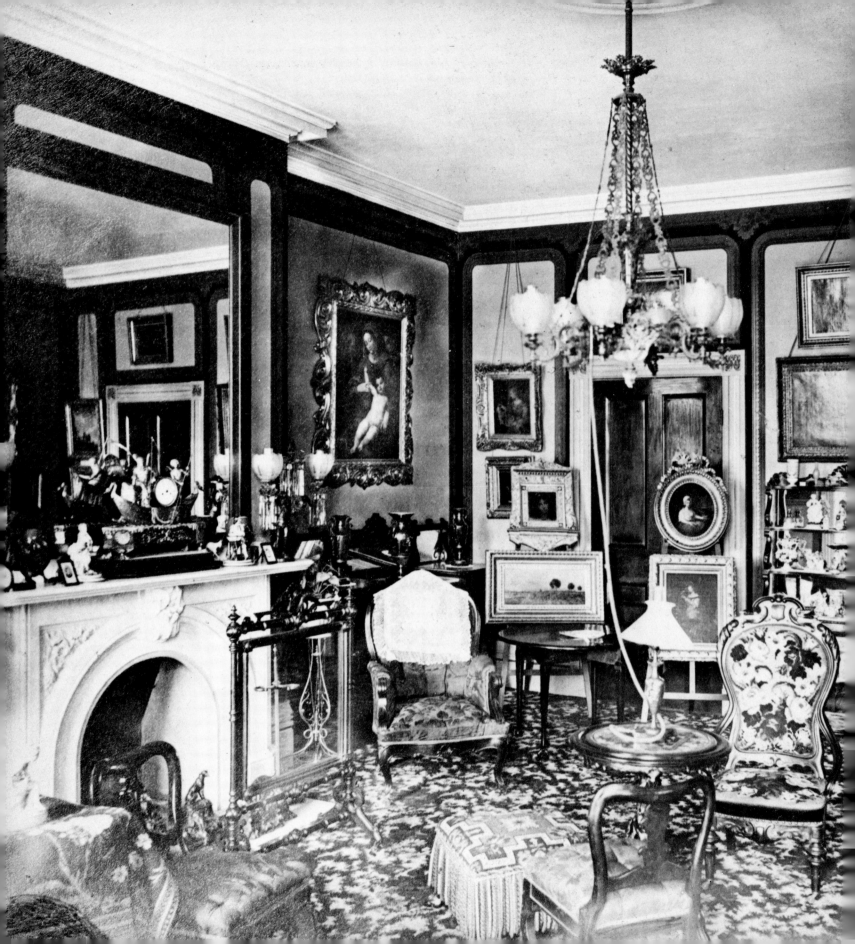

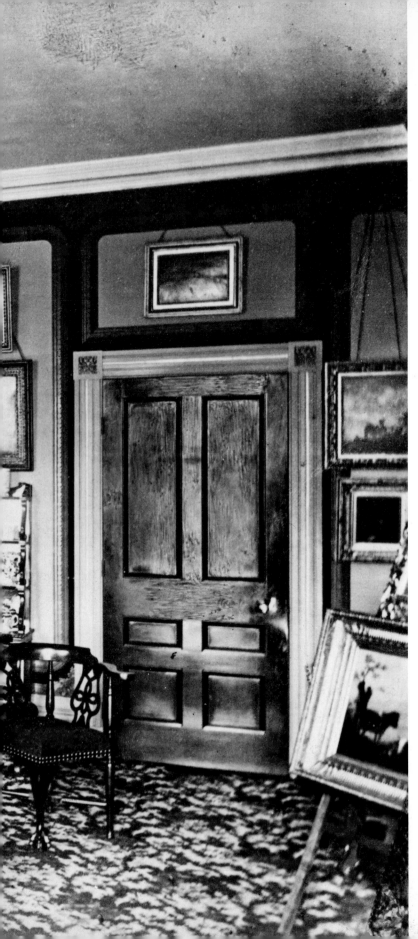

### 58. Parlor, 2 Park Street, Boston, Massachusetts, ca. 1885

This room, originally of the 1830's, was probably redecorated in the 1850's with frescoes and much of the furniture we see here. The house was closed in 1880, according to the Census Bureau, and occupied only by a maintenance man. As it appears in this photograph, one Dr. Warren has reopened it and freshened it up inexpensively in the spirit of the mid-1880's. The gasolier and brackets have been refitted with incandescent mantles, which consist of cotton hoods, soaked in oxides so as to produce an intense white light for little more cost than any other gaslight. The French furniture arrangement might not differ much from the room's appearance in the 1850's, but the easels are undoubtedly new, along with the great numbers of statuettes and framed photographs, porcelains, and artwork, all gathered into careful art units. The Chippendale chair and the Queen Anne table might be colonial heirlooms, or stylish relics recently purchased in a local antique shop.

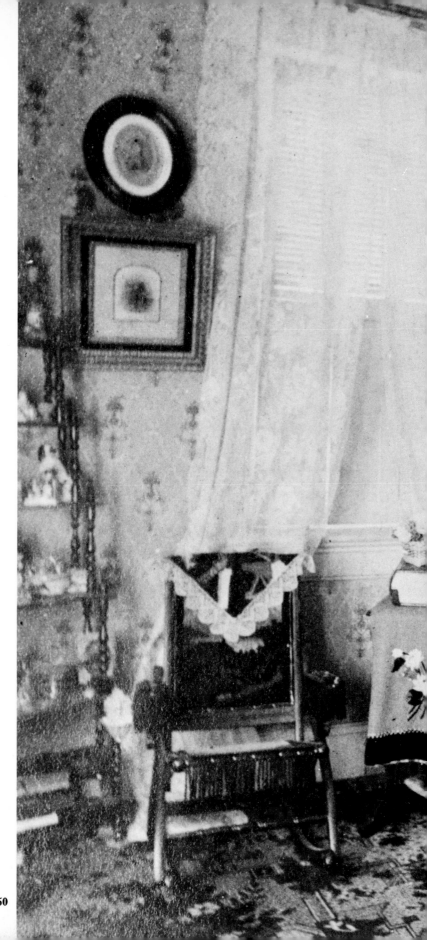

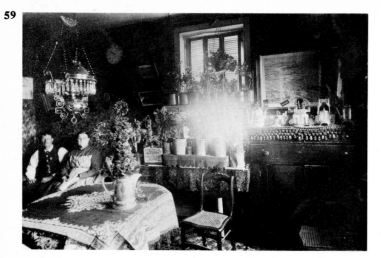

**59, 60. Dining Room and Parlor, Rondout North Dike Lighthouse, Kingston, New York, 1885**

Mrs. C. A. P. Murdock, a widow, was the keeper of the lighthouse and doubtless the source of much of its artwork. She was assisted by her son James. Here they sit together in their dining room, which probably adjoined the parlor. An old-fashioned high sideboard has been trimmed in tied fringe which Mrs. Murdock herself could have made, and she displays her prized silverplate there. The plant steps were common in nineteenth-century rooms and on porches. Mrs. Murdock has made lambrequins out of oilcloth, and with the tin cans of plants lined closely together, the crude construction is hardly noticed. The water pitcher on the table seems to be the justification for the photograph: in it the untiring keeper has arranged something resembling topiary, one of her many tributes to art.

L. P. Conklin, engineer in charge of the lighthouse, was provided with quarters in the dwelling of the keeper of the lighthouse. The parlor of these official quarters has been personalized in a very typical way, at little cost. Photographic portraits suggest a dropped border. China-headed picture pins, costing a penny or so, support the cords, which are sheathed in a colored sleeve and form geometric patterns. The cheap carpeting and the home-made paper ceiling ornament acknowledge Anglo-Japanese design. An appliquéd lambrequin with balanced feather dusters forms a mantel altar to art, surmounted by some pots, artificial flowers, and a seemingly casual row of unframed family portraits.

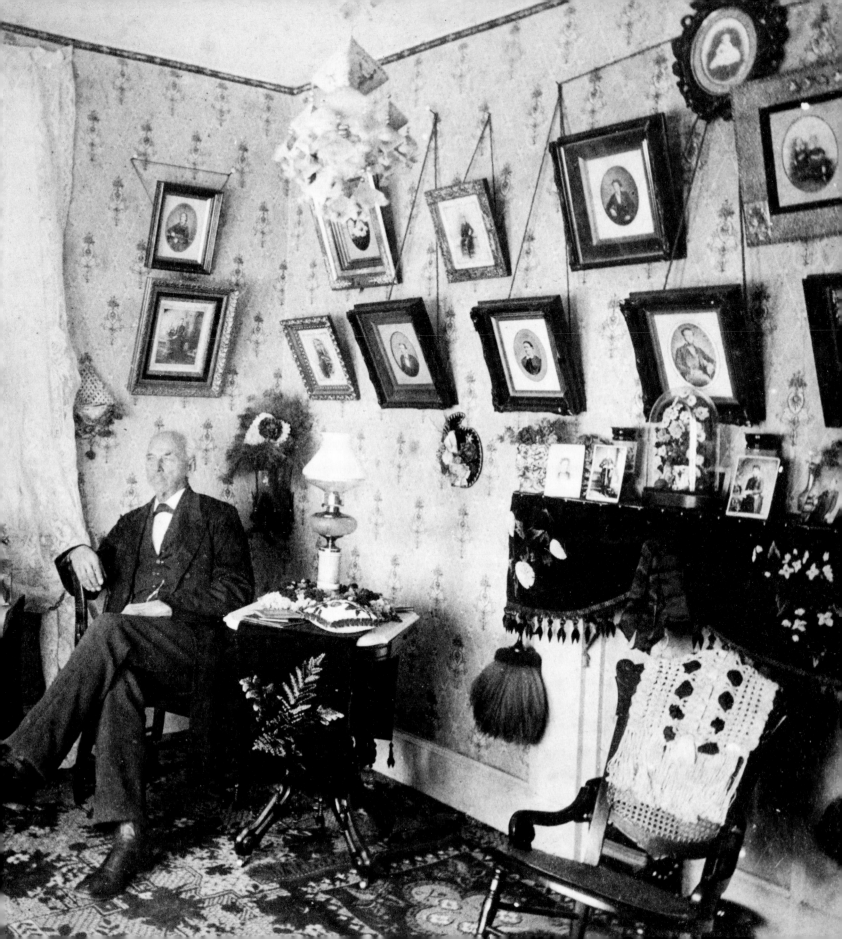

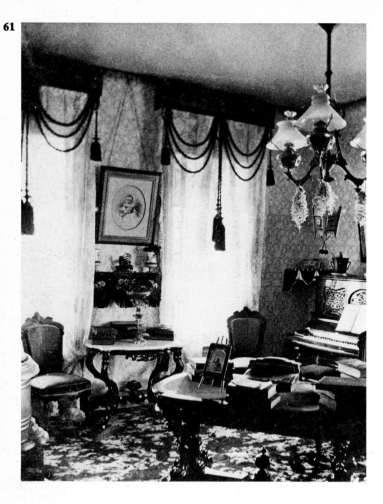

### 61. Parlor, Helena, Montana, 1883–85

Fifteen years after the redecoration of the Leland Stanford house at Sacramento *(20–26)*, this Montana parlor was decorated in a similar taste. The side chairs are probably Louis Seize revival and might have been called Marie Antoinette. Already the creative revivals were in their heyday, but Louis Seize revival such as this was still manufactured and was popular, as were the French Antique table between the windows and the Renaissance one in the foreground. Shelves with lambrequins, pictures, and windows decorated with gilt cornices, swagged rope, tassels, and lace express a sort of calculated elegance found in many middle-class houses. Knowing nothing about the occupants of this house, we are free to guess that what they created in this room was a whole concept remembered from another time and another place, but put together with new parts. The concept is French Antique, and in some of the objects memory served them well; there are differences elsewhere, as in the upright piano and the oil chandelier, which has been enriched in an Aesthetic sense with artificial wisteria and a Japanese lantern.

### 62, 63.  Parlors, Boston, ca. 1885

The first parlor in this anonymous house is in the Renaissance style, its fireplace architecturally enshrined. Having survived the advent of central heating, fireplaces now returned to be household symbols, their main function to be beautiful. The walls are divided into three parts, a fashion only suggested in the previous houses: the paneled dado, above that a foliated material resembling tapestry but probably cardboard or heavy paper serving as a background for artwork, and finally the frieze, or dropped border. Strapwork and stenciled patterns enrich the ceiling. The room seems to have been under the strict control of an architect until it was furnished, and no interior decorator seems to have been at work here. A white and gold Louis Seize revival parlor set with an ebonized and ormulu table mingles with plump overstuffed chairs, probably considered Turkish but here largely concealed by flowered slipcovers.

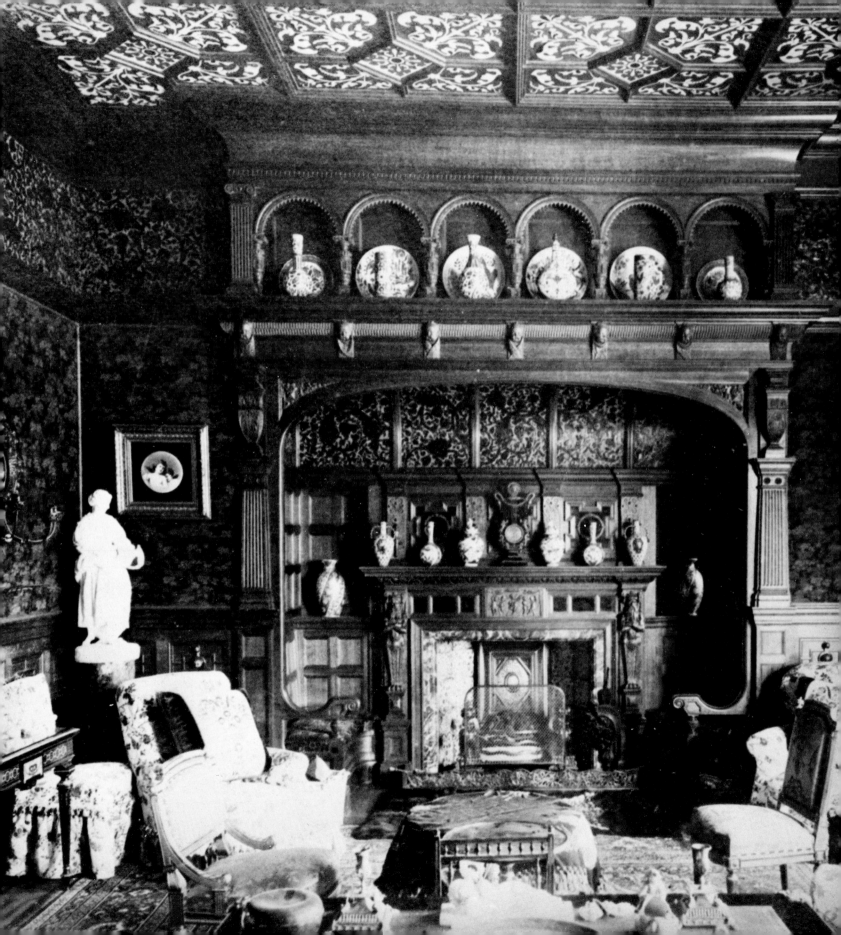

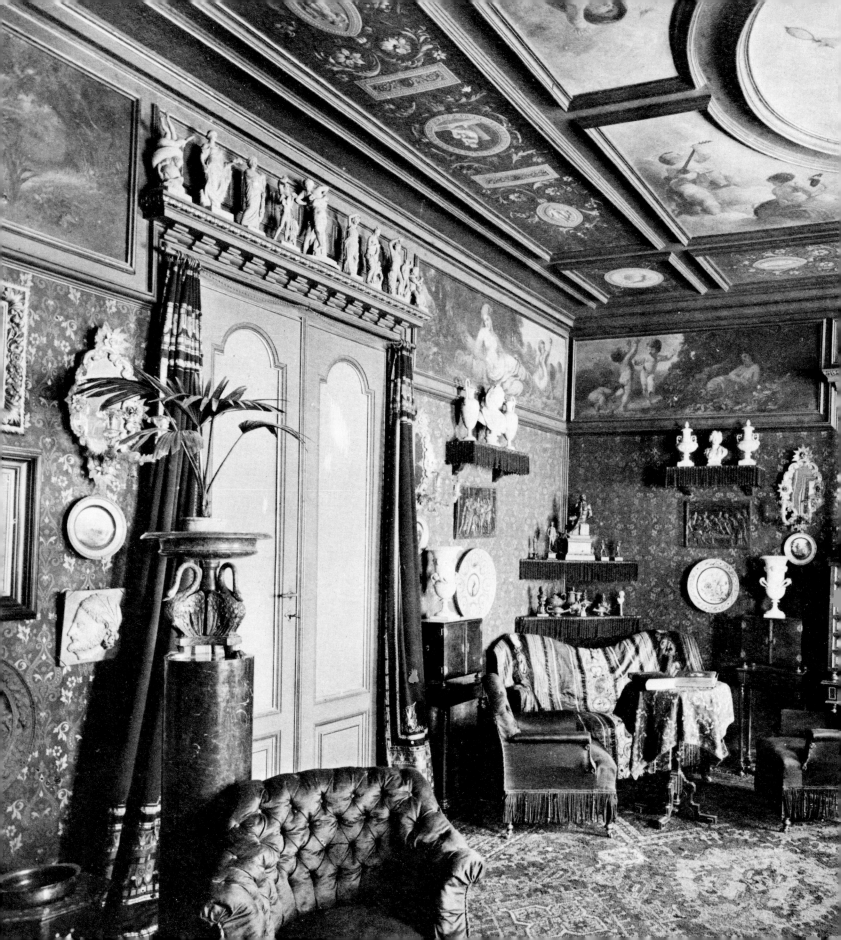

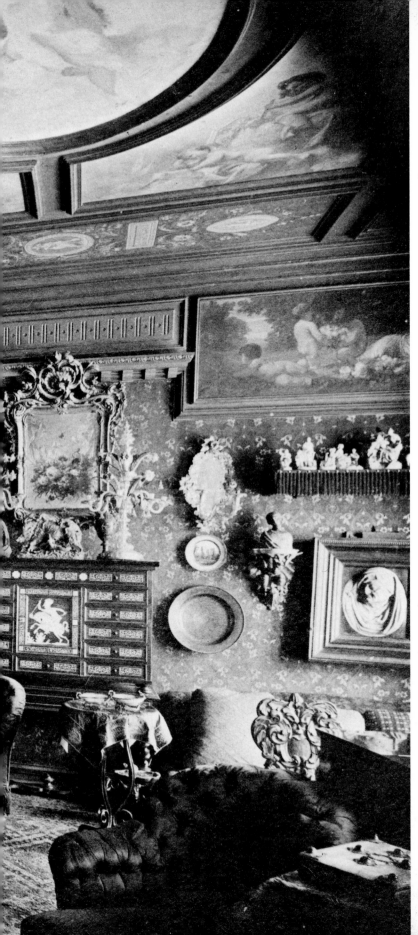

A second parlor in the same house must undoubtedly have been considered Marie Antoinette, with its ceiling decorated in allegories of Venus and its modern upholstered "comfortables," which had been popularized twenty years before by the French court. Little fringed shelves hold small statues and vases; and while the walls seem further cluttered by art objects, the intricate wallpaper and the series of paintings of cherubs that form the upper border, the room is not overloaded with furniture. Three intimate conversation groupings, echoes of the same Napoleon III taste, make this a welcoming setting.

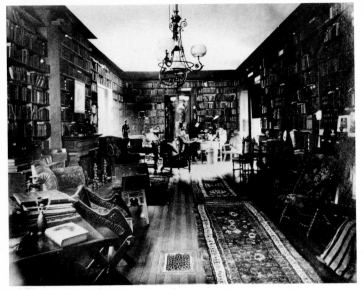

**64. Library, House of Andrew D. White, Cornell University, Ithaca, New York, ca. 1885**

The great private library of the president of Cornell was housed in the official residence built by himself for the university. His books rivaled those owned by small college libraries across the nation. Pine bookcases line the long room, and rise to within a foot or so of the ceiling. At that point the wall is painted a dark color, and the same dark color is carried out onto the ceiling, framing the expanse of white desirable for reflecting light onto books. This is not a costly room, but well-finished. A variety of furnishings, most of them out of style, line the walls in a gallery effect mixed with reproductions of medieval objects and oriental rugs. The sunflower-ornamented gasoliers are a matching pair with convenient center lamps which could be lighted apart from the branches, their light directed downward for reading by the opaque-glass Vienna shades. Polishing and varnishing floors and leaving them bare to look almost like the surfaces of tables was a sophisticated practice in the late nineteenth century.

**65. Homesteader's House, Dakota Territory, 1885**

Whitewashed and simple, this cabin in what is now South Dakota shows the influence manufactures had even on remote places. The stove was brought to the Great Plains with no small difficulty; the French wardrobe, a manufactured piece in walnut and probably from a Midwest factory, was collapsible, as was the stove. Behind the homemade table is a manufactured kitchen chair, while on the walls to the right hang quite a large assortment of store-bought pots and pans. Stark nakedness, as in Sawtell's interior *(19)*, had, by the 1880's, vanished from most of the American frontier. Bureaus, trunks, dishes, lamps, and clothing could be ordered by mail from Kansas City, Chicago, St. Louis, New Orleans, and New York and shipped to the nearest depot, which might be 100 miles away. In comparison with thirty years before, this was one of the most civilized aspects of western life.

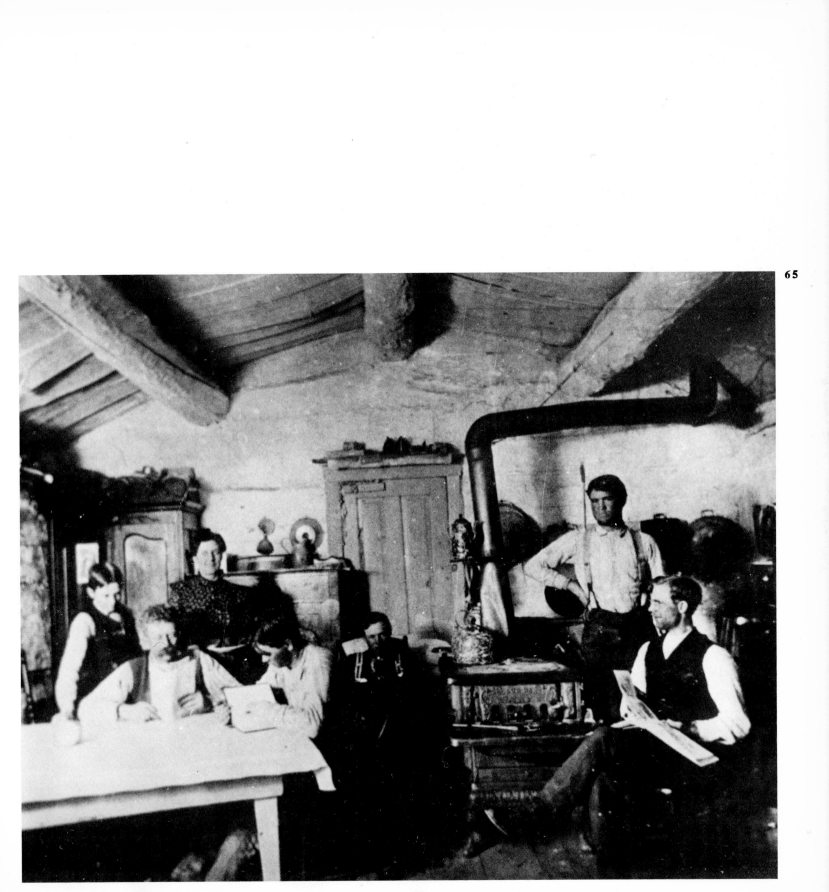

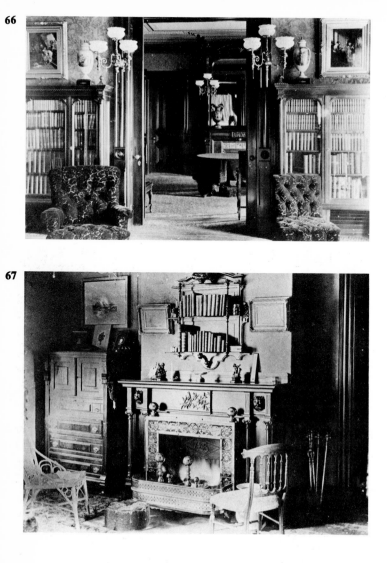

**66**

**67**

Corliss, of the Corliss Steam Engine Company, made a fortune manufacturing machines, the most famous of which was the celebrated Corliss Engine that provided the power for the great Centennial Exposition of 1876 at Philadelphia. The Corliss house at Providence exemplifies a kind of mansion style of the 1870's and 1880's. Although built at a high cost and furnished with expensive sets, it demonstrates no particular interest on the part of the owners in having anything unusual. Here was merely acceptable mansion jargon of the times.

**66.** The Corliss library has a bank of low bookcases of the kind that developed as a direct result of the increase in quantity of household objects through manufacture. Forty years before, a very worthy library might contain no more than seventy-five or a hundred books. Libraries with limited shelving—like those of Le Grand Lockwood and Leland Stanford *(15, 21)*—began to be replaced by ones with hundreds of feet of shelves; rooms were, in a sense, wainscoted with bookcases. The upper surfaces of these low bookcases were perfect places to display photographs, porcelains, and collected objects, while the walls above were covered with fabric or other backgrounds suitable for prints and paintings. These bookcases are handsomely built, probably in walnut, with glass doors. Comfortable chairs, covered in cut velvet, stand in a room otherwise quite sparse. Seen through doors, the dining-room table has a colored silencer and footstools for comfort, and is placed before a mantel adorned with architectural elements in wood and Japanese-style tiles.

**67.** The sitting room and bedroom beyond show Aesthetic ideals by now considerably stilted. Mantels of this kind could be ordered from millwork catalogues; the columns, cat faces, and carved apple blossoms follow the Aesthetic sentiment as do the hammered brass tiles surrounding the stove insert, itself somewhat in the colonial vein. Over the mantel, the art shelf contains books and *bibelots:* vases, a perfume bottle, and, at the top, a model of Hiram Power's *Eve* painted black. Between the fireplace and the window is a manufactured dresser in a creative revival style that came from the Renaissance revival.

**68.** The parlor is bare in this view from the hall. The gas fixtures have been converted to electricity, probably very recently; the electrolier in the hall operates from both a switch on the wall and from pull-chains. Lambrequins at the windows are combined with heavy swags, apparently of velvet, to match the imaginative Louis Seize chairs. The New Grecian pier mirror and umbrella stand, one of the most popular kinds of furniture from the 1850's to the 1890's, matches a New Grecian mantel glass in the parlor. Corliss's grandson Charles Brackett completely remodeled these rooms in the 1920's, substituting flamboyant French Antique furnishings of the 1850's for the, by then, "vulgar late Victorian" of the original.

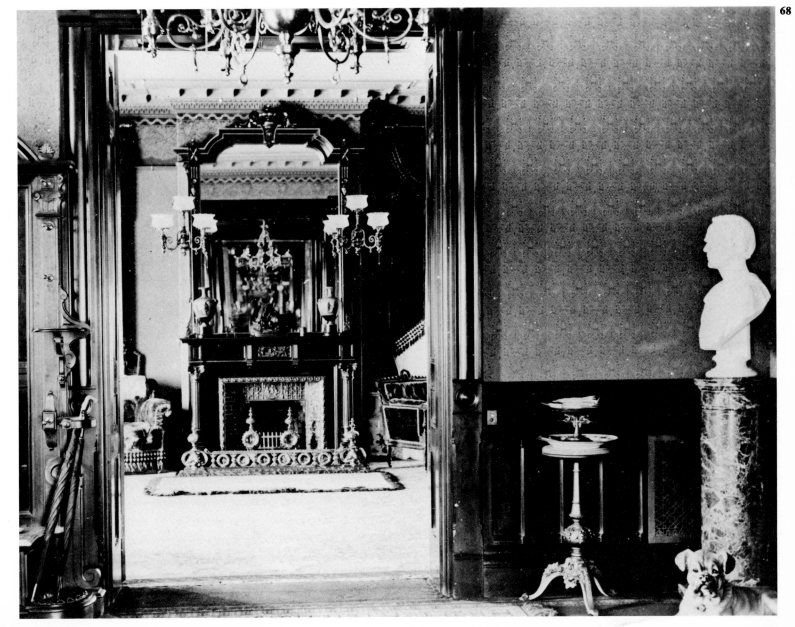

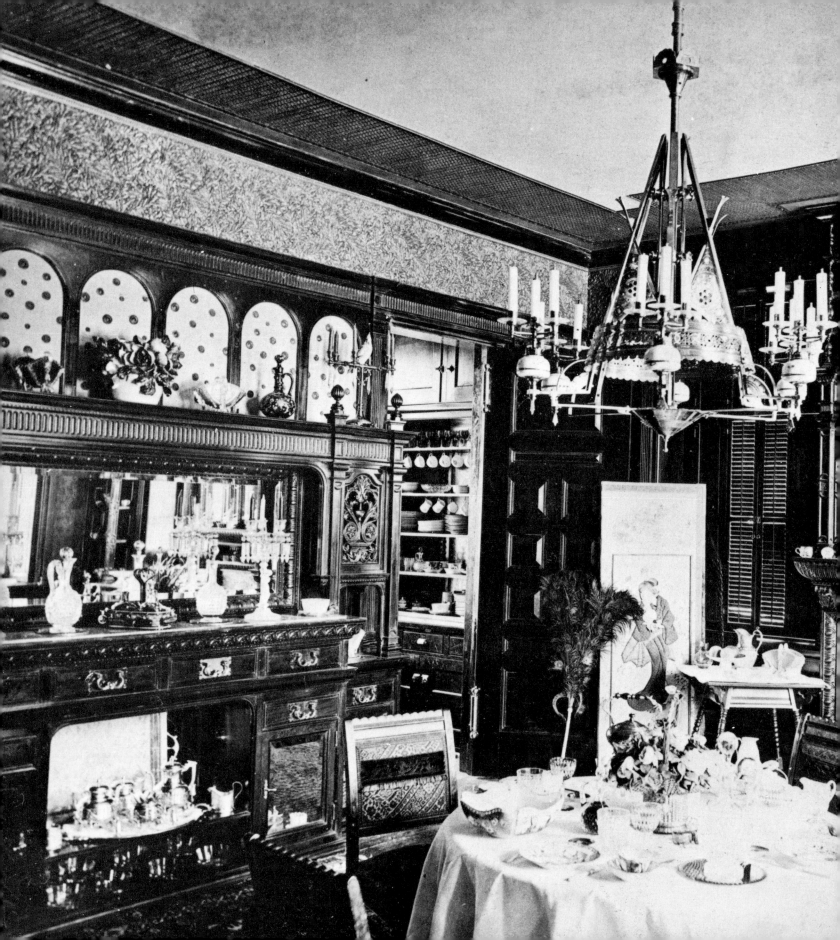

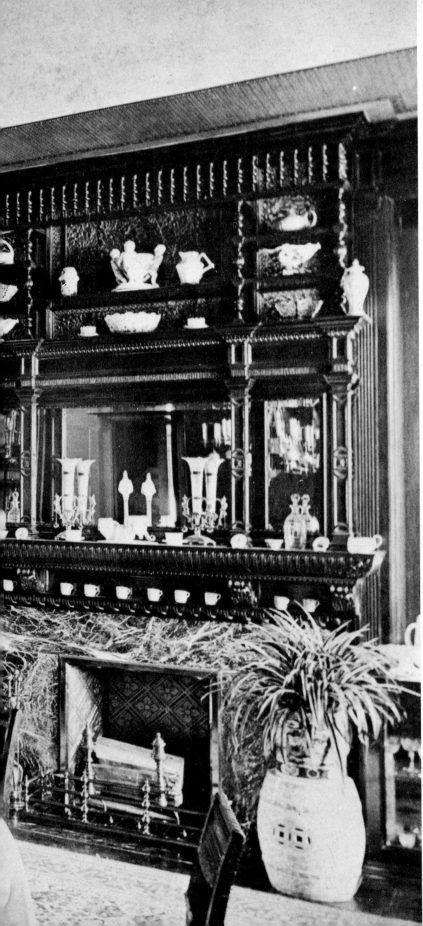

**Dining Room and Bedroom, House of George Finch, 9th and Cooper Streets, St. Paul, Minnesota, mid-1880's**

Finch was about forty-five and his wife Mary about forty-one when these pictures were taken. They lived in this large Italianate house of 1863 with one child, the other three being away at boarding schools, and four servants. George Finch was the most successful wholesale merchant in St. Paul and Minneapolis, and traveled frequently to New York. His exposure to New York shops, hotels, and private houses shows in his St. Paul house.

**69.** The dining room is a creative revival ensemble that seems to come rather directly from the Grecian of the 1840's, with the exotic influences of the 1880's. As though it were their sole purpose, the cabinet and chimney pieces become shelves for porcelains and glass. Mirrors, painted canvas, and embossed wallcovering vary the surroundings of these objects. The opening below the sideboard seems to mimic the fireplace opening, and the polished brasses in the fireplace are further parodied there by the silver, which is omitted from all other surfaces. Matting, carried out into the ceiling as a border, the garden stool in porcelain, the screen, the gasolier, and the general feeling of the room gives it a rich Anglo-Japanese flavor.

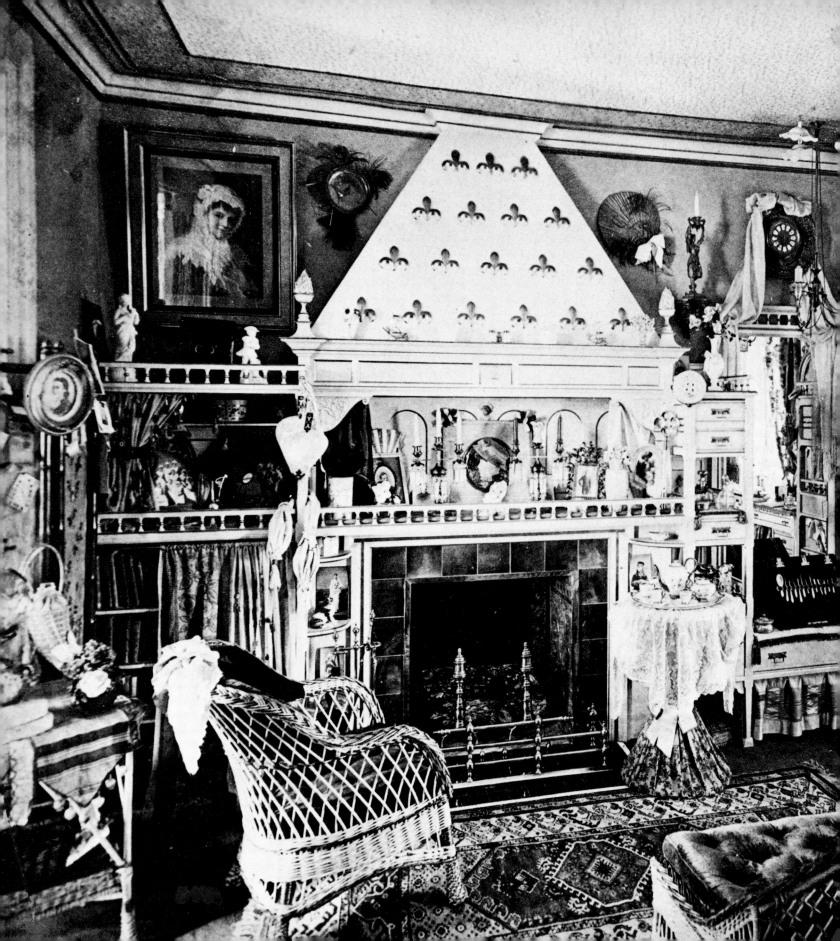

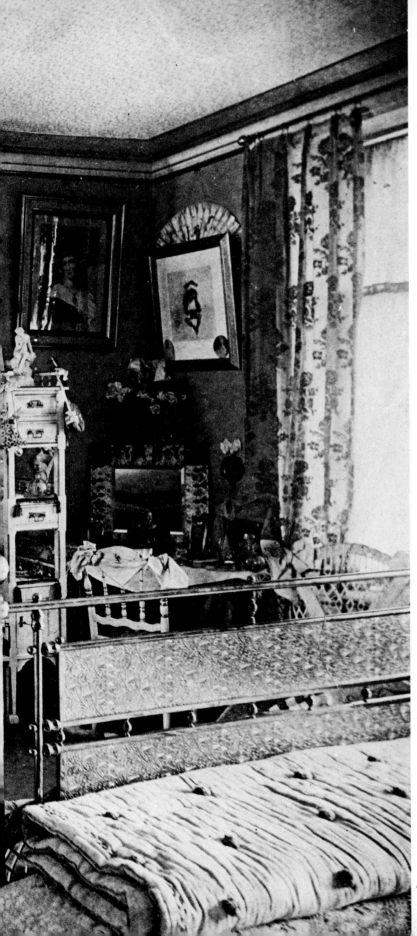

**70.** This bedroom in the Finch house would have been called Queen Anne, with its hooded chimneypiece and quaint little galleries and shelves. Here style was simply not enough, and the room was personalized with transient objects. The whole fireplace wall is a great art unit made up of smaller units. Curtains have been placed in openings, and bows and sashes decorate the chairs. Japanese fan and plumes, pictures, artificial flowers, and countless little everyday things were supposed to connote personal selectivity and taste. The complete treatment of this room is a marked contrast to the dining room, although they came from somewhat the same climate of opinion. It is fairly certain, however, that the dining room was the work of a professional and that in the bedroom the professional's effort was improved upon by some ideas of the owners themselves.

**71**

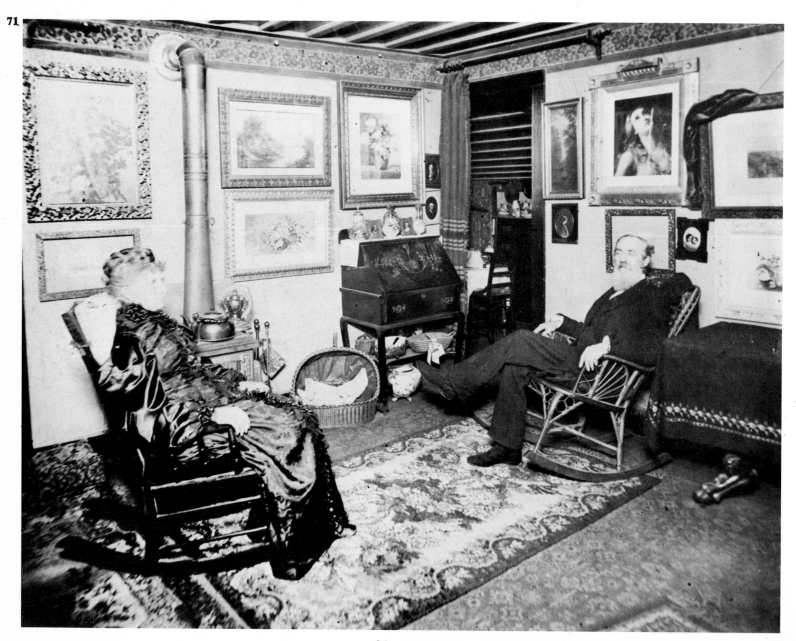

## Parlor and Dining Room, House of Arthur and Mary Foote, Boise, Idaho Territory, 1888–90

There were probably three or four rooms in the Foote house, two principal ones with one or more shed rooms attached by extending the roof to the rear. Nothing else is known about the Footes except what is recorded here, that for a time between 1880 and Idaho statehood in 1890 they cared enough to create this series of personal rooms from things they could order from catalogues and receive through the mail by railroad freight or, indirectly, via the Boise spur of the Oregon Shortline.

**71, 72.** Seated in their parlor, the Footes are not only surrounded by manufactures, but are wearing what is almost certainly mail-order clothing. These scenes visually document statistics which indicate that, by the later 1880's, Midwest mercantile houses did a large trade in the western states. Beside the door to the dining room is a colonial revival desk, which would have been called colonial or Queen Anne. Prints in gilded frames were available from dozens of catalogues of the time, and these are hung with china pins and wires from a wallpaper border that might have come from the same catalogue. Mary Hallock Foote herself must have painted some of the pictures and some of the china plates in the grouping on the parlor table *(72)*. Behind it, art drapery, carefully arranged and maintained, cascades from frame to easel, while a Japanese tea set awaits company on the colonial revival table—in this case a Grecian adaptation —with its rose-bordered cover.

**73.** The dining room seems to contain more of Mrs. Foote's scenes, flower paintings, and china plates, as well as a Renaissance sideboard and common, creative revival versions of Windsor chairs. The Footes probably considered this room colonial; but if they did not, they were simply at a loss for terminology, for the name would have applied in the East by this time. Manufactures have considerably civilized this plain little shed room.

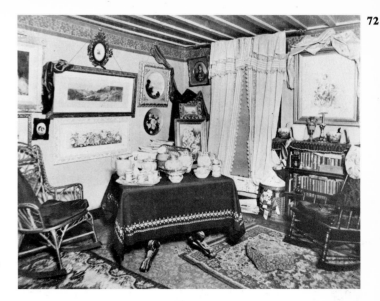

72

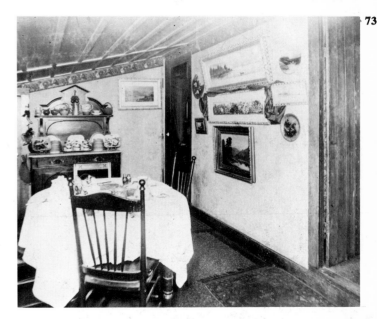

73

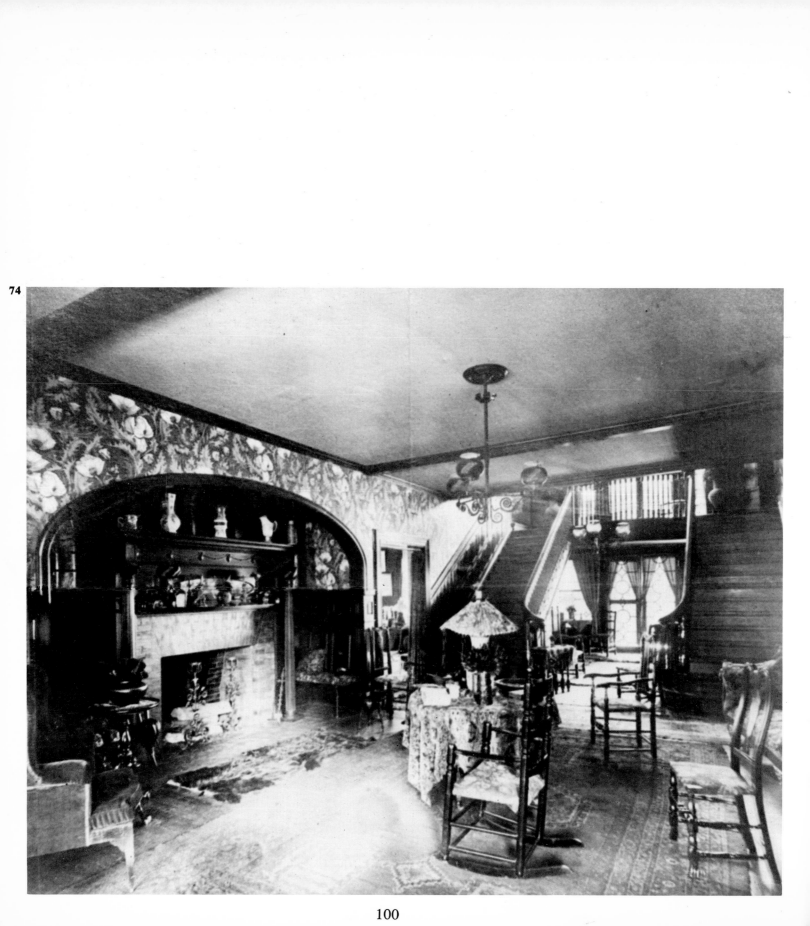

## 74. Living Hall, Massachusetts, ca. 1888

Colonial revivalist Arthur Little wrote in the preface to his 1877 sketchbook, *Early New England Interiors*, "It is thought by many that with the revival of the so-called Classical style in England as the 'Queen Anne,' or 'Free Classic,' we on our side of the water should revive our Colonial style." This hallway might thus be described as American vernacular Free Classic. By no means a reproduction, it is the product of a creative use of Georgian vernacular themes in an otherwise modern house. The grand stair, as it would have been called, rises to a broad landing. A screen of mullioned glass windows resembles the doors on some late eighteenth-century secretary-bookcases and makes the stair appear to be hanging in space. High wainscoting, a characteristic of the Queen Anne, underlines the bright poppy wallpaper. The chimney is recessed into a nook with built-in seats and a window; the mantel is Free Classic and serves as a stage for porcelains. Both colonial revival furniture and "old things" are here assembled casually around a draped center table, which, except for its paper-shaded vase lamp of the 1880's, might have been at home in the 1840's. The many subtleties express what people of the 1880's meant when they claimed to be applying the best of the past to their present uses. Some of what they associated with colonial America was actually much later, well within their parents' era.

## 75. Dining Room, Library, and Parlor, House of A. D. Lytel, 720 North Boulevard, Baton Rouge, Louisiana, ca. 1885–90

Lytel had practiced photography in the lower Mississippi River region as early as the 1850's. In 1880 he lived in this 1845–50 house with his wife, two children, and two female boarders. The arrangement of triple rooms opening to the left off a side hallway was typical of that semitropical area where the breeze was a primary consideration for comfort during at least nine months of the year. In the dining room, the room-size rug appears to be oriental in style, while the other two seem to be art squares, which were nearly always floral and symmetrical, with a center decoration radiating out to borders. There seem to be two kinds of furniture in the dining room: a walnut cottage set in the Renaissance style of the 1870's, its marble-topped sideboard ornamented by high shelves and a mirror, and little cane-bottomed side chairs with

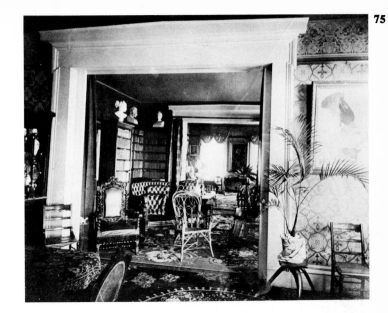

burl panels and incised decorations. A print from the Elephant Folio of Audubon's *Birds of America* is hung on the wall; framing Audubon bird prints came slowly into popularity toward the end of the Anglo-Japanese reign, probably because of the Japanese-like quality of the pictures, as well as an increasing interest in things American. An Elizabethan chair of the 1850's and a new leather-covered library set of chairs are mixed with rattan and wicker similar to that we saw in the Martha's Vineyard parlors *(37, 38)*, against a background of handsome book sets, wallpapers of the late 1870's and portieres, also in a patterned material. The banquet lamp is from the late 1880's. Palms, aspidistra leaves, and whimsical little swags indicate the summer season.

**76. Parlor, House of Richard Peters, Between 4th and 5th Streets, Atlanta, Georgia, ca. 1887–89**

The Peterses were a large and prominent Atlanta business family in the optimistic era of the New South. Only a half-hour away from the door of this house was the Georgia countryside, worlds away from progressive Atlanta, which liked to claim kinship with Chicago, not the neighboring southern towns the Civil War had laid bare. Atlanta had risen from ruins, and its gentry planned an optimistic future in roomy parlors like this one. Wicker and parts of a modest creative revival Renaissance set comprise the main furnishings; the gasolier and gas brackets illuminate a room which has a sparseness common to high-style rooms of the time.

**77. Dining Room, House of Mrs. James L. Morgan, Jr., 7 Pierrepont Street, Brooklyn, New York, 1888**

This house of about 1850 has been brought up to date by the Morgans, owners of a chemical company in Manhattan. The ceiling has been frescoed and borders have been painted to disguise the Grecian moldings in plaster; a picture molding has been dropped and the space above it

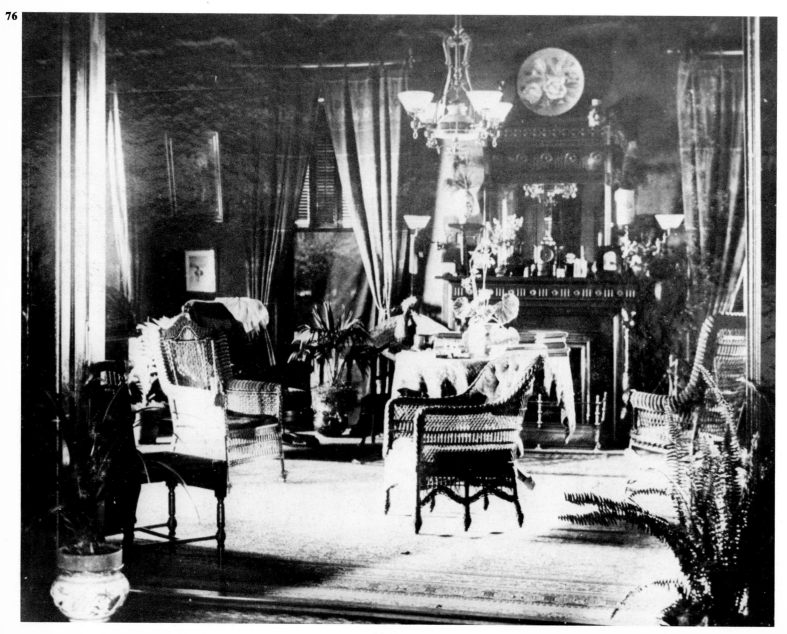

filled with a plaster frieze depicting bamboo shoots. Family portraits weight the walls on either side of the chimney, and the effect of a stylish overmantel with shelves for porcelains has been gained with the asymmetrical art unit of china plates on wires. Fashionable oriental-style carpeting doubtless made a colorful floor for the ebonized furniture—in a creative revival mode that came directly from the Louis Seize with the curiously stable look of the Elizabethan carried out in the heavy stretchers. The gas fixtures are in the New Grecian style, with wine pitchers as finials, and Grecian wine craters as counterweights on the arms of the gasolier. Theatrical portieres conceal the last vestige of architectural character from the 1850's and dominate, almost like huge cabinet pieces, forming a grand archway between the dining room and the parlor.

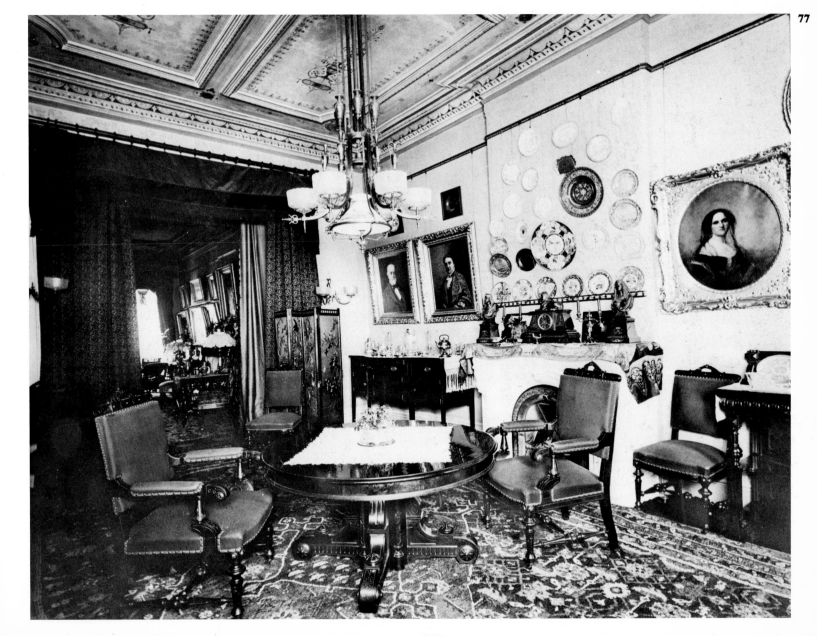

77

**78, 79. Double Parlor, House of Mrs. Frederick Tudor, 34 Beacon Street, Boston, Massachusetts, 1888**

Euphine Tudor was the seventy-three-year-old widow of the famous New England ice king, Fenno Tudor. Their urban mansion had its heyday in the 1840's; left with an immense fortune, Mrs. Tudor was able to maintain her style of living until her death. Here she remained for the balance of the nineteenth century with her four servants, an aging butler, and three maids. If she was set in her ways, her house was ruled by the calendar, and on a certain day in May her rooms were disrobed for summer

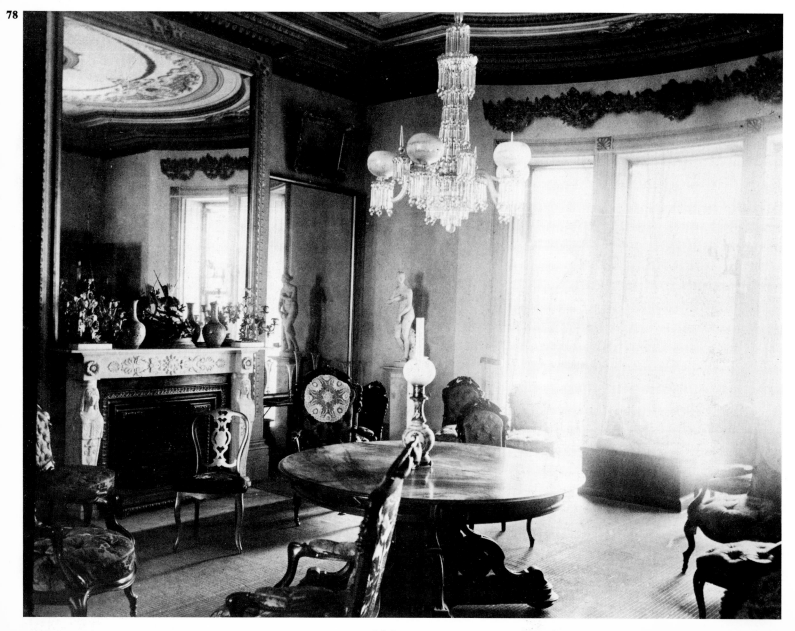

78

and left as they appear here. Curtains were removed to the attic and laid out flat in a long cedar box, a candle being lit in a nearby sandbox to attract moths away from them. Carpeting was taken up and straw matting laid down. This double saloon, two rooms connected to one another by doors that folded between the Corinthian columns, had, by 1888, probably changed very little. The French Antique parlor set and the Renaissance dining room set had once been quite expensive, and could have been made in any one of a half dozen or more excellent manufactories in Boston. These styles were mass-pro-

duced by the later 1860's and were still being produced in the 1880's. Time had hardly faded the stenciled Grecian borders, or dulled the gilding on the woodwork, yet the widow Tudor did not ignore changing tastes. Her parlor mantel and her sideboard have been decorated with art-painted and oriental porcelains, and the matched pair of banquet tables, necessary for large gatherings in times past, are reduced to center tables and ornamented with the latest pretty vase lamps on the market.

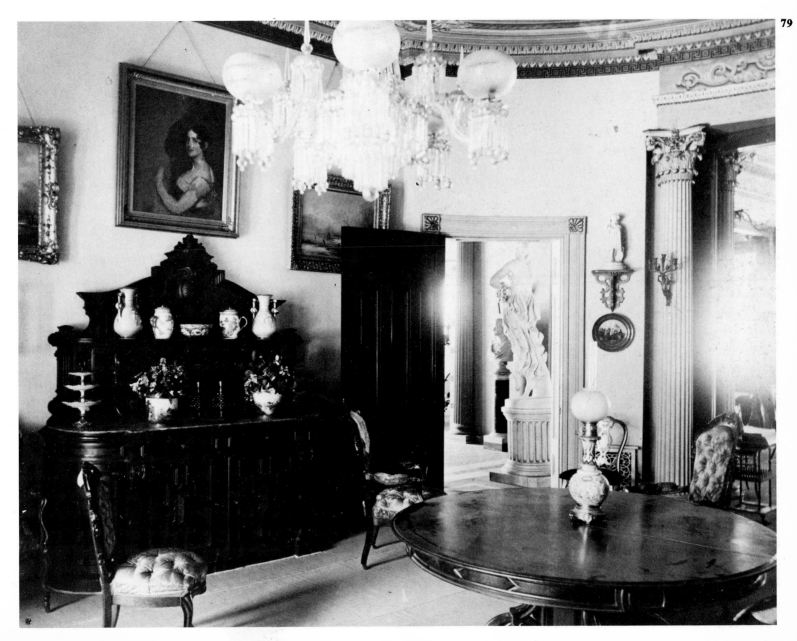

**Parlor and Bedroom, House of the Emerton Family,
Salem, Massachusetts, ca. 1886–88**
By the later 1880's, the colonial revival was well under
way on the East Coast. Colonial motifs, which had once
been merely decorative, were now becoming foremost in
the design of houses, making them more nearly resemble
actual historical models. Reproduction, however, was
still a long way off. The Emerton house, remodeled and
expanded in 1885–86, was an eighteenth-century house
in the Georgian vernacular of New England. Arthur Little's bold designs brought to the orderly existing struc-

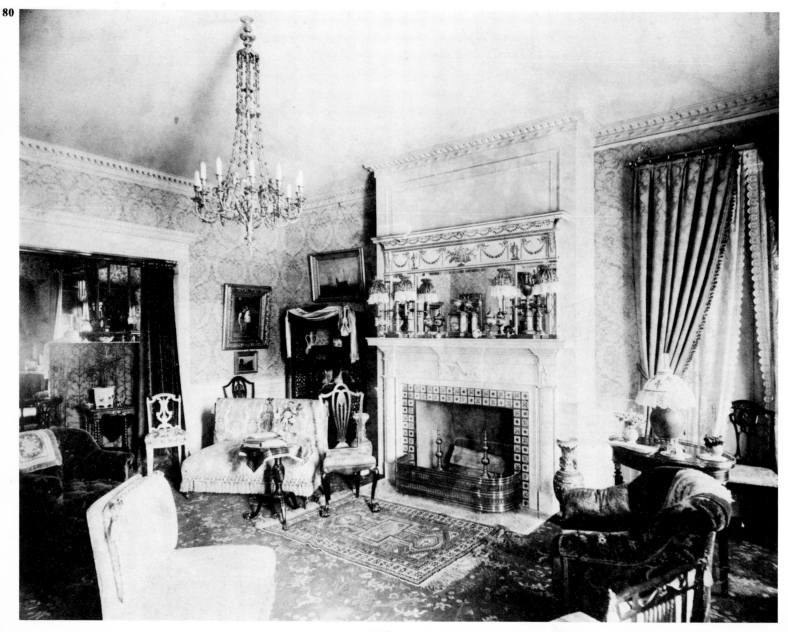

80

ture additions that had a picturesque effect. He used the old house merely as a point of departure for what can be considered today a transitional composition, and he was quite consciously building a modern living environment in the mood of the colonial past.

**80.** Adapted neoclassical style woodwork in the first-floor autumn suite, as Little called it, demonstrates how little the early colonial revivalists bothered about whether their motifs were technically colonial or not. White woodwork and intricate modern wallpaper are the backgrounds for new furniture, much of which was in the colonial revival style. These furnishings were not exact reproductions, but were far closer to being so than colonial furnishings had ever been before—or, for that matter, than any revivals had been since the first Louis Seize of the 1860's. Argand lamps have reappeared here, dressed up with fancy shades and perhaps piped for gas, for the particular sort of chimneys which we see indicate that incandescent mantles are in use. Colored tiles set around the fireplace opening had been popular since the early 1870's, and were readily accepted as being colonial.

**81.** In this upstairs bedroom, Arthur Little's work lingers in the picturesque far more than in his parlors below. More than colonial revival, the mantel wall is like some of the English Queen Anne of the 1880's when it took on a heavy Georgian flavoring: here is a little gallery to hold whatnots, a long and extended mantel shelf and oval mirrors, all decorated with Adamesque ribbons and garlands probably in plaster and painted colonial ivory, or Old Virginia White, as one trade catalogue had called it for a decade. There is considerable kinship between this and the bedroom mantel in George Finch's house in St. Paul *(70)*. Both were built in the same decade; yet this one in Salem is much more advanced toward what the late nineteenth and the twentieth centuries would produce. While the Emerton parlors were probably furnished by an interior decorator, or Little himself, this bedroom contains furniture that is already fifteen years old.

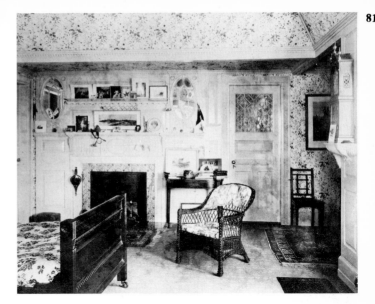

81

**82. Sitting Room, House of William Glasgow, Jr., 3024 Glasgow Place, St. Louis, Missouri, ca. 1888**

Nearly everything in this room would have been considered outmoded in 1888, but Glasgow has nevertheless attempted to update the setting. The four pieces of Grecian furniture of the 1830's include three chairs patterned on Ionic column capitals and an overstuffed sofa with great cushions, early and quite handsome expressions of the creative revival movement. Pushed against the left-hand wall is a French Antique center table covered with a modern embroidered cloth, while in the cen-

ter of the room a cheap little tea table, neither new nor old, replaces it, and is adorned with a tea cloth, vases, and a statuette. The armchair is of a creative revival mode which evolved from the Renaissance revival, and the other overstuffed chair is a Louis Seize brand of the creative revival, with an even more creative mate in the hall table. The oriental rug and the porcelains on the French Antique *étagère* are a tribute to the exotic. A modern piano lamp, forerunner of the floor lamp, a gasolier of about 1875, and a mass of art pictures on inexpensive new wallpaper complete the consciously stylish

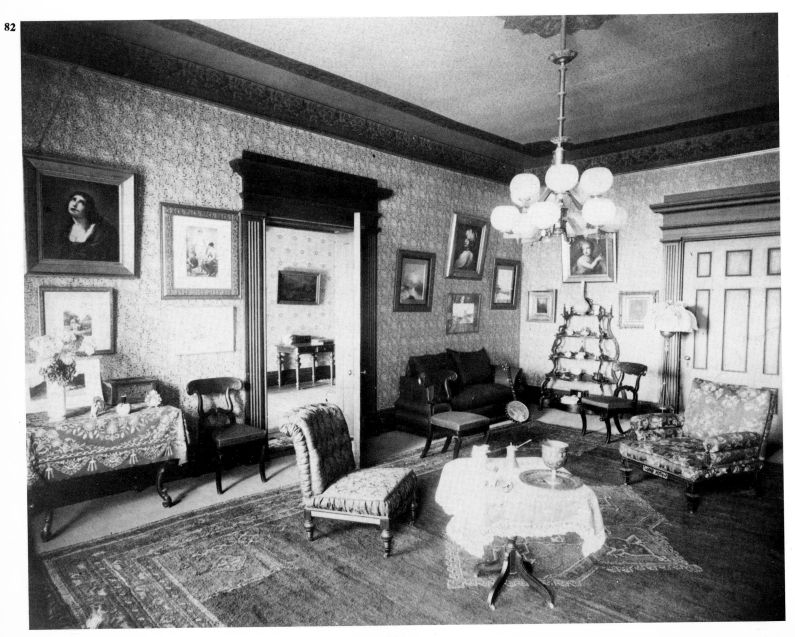

82

108

treatment of this middle-class sitting room, in which most of the furnishings have probably been spared the second-hand wagon only by the limitations of their owner's pocketbook.

### 83. Library, House of Chief Justice Melville Weston Fuller, Washington, D.C., 1889

Without going to much expense, Judge Fuller has created a comfortable retreat from his public life. Low bookcases which seem to be the work of a carpenter hold his library and display his pictures, porcelains, and plates against modern colonial revival wallpaper and white woodwork. Plush portieres, here only panels for appearance, hang from white rods. The floors are bare around the edges, though not yet stripped of their dark paint and wax, and varnished. The room is adorned with arrangements of real roses instead of amateur paintings of them. Over the door is a little art affectation consisting of an oriental rug with an Arab's portrait hung upon it. The big easy chair covered in tapestry was a model that developed in the 1870's and knew great popularity on all levels until World War I, after which it took other forms.

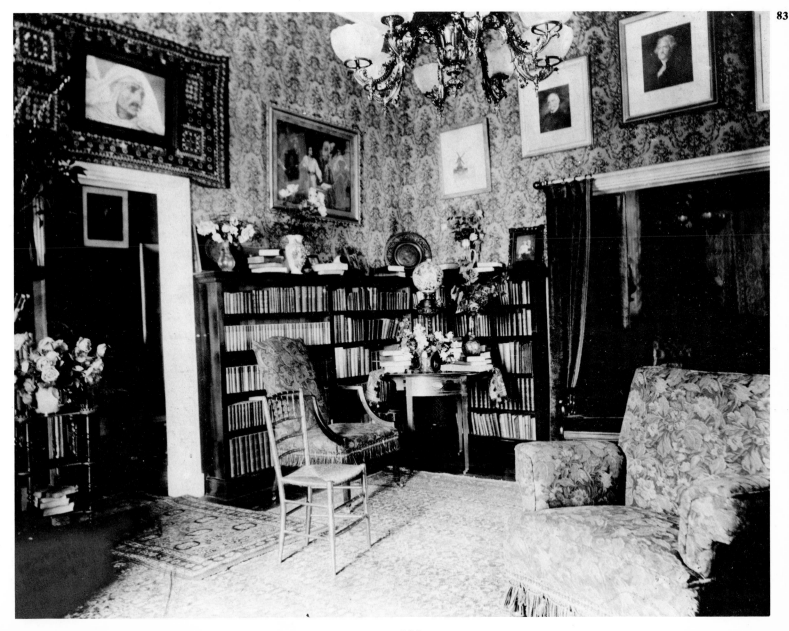

83

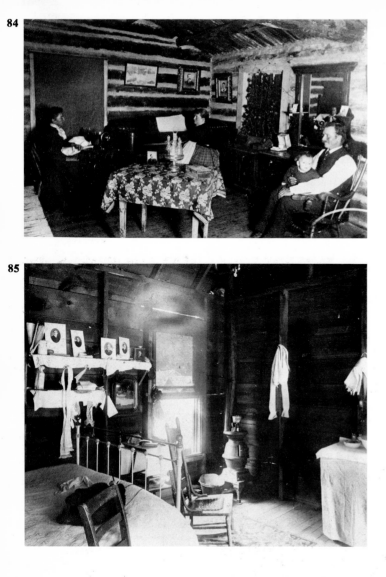

**84. Living Room, House, Dakota Territory, 1888–90**

Manufactures have asserted their authority dramatically in this plain log-walled room, which might otherwise be a room of the early nineteenth century. Close together are the parlor, or square, grand piano so coveted by pioneers and the marble-topped washstand and dresser. The latter two, undoubtedly in walnut, are creative revival pieces based upon Renaissance revival predecessors. To the left is a sewing machine, one of the earliest machines to enter the realm of domestic art, and initially designed to resemble earlier sewing tables. Over a rough and homemade center table has been thrown a cheap piece of printed goods, and on that is placed the silverplated Japanese-style cruet set, a popular item in the catalogues. The man is sitting in a colonial revival rocking chair; rockers grew to great importance in the 1880's and middle-class houses without them were rare even until World War II. Vines have been trained up one window in a very old-fashioned way, while the other window, with its white trim, seems to be covered by a painted cambric shade.

**85. Bedroom, Miner's House, Colorado, ca. 1888–90**

The diggings had become mines, and something of the aura of company communities settled over them. Tents and shacks disappeared and were replaced by permanent houses, like this one, of milled lumber. Unceiled houses were more common in the United States during the nineteenth century than is usually supposed; nor were houses such as this considered shacks. Shelves substitute for a mantel. There are many conveniences such as the gaslight and the stove. A flowery cotton skirt has been fixed over a box or table, making a washstand. An inexpensive rug and colonial revival rocking chair are at the foot of an iron and brass catalogue bed which, in 1890, cost about $4, delivered from Chicago to the Rockies.

**86. Ranch House, Eastern, Montana, ca. 1888–90**

Sold through mail-order catalogues, manufactured goods rolled westward on railroad trains or wagons. Many family legends of beloved heirlooms that made the trip to the West have been told, and this picture seems to confirm that it might have happened, at least in this instance, with the Renaissance bookcase, a harbinger of about 1855 of the creative revivals. The whitewashed log interior, with its bare ceiling of cedar poles, is filled with manufactured transient objects—pots and pans, particularly. American cookstoves like this one were shipped dismantled to any place in the world. The Windsor, considered a kitchen chair in most catalogues, cost less than a half dollar at this time in Chicago, but was probably somewhat more in Montana. Only the table and bench here are homemade; packing crates serve as tables. On the wall to the right is a Winchester rifle, and to the left a Colt revolver hangs in its holster. Designed to use interchangeable bullets, the Colt and Winchester are known as "the guns that won the West," and are examples not only of another kind of manufacture but another kind of

transient object ever-present in the nineteenth century American home.

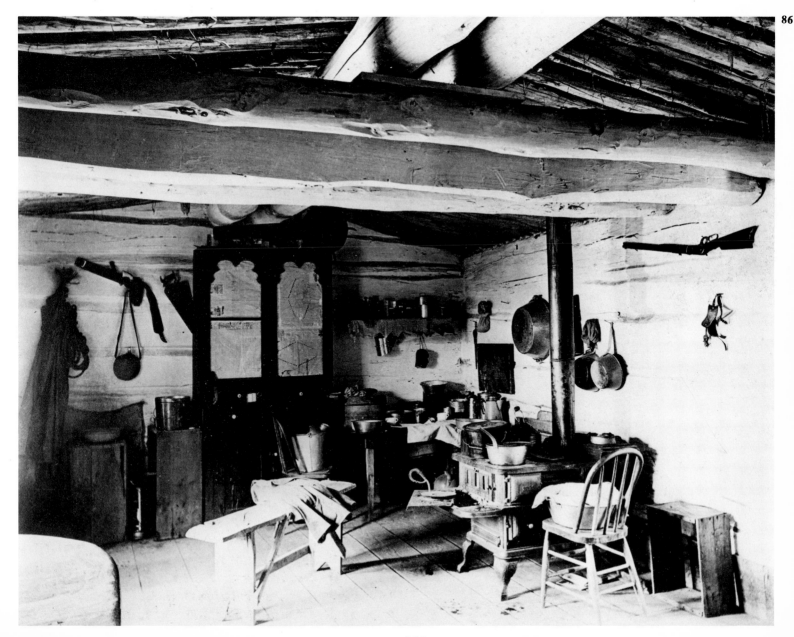

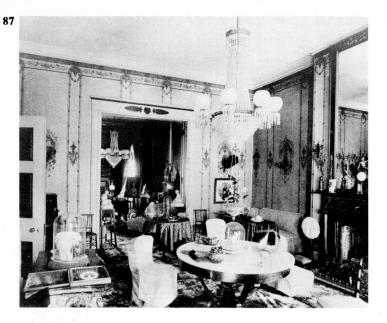

87

**87. Double Parlor, House of Judge John Cadwalader, 240 South 4th Street, Philadelphia, Pennsylvania, 1890**
Little has changed in this Grecian and French Antique setting, perhaps put together first about 1848 and 1850. To the eye of a visitor in 1890, the rooms must have been greatly improved when the furniture styles fell into anonymity beneath the white linen summer covers. French Antique wallpaper—which might actually have been French—dating from about 1850 is about contemporary with the Brussels carpeting, while the Grecian mantels, like the motifs on the double doorway, seem slightly pre-1840. It is true that everything here seems to be intact, but there have been changes. A gilded French Antique card table is now serving as a Japanese tea table in front of a sofa in the left foreground, with objects of art, placed about with studied casualness, but no more so, of course, than those on the three center tables that, chain-like, stretch from one end of the double space to the other. Rich mantel garniture of the 1820's and 1840's in both rooms has been punctuated by the addition of oriental porcelains. China tea sets are placed here and there—a pot, a stack or two of cups and saucers. In the foreground appears the edge of what seems to be an eighteenth-century Philadelphia Chippendale chair, returned from exile perhaps around the time of the Centennial of 1876.

**88. Parlor, House of Judge Augustus Macon, Canon City, Colorado, ca. 1890**
Macon, a lawyer born in Kentucky, lived with his wife Virginia and three children in this house, which was considered one of the very best in Fremont County. The chandelier is made to look as if it might burn gas, but the cocks are useless, as oil lamps have been installed on the branches. Alternating panels of two slightly different designs of wallpaper ornament the wall over the mantel; breaks between the panels are framed in what seems to be gilded half-round molding. The floral carpet, ordered in strips and sewn together with a surrounding border, presents only a small variance on the pattern of the wallpapers. Art pictures, family photographs, and pastels adorn the walls and the top of the low bookcase where a stuffed eagle stands guard, binding the diverse elements

together. The center table is creative revival with Renaissance revival background, although it might possibly have been called colonial in its day because of its vague resemblance to early nineteenth-century library, or sofa, tables. With the exception of the rattan rocking chair, the other furniture is also creative revival of many sources. The desk in the right-hand corner is based upon the Louis Seize revival, while the chaise longue and the armchair in the left-hand corner have Grecian roots. A secretary-bookcase of the mid-1870's is the earliest object in the room.

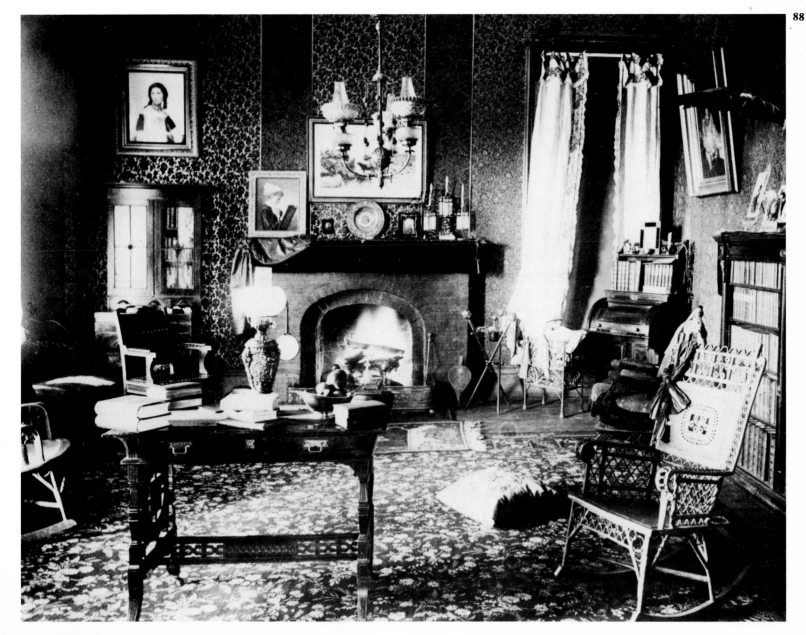

88

**89. Parlor Musicale, Tallahassee, Florida, 1890**

A. S. Harper, the photographer, was very successful with this long exposure but he failed to record the names of his subjects. Banjo, guitar, and piano comprised many a home band, and such family amusements were heartily encouraged by the ladies' magazines. Perhaps such a magazine gave the instructions on crocheting the lambrequin that beautifies a crude old mantel. New wallpaper in some dark color with gilt figures doubtless covers old wooden walls. Tasteful geysers of pampas grass, with the bust, pictures, and hammered copper ornament framed in black velvet, give the room a tasteful art look, which the younger of the two women may have learned at school and is teaching her mother.

**90. Parlor, Shirley Plantation, Charles City County, Virginia, 1890**

The piano lamp and rattan chair are about the only new objects in this parlor; but because of the room's arrangement, and the growing acceptance of American antiques in the 1890's, it is not wholly out of date. It was not, however, any more sophisticated or fashionable than it

89

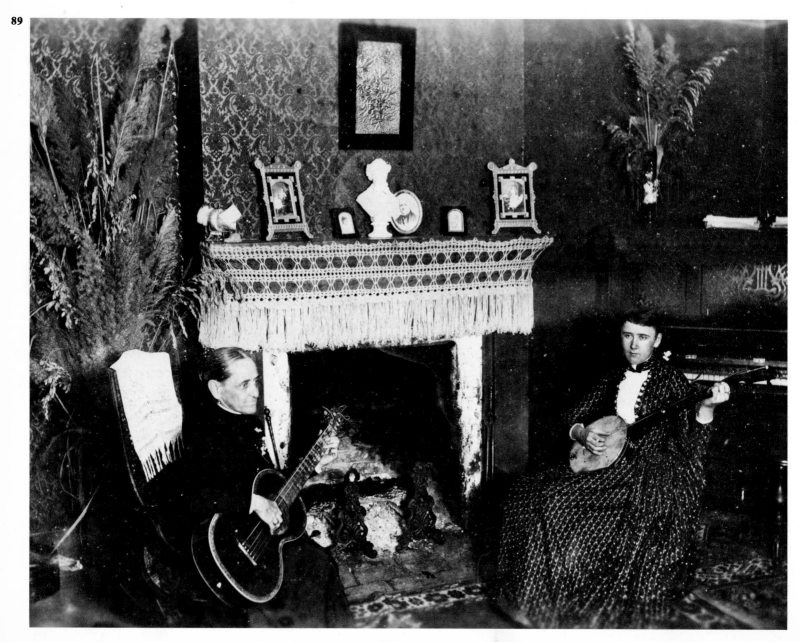

probably would have been to an Englishman's eye when it was originally built. Completed about 1770, Shirley was already, in the 1880's, recognized as one of several major colonial monuments on the James River, and this parlor was only the second most important in a series of paneled rooms, the best of which was a stair hall. Notwithstanding the presence of an abundance of family things from the past, the descendants of Shirley's builders felt no more compulsion to attempt period interiors than anyone else did in 1890. Banquet ends of about 1820 are pulled together to make a center table to hold an art unit composed of bouquets and pieces of china. The symmetrical mantel arrangement and tilted mirror may represent a conscious effort to appear old-fashioned. The fine group of early nineteenth-century portrait sketches includes, in the center, a profile by Saint-Memin. No eighteenth-century furniture appears here.

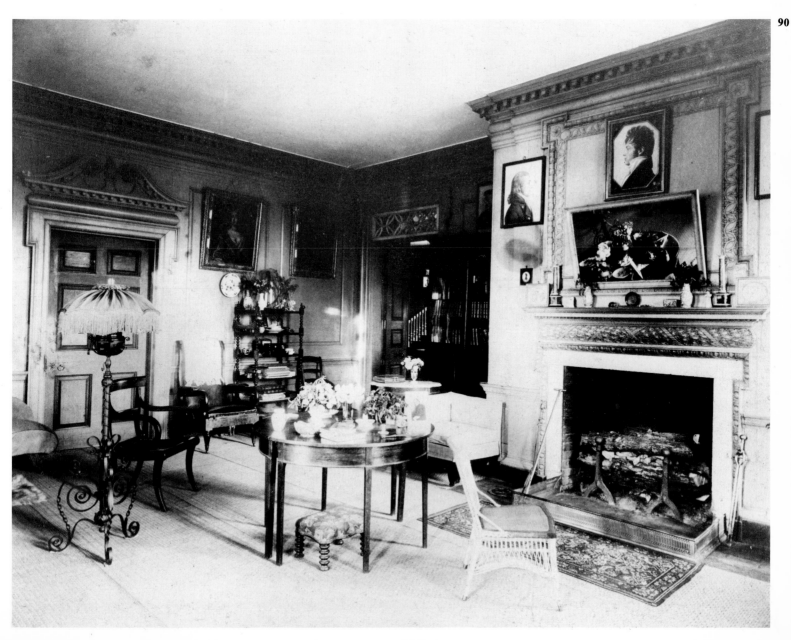

**Parlor and Dining Room, House of Lady Mann, Boise, Idaho, 1890**

**91.** Lady Mann, whose name survives simply as that, had a small music school in Boise, and here she is shown in her parlor with some of her students. The curtains seem to have been adapted to fit these windows, and are dramatically tied back low to the floor. Between the windows is a shelf with a fringed lambrequin, treated as a single unit, just as though it were a mantel. The composite lamp, an innovation of the 1880's, was one that did not require a chimney and therefore cut down consider-

ably on cleaning. All the Mann furniture is mass-manufactured in creative revival styles. On the floor beside the platform rocker, a photograph album has been "tastefully" propped open and its contents seem to rise by magic from its pages. The pictures on the walls, it can be suspected, are the works of Lady Mann.

**92.** In the manner of the entire nineteenth-century, in houses great and humble, the dining room doubles as a sitting room. White walls, by no means unheard of late in the century, set off the room, which is decorated with a lambrequin-draped shelf and art unit and a variety of

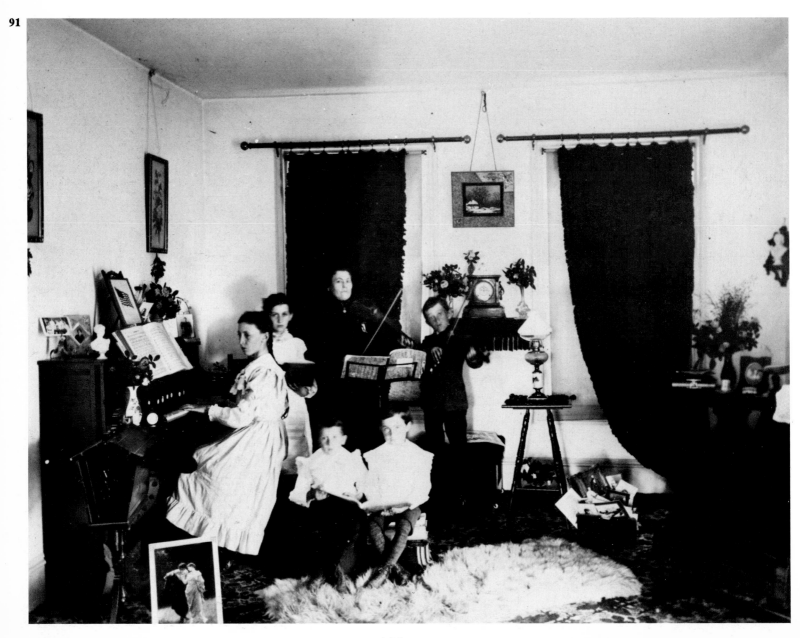

91

pictures hanging from china-tipped pins. Perhaps some objects, such as the fur rug, have been moved to this room for the photograph. In the doorway, a heavily embroidered and appliquéd portiere is made to fit by draping it over a rod; called a queen's curtain, it was often meant to pile up deep at the hem and could be ordered from dozens of mail-order houses all over the United States much as one ordered plush, damask, or lace window curtains. Instead of wallpaper borders, Lady Mann has taken leaves and pasted them in artistic rows on the wall and over the door. Her table is not a center table, for lack of room; but she has not surrendered the idea, and has made the table top an art unit for the display of the interesting and the instructive.

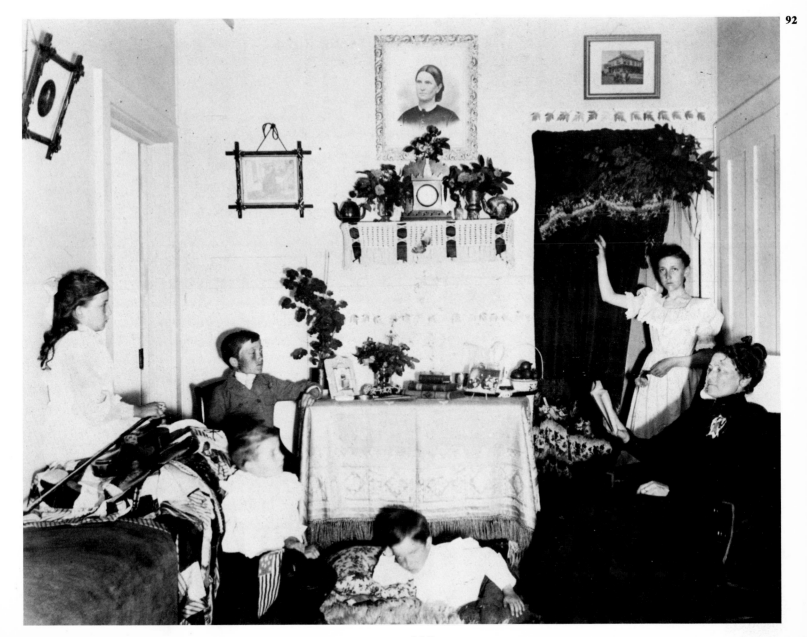

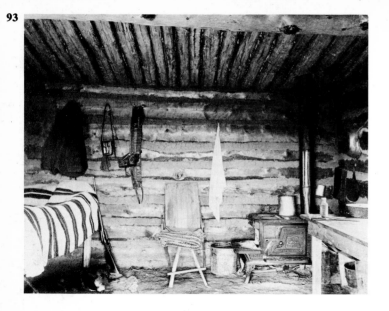

### 93. Wolfer's Roost, Montana, 1890

A wolfer was a man who hunted wolves for a business; when he killed them, he cut off their heads and brought them to the nearest state agency where he collected a bounty in cash. This anonymous roost, in the era of lambrequins and art units, expresses a lonely and temporary existence. Basic necessities—binoculars, rifle, pistol, a jacket, and a few pots and pans—comprise the decoration. The iron stove rests on a dirt floor not even packed hard with use. Rude table, bed, and chair, built against the wall, show an effort to provide elementary comforts. Even in this barren roost, the majority of the objects are mass-manufactured goods.

### 94. Drawing Room, House of Benjamin B. Comegys, 4205 Walnut Street, Philadelphia, Pennsylvania, ca. 1890

The house of this Philadelphia bank president was not a new house when he bought it, a villa of perhaps 1845. During the 1870's, he added a large library to one side in a style that might be called Cedric the Saxon, and there he filled his idle hours meticulously taking apart folio volumes of Shakespeare and Scott, pasting in appropriate prints he had collected, and having them bound to match, with his name and the date. When the house was demolished nearly a century later, the library was removed to the Smithsonian Institution's Hall of Everyday Life in the American Past, where it remains today. Mr. Comegys's daughters were brought up to be cultured ladies. After attending the right schools, and with no matrimony in sight, they began what amounted to a career of traveling that lasted until their deaths in the middle of the twentieth century. Their drawing room, looking out on Walnut Street over a porch shrouded in wisteria, was a museum of their genteel adventures in foreign lands. Little of the old Italianate feeling was left there when this picture was made. The fashionable three-part wallpaper treatment had been added probably about 1878–80; Japanese fans and other orientalia must date from the same period. Louis Seize revival and Grecian seem to be the sources for most of the furniture that can be seen, excepting, of course, the Philadelphia Sheraton-type chair, the room's only colonial piece.

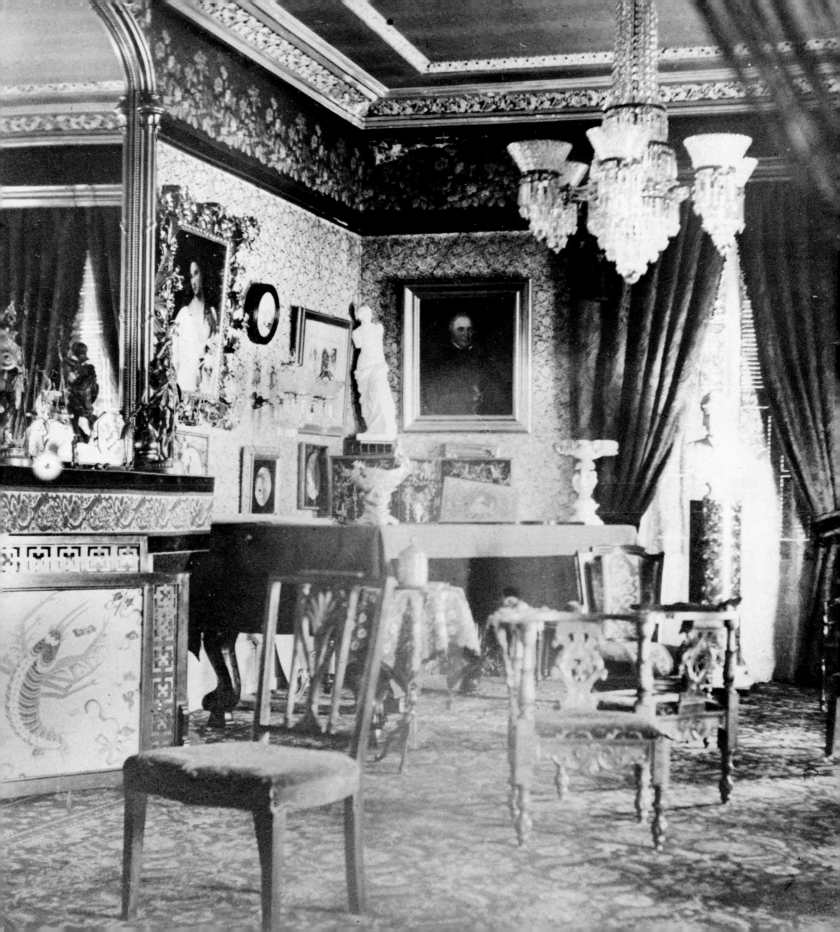

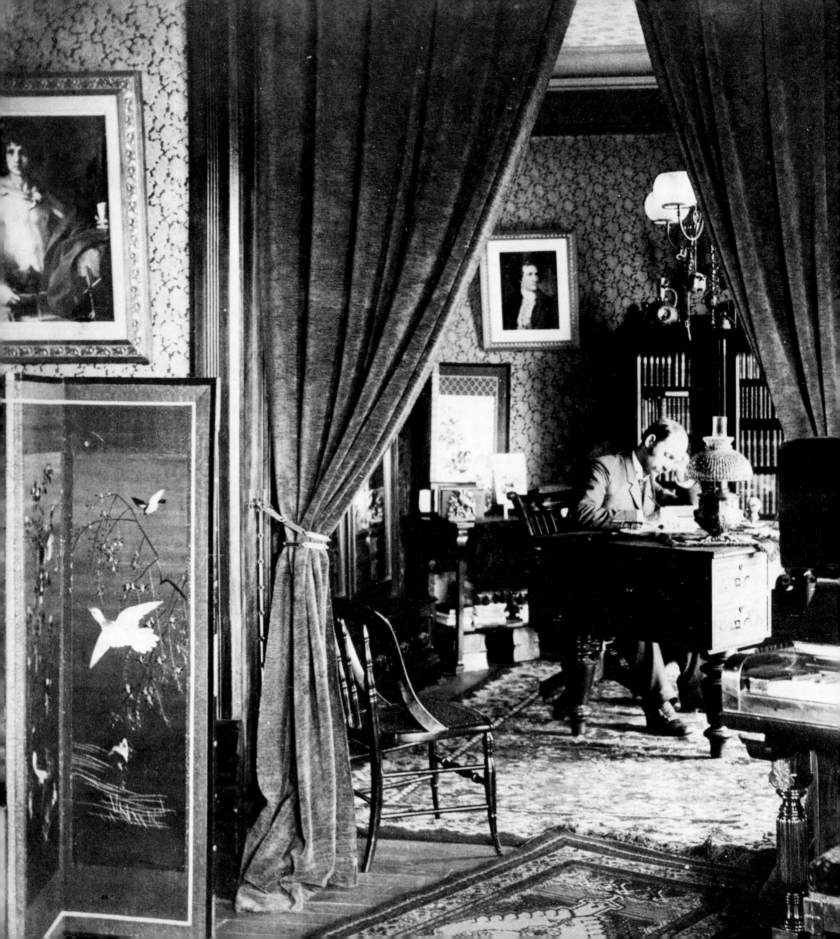

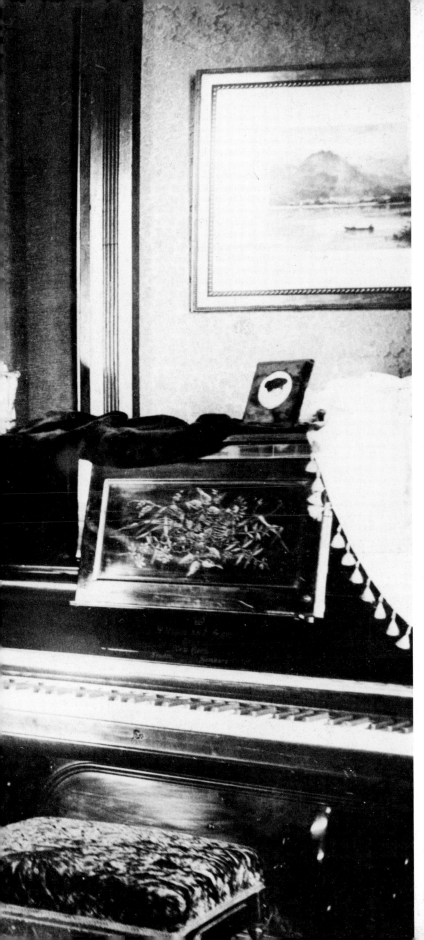

**Apartment of Arthur Dana Wheeler, Mentone Apartment House, Erie and Dearborn Streets, Chicago, Illinois, April, 1891**

In the Midwest and West, the pace of style was set by Chicago. Particularly after the fire of 1871, apartment houses were built in great numbers, echoing, and even anticipating, trends in other major cities in the United States. The Mentone was an upper middle-class apartment house eight stories tall which presented handsome views of Lake Michigan. While the exact nature of the plans of the individual apartments is unclear, this particular apartment seems to have contained a series of three connecting main rooms which led into one another around the corner of the building. Probably the kitchen and service entrance were at one end and the bedrooms at the other. It amounted to a small house for, unlike most apartments of the time, which were divided former single-family dwellings, the Mentone was built as an apartment building, and every convenience was taken into consideration.

**95.** The library was situated off the central parlor. The man is seated at a colonial revival desk, a two-sided, or partner's, desk with Grecian legs of the sort that had supported parlor grand pianos forty years before, and colonial revival brasses. There has been careful coordination of varnished walnut woodwork, flocked wallpaper, dark banding above the picture molding, fawn-colored plaster cove, and the ceiling which is covered in a light, and entirely different, pattern of printed wallpaper. Paper and wood screens heighten the Japanese flavor, while on the walls hang art pictures. Carved panels on the upright piano show the Japanese taste of the Aesthetics. Such piano decorations were becoming prevalent as stoves and central heating made fireplaces luxury items in many new houses, and a substitute was sought for the fireplace mantel.

**96.** The view from the parlor to the dining room shows an easel, a self-contained tableau; an ivy plant has been trained over it as an apartment dweller's tribute to nature. The portieres here, as the others in the apartment, are velvet and held back with chains, and their value in the bitter Chicago winters was more than decorative. Beyond the colonial revival rocking chair and lushly organic table with carved serpent and leaves, the dining room seems very plain, containing little more than a table with a cover, a gasolier, and a silver basket of fruit. To the left of the doorway, the wooden overmantel is decorated with bronze, glass, china, and a wisp of silk, a fully developed art unit, as clearly symbolic an offering of its kind as are wreaths at the door of a tomb.

**97.** This view from the dining room back into the parlor reveals the spaciousness of the apartment. Situated in a corner of the building, the parlor has a bay window, crisp lace curtains, and various kinds of chairs, including the Turkish overstuffed one with its Grecian legs, a colonial revival rocking chair, and in the doorway, decorated with a bow, a plain little chair which might also have been called colonial. The dining room has a

96

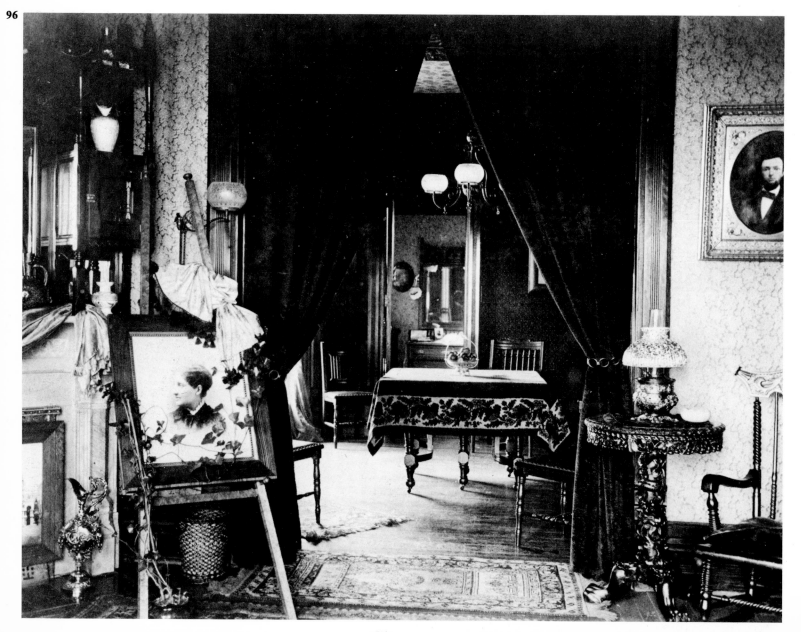

corner sideboard that comes close to following Charles Eastlake's medievalized tastes of twenty years before; but it is not so with the chairs, which are creative revivals coming, by and large, from the Grecian. A heat register, located immediately behind the parlor's corner mantel, proves the fireplace is merely an ornament.

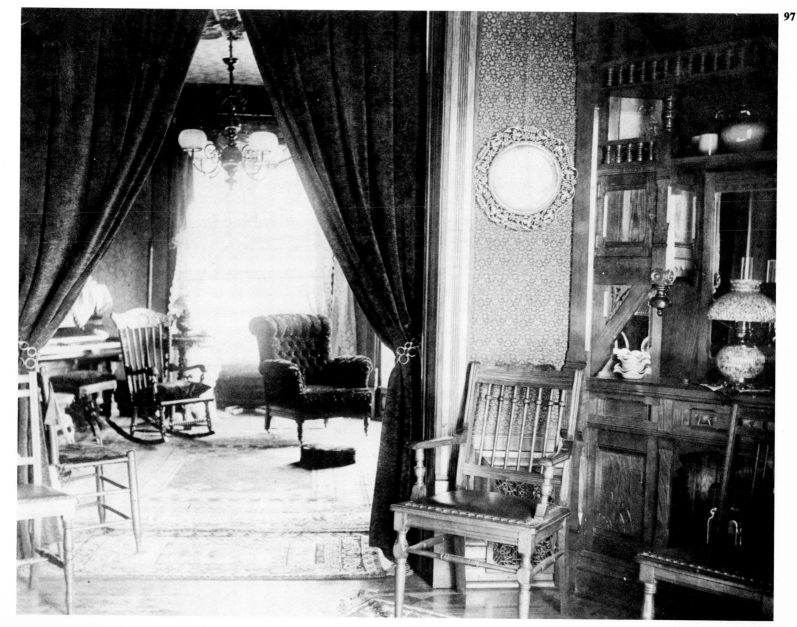

## House of Eugene A. Fiske, Santa Fe, New Mexico, August, 1891

**98.** The parlor, with its lambrequins, side panels, and lace curtains, its mantel, and ebonized overmantel laden with porcelains and statuettes, its oriental runner laid over a wall-to-wall Brussels carpet, and its profusion of little things, is very much up to date in expressing the personal taste of its owner. It seems that personalizing took on a greater significance and lasted longer in the West than anywhere else. This is not necessarily because style lagged in the West, although it did lag, and did also

98
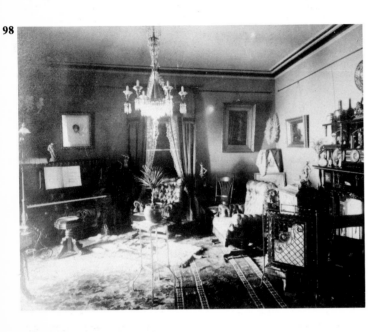

99
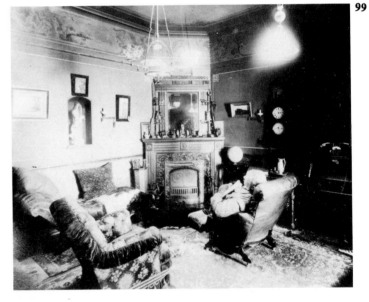

100
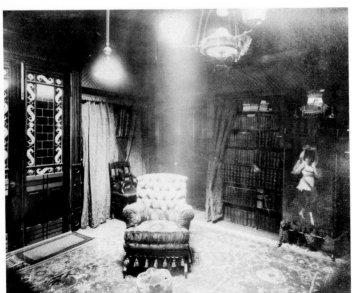

101
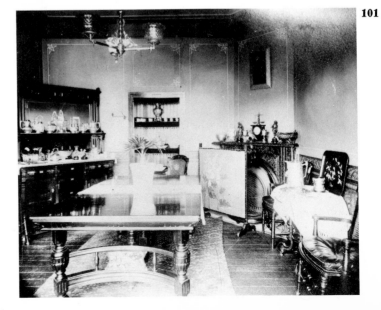

in middle-class houses nearly everywhere, even a few blocks away from the most fashionable residences in America. Personalizing, in particular, had a long duration perhaps because the West was new country; while westerners proclaimed their newness, there seems to have been a certain quest for identity in the decoration of their houses. Fiske carefully recorded his rooms that summer day, and did so again when he redecorated them nine years later, as will be seen *(157,158)*.

**99, 100.** The man sleeping in the massive-mode chair has been reading beneath that new innovation, the electric light, which was not entirely dependable and would not cause the removal of gasoliers until some years later. Most of this furniture would have been called Turkish for its cushioning; such stuffed furniture is an important link in the history of American furniture because it represents a virtual abandonment of wooden style and a conscious freedom of form through upholstered masses. The mantel and overmantle, with Queen Anne and Grecian motifs, was probably considered colonial. What appears to be a painted frieze surrounds the room, with pin striping on the ceiling, in the molding, and on the walls in a manner first popularized in the 1860's. To further minimize wood, the old custom of draping the fronts of bookcases has been revived here. The double doors have stained glass lights; they and the woodwork are catalogue products of the kind shipped nearly anywhere from mills in the Midwest.

**101.** Besides the pin striping, dark coves, and touches of gilt, the dining room also appears to have a three-dimensional dado, perhaps of cardboard or plaster, and painted. The mantel is marbled iron, its outdated unsightliness covered up by a screen in the Japanese taste, its shelf laden with new art objects. Perhaps the massive-mode dining table was called Jacobean by this time; its inspiration, however, was the Elizabethan revival, just as the chairs are creative revivals based upon the Grecian and the sideboard a creative revival from the Renaissance.

**102. Company Cottage, Kohinore Coal Mine, Shenandoah, Pennsylvania, 1891**

Modest but often pleasant housing was provided by many different kinds of companies, from large agricultural establishments to mills, factories, and mines. This miner's parlor, decorated from mail-order catalogues and perhaps

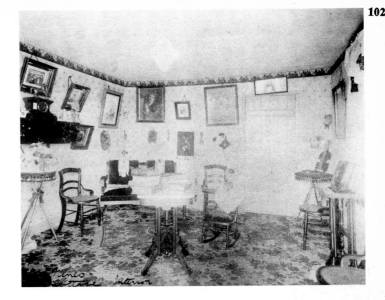

102

the company store also, shows what an ambitious family could do with a plain company house. Diapered wallpaper, daringly light in color for a coal-mine town, is bordered in a floral motif. The stove has been taken down, probably for the summer, and the hole for the pipe has been plugged and covered with wallpaper. Four inexpensive caned chairs and a sofa, creative revivals with Grecian sources, are mixed with fringed gypsy tables and walnut tables with marble tops. Nearly everything here appears to be new, yet the taste of the owner is confined to the past. A center table is piled with books, and chairs are lined around the walls in the mid-century manner; pictures are hung high with cords and pins, and the absence of a mantel has been compensated for with a long lambrequin-covered shelf, garnished with a mantel clock and curios. The miner has created, with new furnishings, a room setting which is, in most respects, forty years out of date.

**103, 104. Parlor and Sitting Room, House of William A. Finch, 137 Hudson Street, Ithaca, New York, 1892**

Professor Finch taught at Cornell University. The absence of books in this part of his house is surprising, and indicates that there was probably also a library. Different carpeting denotes that one of these rooms is for a different purpose than the other, the sitting room being that with the piano, the creative revival credenza with its Grecian and Elizabethan revival sources, and the colonial revival rocking chair. In the parlor, the center table, by now out of style, has not been abandoned by the professor, but pushed into a corner to serve its usual purpose as a place upon which to display things. On the walls of both rooms hangs a mixture of prints and flower paintings doubtlessly executed by a female member of the family. Bows and antimacassars on the chairs, cushions here and there, and artificial flowers over the picture frames are strange instances of personalizing in rooms otherwise rather gaunt.

103

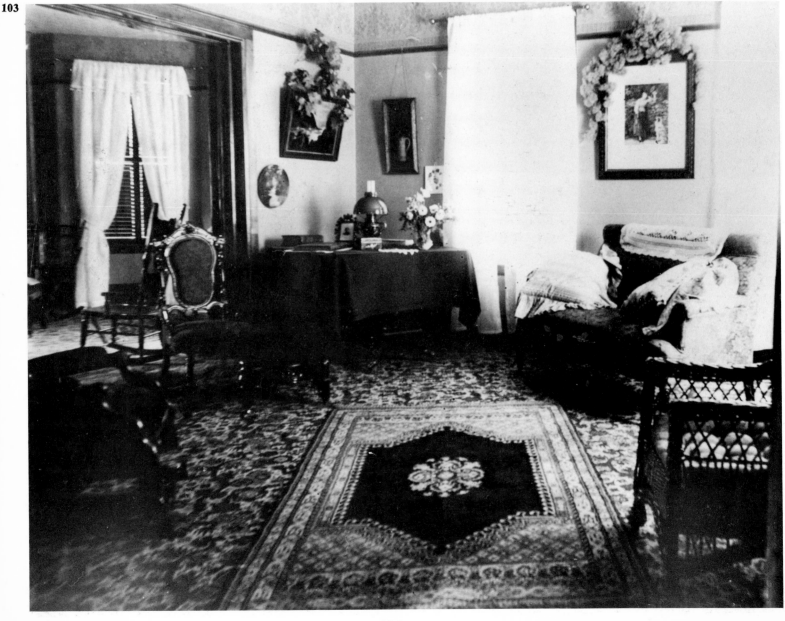

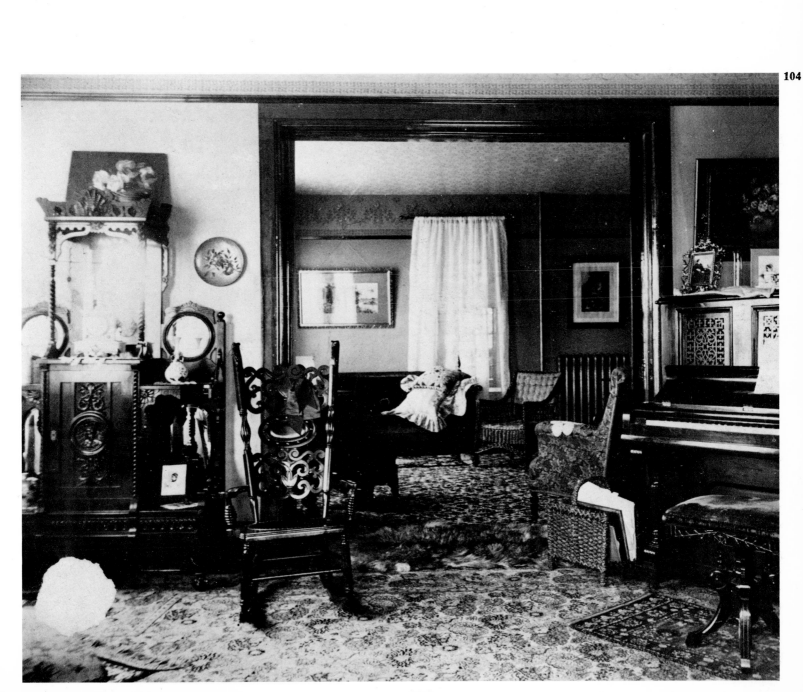

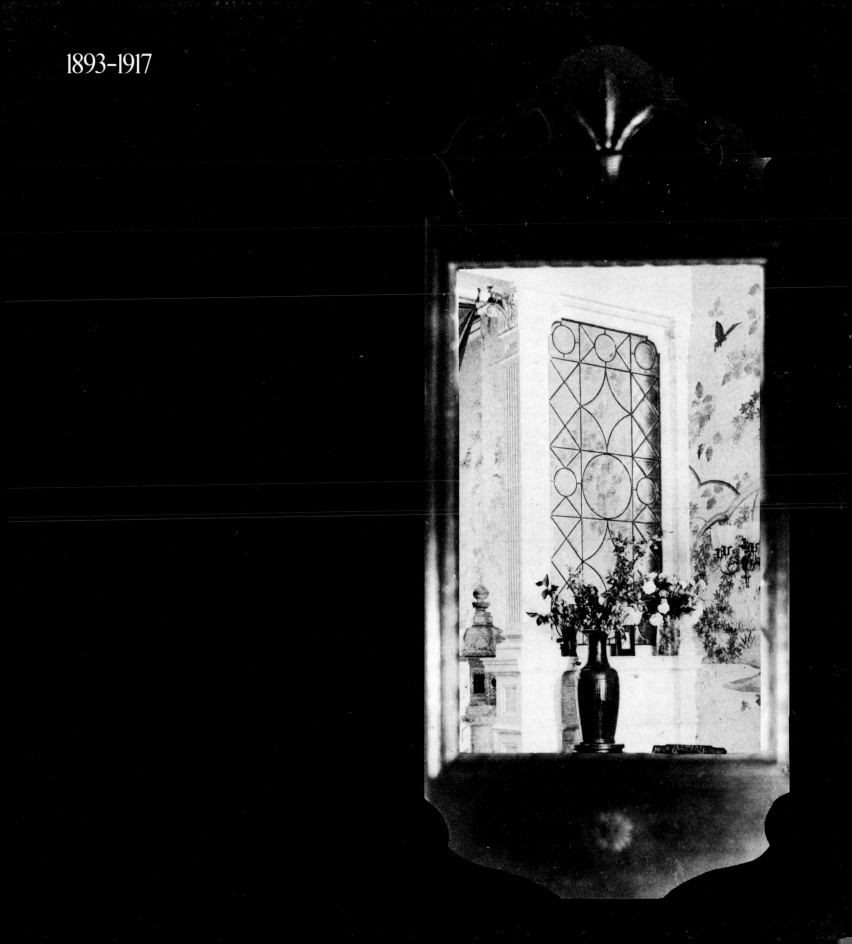

1893-1917

## 105. Library, House of Charles L. Dahler, 212 South 8th Avenue, Helena, Montana, 1894

The treasurer of the Iron Mountain Company lived in one of the handsome Queen Anne houses built by Minneapolis and Chicago architects in Helena since the late 1870's. Dahler's library has kept abreast of the times, with its overstuffed leather library chairs, oriental-pattern portieres, and Quaint, or Fancy-shaped, armchair which had only very recently made its appearance on the American market. The popular creative revival table in the foreground has Elizabethan revival antecedents; while it is still kept away from the wall, its place as a center table has been usurped by a flax wheel, equipped with flax and lending a desired colonial air. Efforts at personalizing are more orderly and spread out here than in many other rooms of the period, and that reflects a new tendency, which eventually led to a revision of the role of transient objects in such rooms. The library and parlor beyond it are, architecturally, products of the 1870's; it was perhaps in the 1880's that the scroll fancy-work screen was inserted in the double opening, and even later that the woodwork and floors were stripped and var-

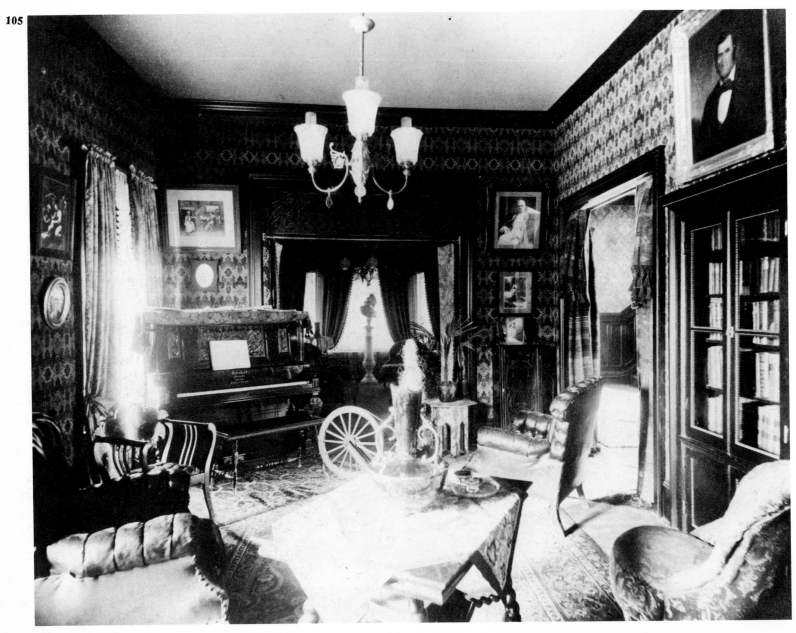

nished. Popular art prints and religious pictures complete this comfortable middle-class setting, which could have been located nearly anywhere in the United States.

### 106. Sitting Room, House of Miss Mary Russell, 72 Beacon Street, Boston, Massachusetts, ca. 1894

At fifty-four, the daughter of Nathaniel P. Russell lived alone in her family home and was considered an old lady. The room was probably wallpapered in the 1880's, although the border might be earlier, if not simply un-stylish. Intermingled with portraits and photographs of

her family and friends, Miss Russell has decorated walls, fringed mantel, and easel with art pictures of famous paintings and statues. Potted plants stand ceremoniously on stools beside the fireplace. The chintz slipcover on the chaise longue matches the covers of the stools, which may contain chamber pots. It is a sitting room filled with the familiar, where Miss Russell lives with the past, and whatever of the present that comes to call.

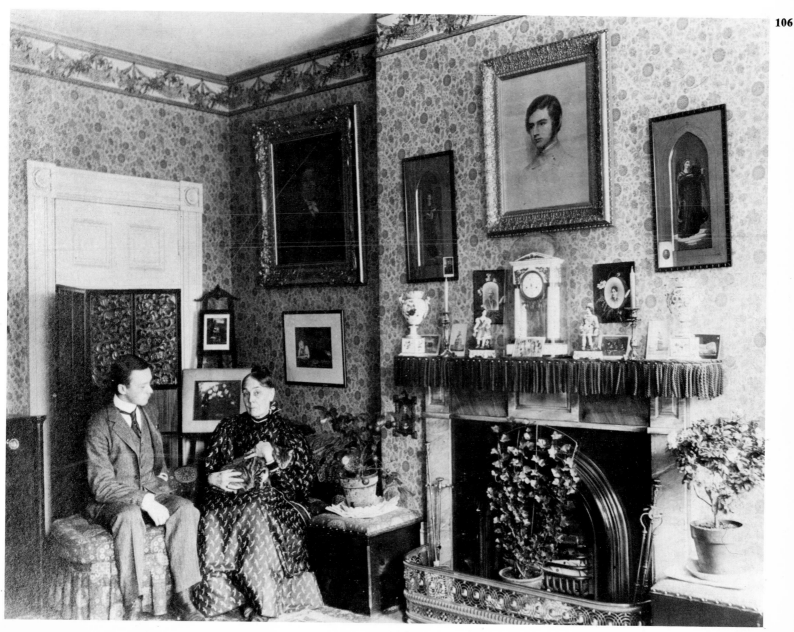

## 107. Parlor, House of Louis Melcher, La Grange, Texas, 1893

Written on the back of the original of this picture is "Living room of Louis Melcher showing furniture made by himself." The interest in organic furniture reached its peak in the middle 1890's; the twigs and vines once imitated for furniture in iron and wood had by then long been familiar in forms made from the actual materials. In the 1850's the rockwork from which rococo gets its name was popularized in various ways, from the introduction of polished sea shells and rocks on mantels and center tables to the cementing of shells and little rocks as crusts all over pieces of furniture. Melcher, a photographer, has created here an organic parlor with horns from Texas longhorn cattle; his settee could be called creative revival, so obvious is the origin of its form in the Renaissance revival, just as the center table of horns, here pushed against the wall, is in form Louis Quinze revival. The wooden walls, painted a light color except for the simulated washboard, and a real but very low chair rail, are decorated with other evidences of Melcher's horn creations, arranged beneath a crowning band composed of framed photographs. Both the glass vases and the ill-fitting mantel lambrequin have close identities with the German origins of this Texas family. To the right, the manufactured platform rocker has been given a patchwork seat.

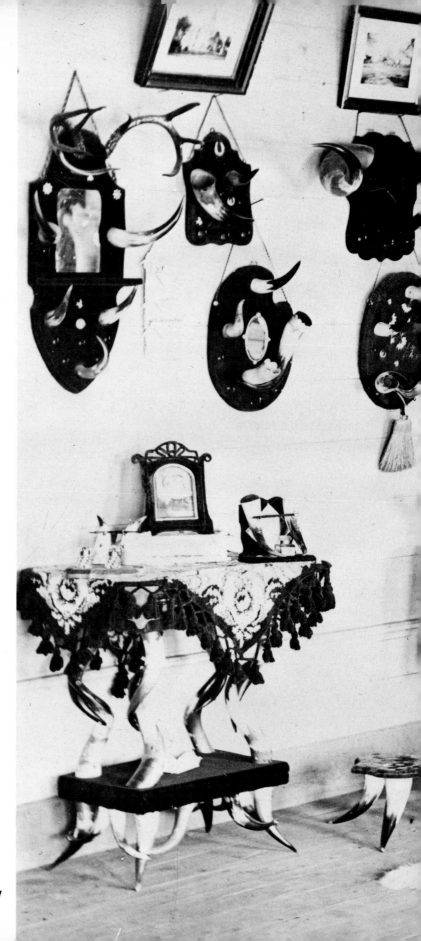

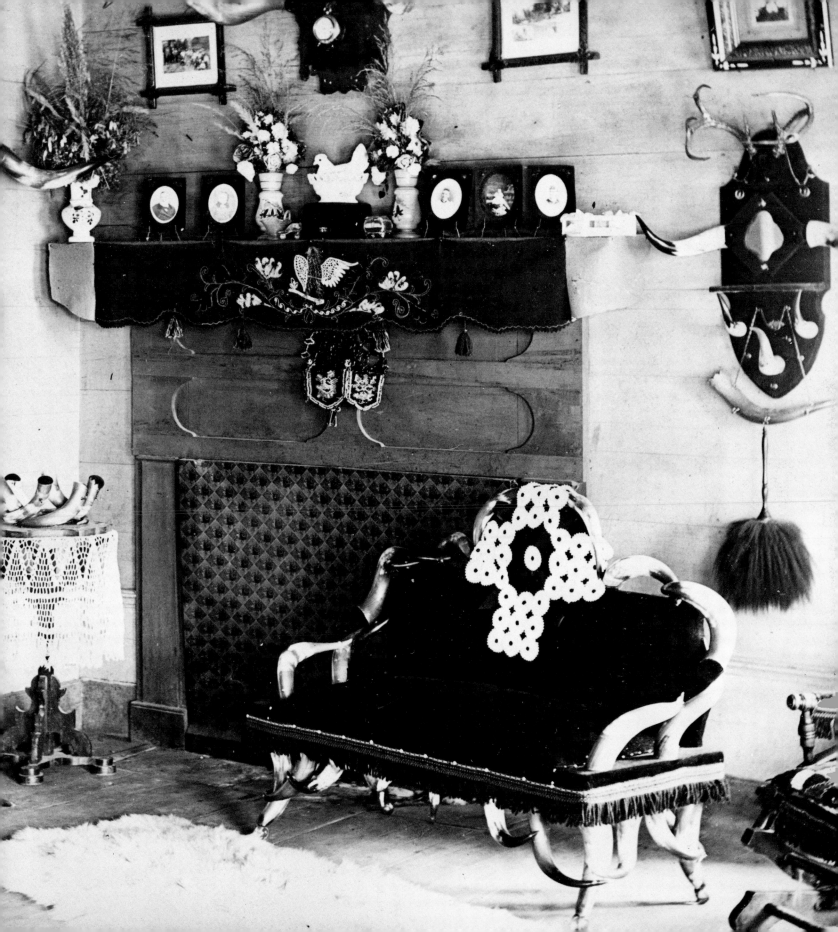

**Clonniel, House of Dr. T. G. Morton, Strafford, Pennsylvania, 1895**

The expansive room arrangements possible in houses built to be used only during the warm season anticipated the open planning commonly found in twentieth-century residential architecture. Clonniel, with its views of forests from deep porches, and its freely connecting rooms, epitomizes that American fondness not only for the pastoral but the homey. Comfort was an important element in American room decoration from the start, but it was not until the 1870's and 1880's that the houses them-

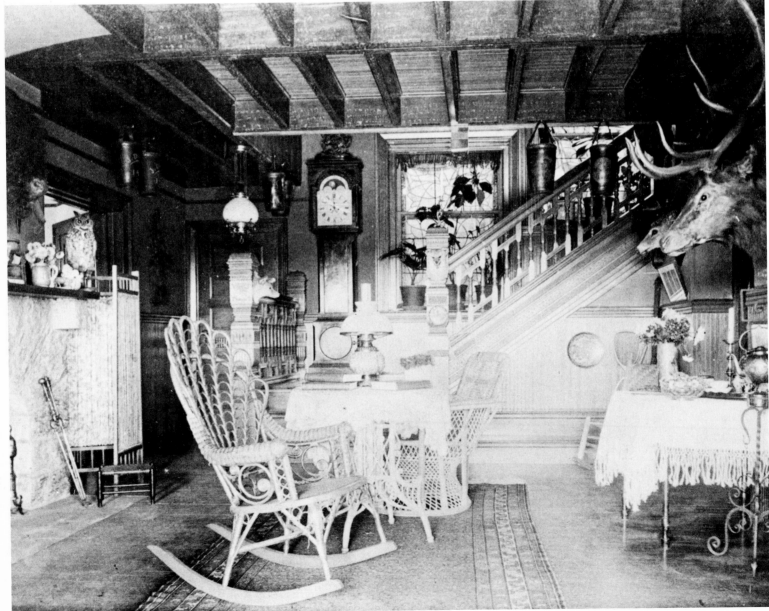

selves began to take on that special kind of comfortable look. The tight art units were broken up and spread out. As the use of central heating became widespread, connecting series of rooms began to characterize American domestic design. With ancestry in the double parlor and in the multiple use of rooms found in vernacular houses, this planning brought a built-in quality of livability to houses, and gained the almost universal approval of the middle class.

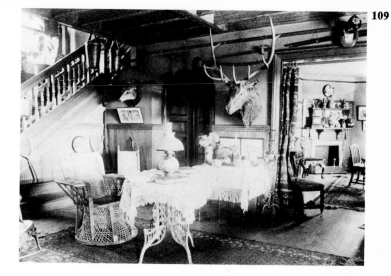

**108, 109.** The living hall served both as entrance and sitting room. One was prepared for it already having crossed a furniture-strewn porch, which might be further defined by awnings and potted plants. Heavy polished beams grid the ceiling of inexpensive railroad-car siding. Pictures, animal heads, rifles, and plates ornament the walls, which appear to be covered with painted burlap, a popular and practical sheath for plaster, while reproductions of colonial fire buckets hang from the beams. A big stone chimney and floors of varnished narrow boards set the stage for the wide staircase which might ascend to a very narrow upper hall. Tea set, rattan furniture, and white table covers enliven the airy space, into which light floods from all directions.

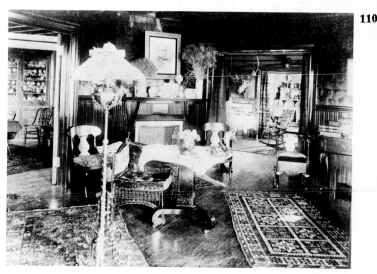

**110.** The sitting room, adjoining the dining room and living hall, is furnished in colonial revival furniture of a type relatively new on the furniture market in the 1890's. Grecian chairs and center table are in a colonial style marketed somewhat later as American Empire. More believable colonial revival is seen in the sword chair and in the low table to the right. The walls are shingled and either painted or stained. Oriental rugs are scattered over the polished floor. In the 1890's, oriental rugs were essential to the proper colonial interior, although the practice was largely an inheritance from the exotic Moorish, Turkish, and Anglo-Japanese.

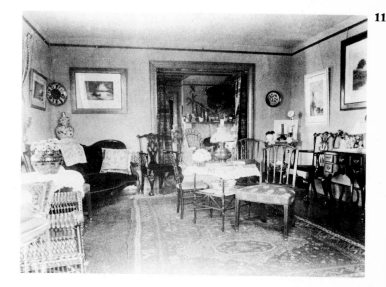

**111.** Pairs of reproduction Chippendale chairs ornament the parlor with rattan, an old French Antique sofa, and simulated Sheraton bamboo table and chair. It was to this sort of reproduction that the historical revivals began to turn in the late 1880's, and more noticeably in the early 1890's to counterbalance the abstractions of the creative revivals. It is interesting to observe that there are no creative revival pieces in these rooms, except for the rattan furniture.

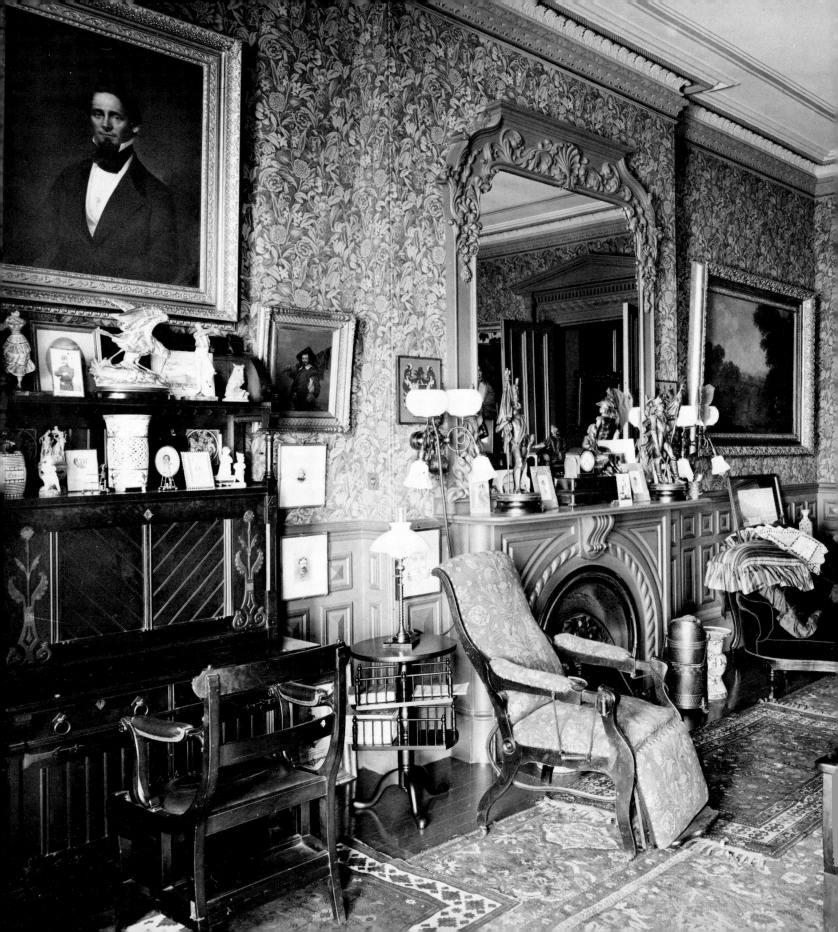

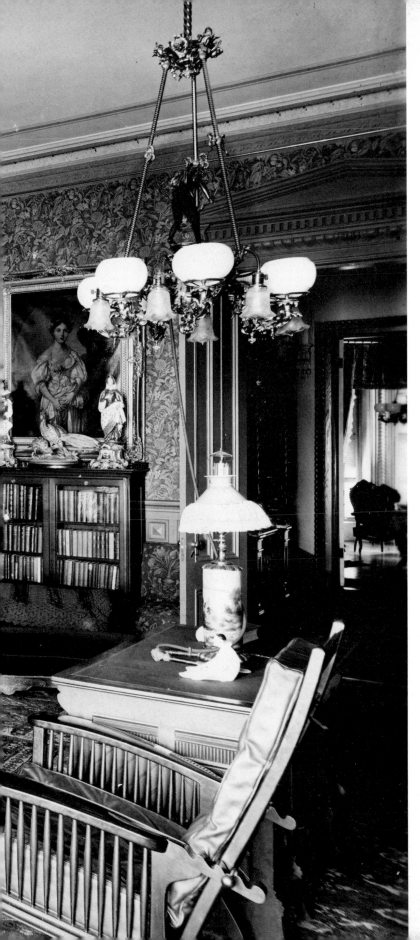

### 112. Library, House of T. B. Winchester, 138 Beacon Street, Boston, Massachusetts, 1894

This room of the 1840's has been recently modernized by the addition of electricity to its gasolier and brackets, new wallpaper and much paint, applied over the gilded French Antique mirror, marble mantel, and woodwork, including a wainscoting of about 1875. Old Brussels carpeting has undoubtedly been pulled up, and the painted and varnished floor is allowed to show around the edges of the oriental rugs. Portraits and landscapes from another time now share the walls with photographs, an art picture, and that sure sign of East Coast affluence in the 1890's, the family coat of arms. To the right of the fireplace, the Marie Antoinette chaise longue has been recovered perhaps in imperial blue with cording in a light color and fluffy pillows with ruffles. The invalid chair of about 1860, to the left of the fireplace, had once been considered Grecian; it is the progenitor of the creative revival Morris chair across from it, which might have been called colonial at the time, rather than being named after its Grecian ancestor of nearly a half century before. Released from their formal units, the objects here bank the room and visually intermingle with its architecture.

**113. Hallway, Norfolk or Richmond, Virginia, 1895**
Secluded cozies and nooks were often composed of plants, various kinds of fabrics, and cushions, and decorated as elaborately as one might wish with porcelains and brasses. Sometimes an inglenook, of wood and tile, was built into a house, forming a cave around the fireplace. But simpler, and more widespread, were such bays full of ferns and pots as this one, attesting to an affection for such altars, but not an obsession. Here snowy lace curtains form a backdrop for the green plants, and hang loosely from brass rods in deep folds, cascading to the floor. The oriental-type carpeting has been covered with an actual oriental rug and some fur rugs. Hall trees, nearly always present after about 1845, became informal art units, displaying personal objects, like hats, gloves, umbrellas, and scarves, which, in more sophisticated houses, were already being hidden away in coat rooms and closets. This hall tree is a creative revival type based upon the Elizabethan revival and has some colonial overtones. On a commonplace wallpaper, borders have been used cleverly to create a Japanese-style ceiling. Hardly the work of an interior decorator, this hallway,

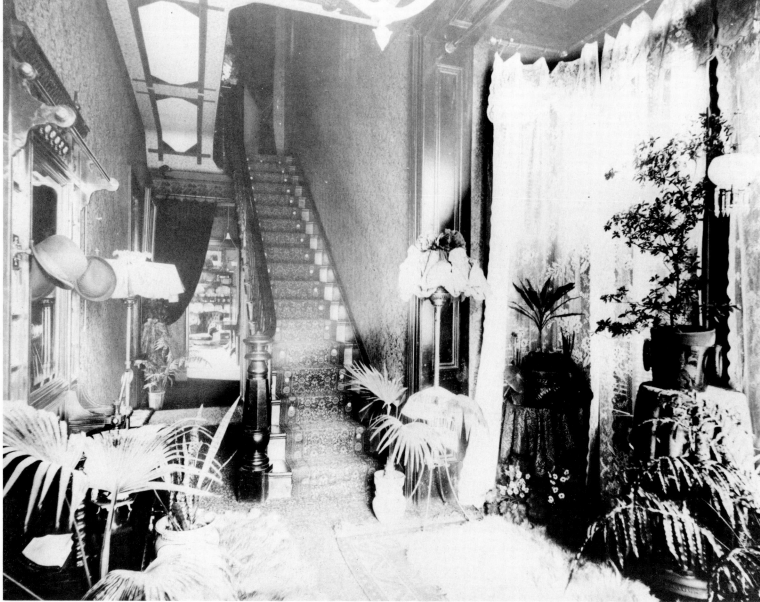

113

we can suppose, reflects an avid reading of magazines and some familiarity with decoration in public buildings of the day.

**House of James E. Sullivan, 245 Wayland Avenue, Providence, Rhode Island, 1895–97**

The colonial revival house of James Sullivan was completed on one of the suburban streets of Providence in 1893. Colonial indeed, but still picturesque with its Georgian rooms installed in a structure largely in the Queen Anne style, the Sullivan house might be called transitional. By the close of the decade the Sullivans would have demanded a more believably colonial form.

**114, 115.** Corner fireplaces permitted more windows and broader openings, which minimized the ponderously grand scale from without, and made rooms sunny and cheerful. The two views of the Sullivan parlor show a colonial revival room embellished by gilt-frosted French ceilings of applied plaster ornament, with some bouquets of flowers painted on in pastel colors. The white woodwork follows colonial revival lines, but the furniture was considered French.

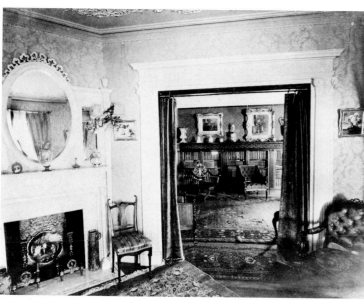

114

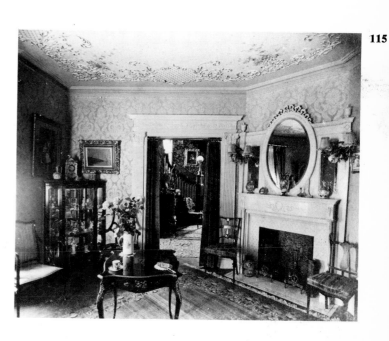

115

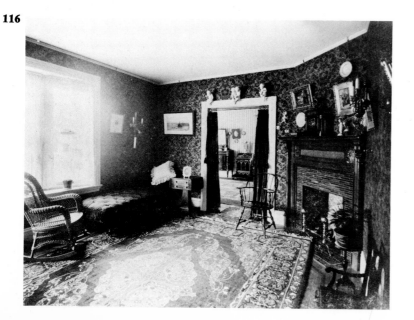

116

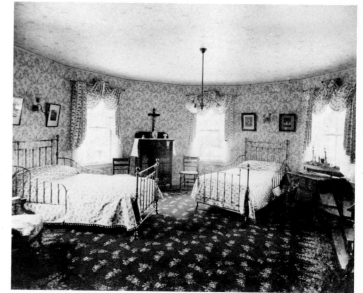

117

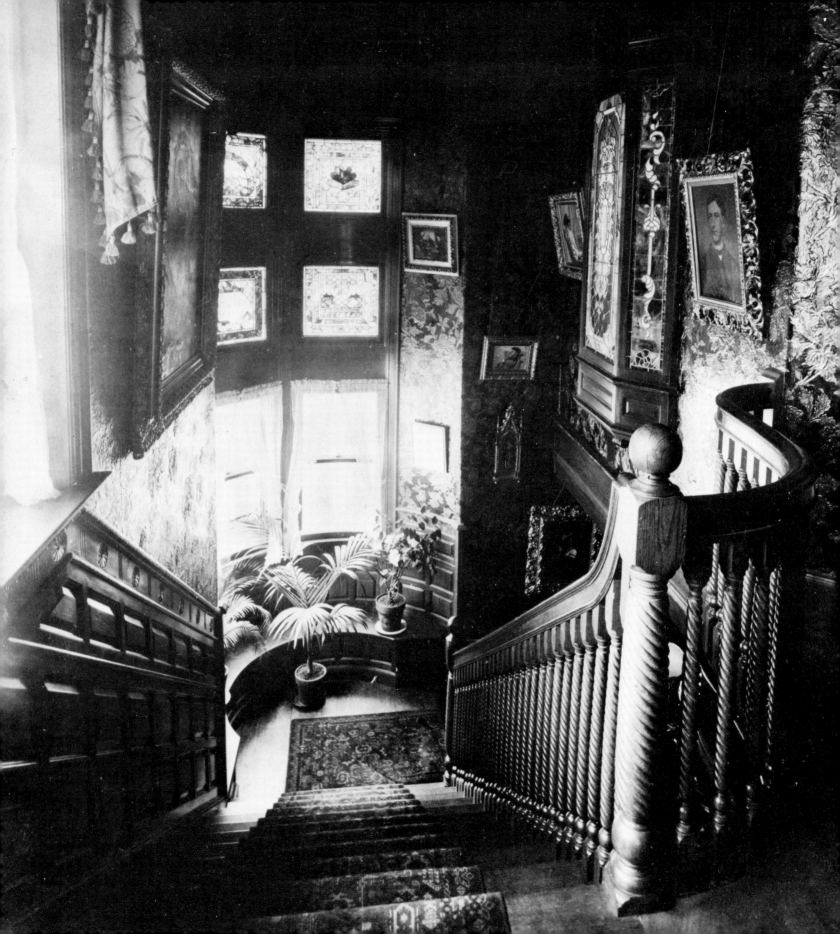

**116.** The sitting room, or den, is another pause in the open and rambling plan of the Sullivan house. A colonial revival Windsor chair shows the sort of reproduction available on the furniture market by the late 1890's. While the style was most readily accepted in New England at first, it would be so nationwide by the turn of the century. A Grecian sewing table and an old chaise longue have been revived for use here. Sheer, or "glass," curtains at the windows, rich wallpaper, and polished parquet floors, set off by white woodwork and the varnished mantel with its glazed tiles, make a modern setting in the colonial taste. The cherubs over the door are very new, and represent the growing French taste that began in the late 1880's and entered the mainstream in the mid-1890's.

**117.** The semicircular outer wall of this upstairs bedroom shows clearly the external picturesque effect the Sullivan house must have presented. Several of the bedrooms extended this way into towers or bays. Here brass beds with side guards for children are the main feature. The general decoration is colonial revival, with swags to match the bedspreads and glass curtains on the windows, another pattern on the walls, and still another in the wall-to-wall carpeting.

**118.** To the taste of the late 1880's, the Sullivan staircase was colonial. The little oriel window with stained glass aglow at night from the gas and electric light in the adjacent room, together with the other windows and the narrow channel that spread open as one descended, contributed to a mood of romantic nostalgia. On the landing is a bay with potted plants and a seat. The walls gleam like porcelain with their shiny cardboard wallcovering made to simulate morocco.

**119.** An attic room served the Sullivan children as a study and might well have been over their bedroom. A mantel has been simulated with a shelf, and on it are placed a crucifix, photographs, and statuettes. The Renaissance chair to the left is the only old object in the room, which otherwise has office furniture and perhaps a few castoffs from downstairs.

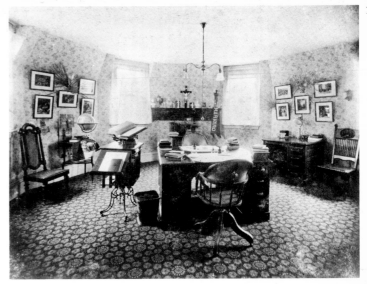

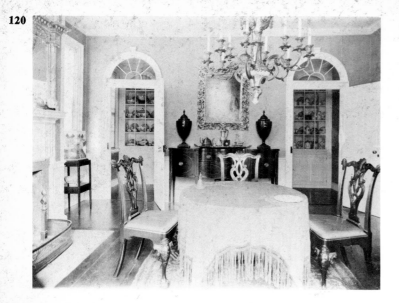

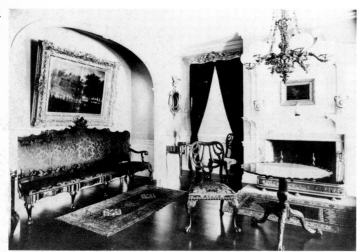

deep fringes, French gilded garniture, floral carpeting, and walls covered with pictures. Here the floors have been sanded and polished to a furniture-like finish, as was never done previously. The woodwork is colonial white, and the walls seem to be the same color in the parlor and dining room, only several shades darker in the latter. Overhead, the parlor gasolier of about 1850, complete with Bohemian glass vase, has been allowed to remain, while in the dining room a china and gilded metal fixture has been installed at a recent date. Few if any of the furnishings in either room are antique. They demonstrate the self-assurance of the new historical revivals of the 1890's—not yet reproductions but closer to being so than furniture had been since the Civil War. Barren rooms like these, even for the most impassioned colonial revivalist, were very unusual for the 1890's, but they had become rather common in some places on the East Coast by the time of World War I. The effort very seldom represented conscious restoration, but was still looked upon as modern improvement in the spirit of the past.

**120, 121. Dining Room and Parlor of E. W. Blake, 72 Waterman Street, Providence, Rhode Island, ca. 1895–98**
The hastened interest in colonial correctness is seen in these two views of what was known as the Edward Dexter house, which, though moved from its original site, was about one hundred years old at this time. In 1895, it was occupied by Professor Blake of Brown University. One can imagine the quantities of objects that have been stripped from these rooms rather recently; earlier photographs of other parts of the house show velvet curtains,

**122. Parlor, House of Blakeley Hall, 11 West 45th Street, New York, New York, 1896**
Old directories indicate that people in the biggest cities were constantly relocating; such changes of address might represent an economic step up or down, or merely a whim. For nomadic lives, the enormous furniture of the 1870's and 1880's was becoming obsolete, for not only was it in danger of getting broken when moved, it was costly to transport. There arose in the 1890's a great fashion for the temporary, or at least the temporary-looking. Mr. Hall must have dazzled his guests with this Japanese parlor, most of which could be folded away on not much notice. Against one basic background pattern of fabric many other patterns and textures fall and drape in many different ways. By this means of decorating, a dramatic effect could be achieved in a hurry, no matter what the nature of the apartment or house. Hall has placed in his tent a mother-of-pearl gypsy table, a long curving seat, a china tea set, statues, and porcelains. While nothing here was expensive, the effect of it all in the dim gaslight must have been overwhelmingly rich.

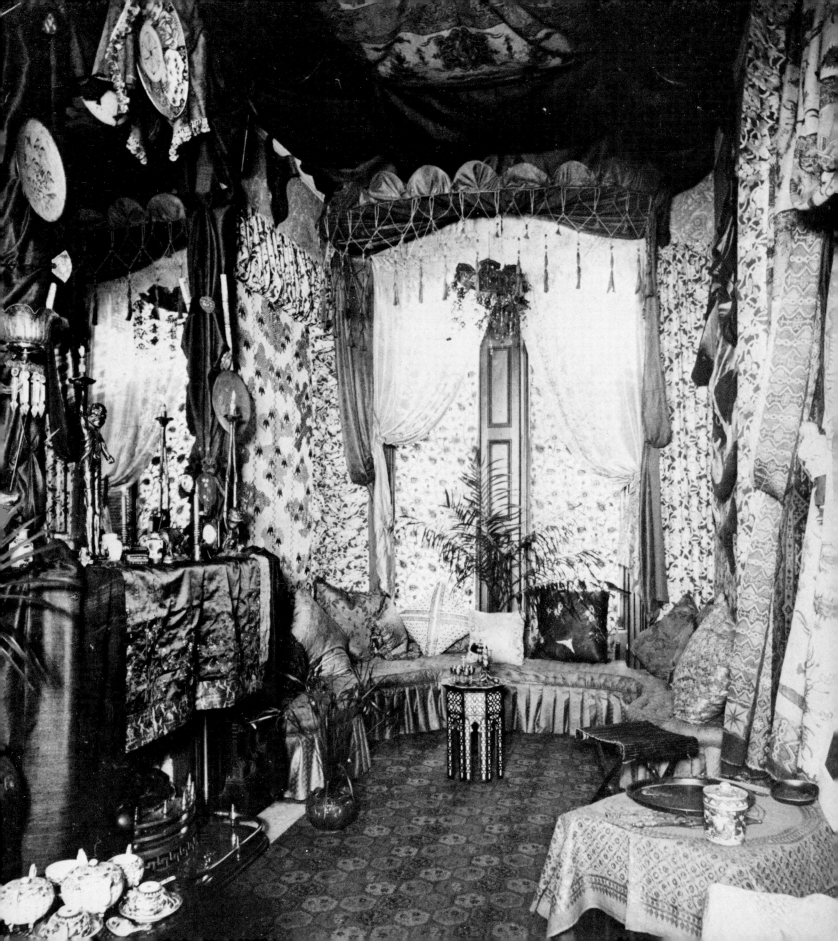

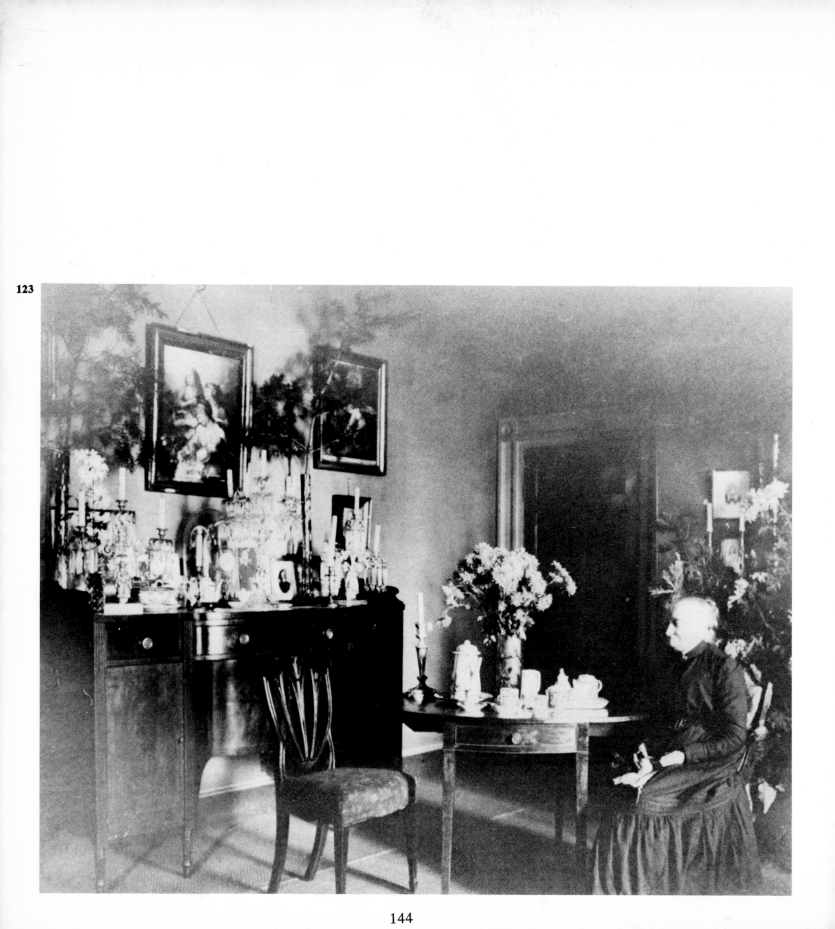

123

**123, 124. Breakfast Room and Bedroom, Bolton Farmhouse, House of Effingham B. Morris, Tullytown, Pennsylvania, ca. 1895–98**

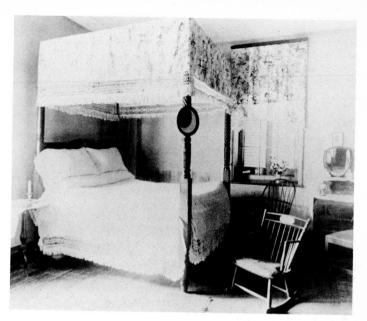

The interest in old American houses was largely restricted to New England in the 1870's and 1880's. By the 1890's, however, an antiquarian spirit was very evident in every part of the United States, but especially in regions where the vernacular architectural traditions fit in nicely with the colonial revivalists' preconceived ideas of good colonial taste. This kind of antiquarianism is, of course, still very evident in the United States; more or less the same value judgments too often determine the fate of endangered buildings today. The reigning preference in the 1890's was for things classical, as this house was in part; hence the term colonial was applied to the late eighteenth-century classical and the Greek revival that followed it, as well as, more accurately, to the Georgian vernacular. These Bucks County rooms show a conscious fascination with the antique and an effort to omit nearly everything which might appear to be modern. The old lady has been seated with her sewing beside a breakfast table set up for tea. In spite of the photographer's best efforts to be historical, the subject, surrounded by blossoms, looks far more in step with the Japanese craze of the late nineteenth century than with anything colonial. She would doubtless agree. On the sideboard, favorite kinds of nineteenth-century heirlooms appear on display—all were called colonial. Straw matting and the light walls here, as in the bedroom, convey a touch of "historical" simplicity. Flowered fabric with crocheted borders is fixed to the tester of the early nineteenth-century bed and to the deep-set window. A fancy rocker, a Windsor chair, and a neat little dressing table fixed up, in true antiquarian fashion, from a chest, and a shaving glass lend a tasteful flavor all too familiar to us today in historic-house museums and decorative arts galleries. The effect, however, is more a colonial affectation of the 1890's, reflecting the matched sets of mass-manufacture than a careful re-creation of history.

### 125. Hallway, Cohasset, Massachusetts, 1895

By the mid-1890's the colonial revival was dropping its picturesque Queen Anne and Free Classic form, and showing more evidence of the Georgian vernacular. The colonial revivalists, in borrowing motifs from the houses of the very richest and most extravagant colonial Americans, were not even yet trying to copy exactly. Middle-class patrons of the revivalist architects needed far more space than a copy of an old house could provide. Room functions were now far more specialized; there were breakfast rooms, sun parlors, dens, libraries, pantries,

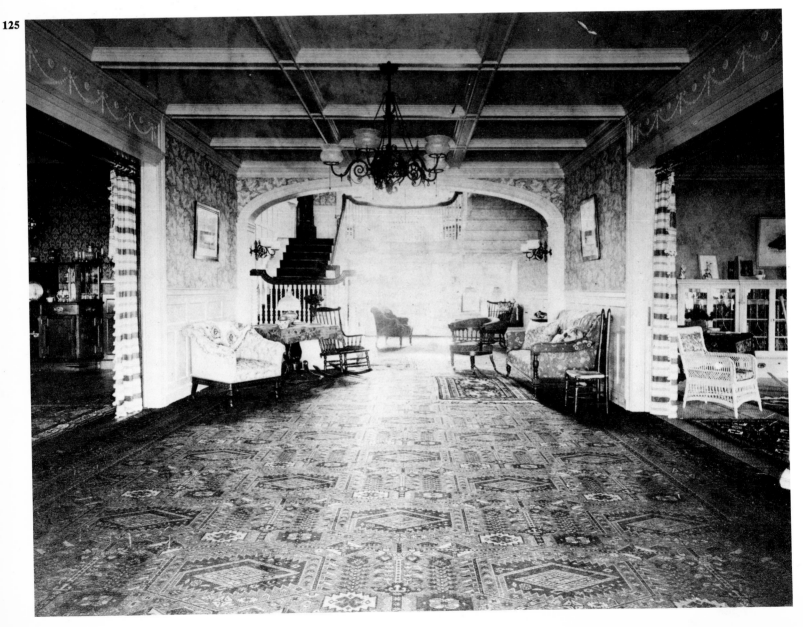

bathrooms, sewing rooms, laundry rooms, playrooms, dining rooms, morning rooms, bedrooms, and kitchens in greater or lesser numbers according to the class of the house. This view is of a living hall that has been designed to suggest the hallway of a late eighteenth-century house. It is too broad to be mistaken for the real thing, and its various openings are too wide. The squat staircase and white woodwork capture the flavor of the colonial; and the achievement of this hall is twofold, as a bit of romantic architecture and as a convenient and welcoming central space in a house built to be lived in on modern terms.

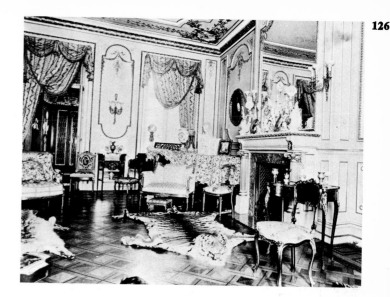

### 126. Parlor, House of George Finch, 9th and Cooper Streets, St. Paul, Minnesota, ca. 1896

The George Finches, whose superb Queen Anne dining room and bedroom we saw earlier *(69,70)*, had the parlor of their mid-century Italianate house redecorated in the 1890's in the French style. As the chief rival of the colonial, the Louis Quinze and Louis Seize revivals of the end of the nineteenth century appeared in many different kinds of American houses both piecemeal and in entire ensembles, as seen here. At one extreme was a creative revival called variously Fancy-shaped and Quaint, and at the other was the concerted effort to appear historically authentic. The latter was seldom attempted except on the upper economic levels, with people like the George Finches, who, as we see, went all the way. Imitation *boiserie,* trimmed in gesso ornaments, covers earlier plaster walls, while the old flooring has been covered with manufactured parquet. The walls are off-white, their ornaments picked out in gilt. Light-colored silk curtains with garlands and stripes are tied back on two levels at the window and door; similar fabric is used for upholstery and for a piano cover, upon which family photographs are displayed. Porcelains and pictures on the mantel in company with paper roses continue a twenty-year-old custom of personalizing, as do the arrangements on the cabinets, piano, and tables. Curiously there is no electric light; the sconces are apparently piped for gas, and on the piano, banquet lamps await the evening cutoff by the gas company.

The couple's wooden cottage is perhaps thirty years old, opening from the street into a parlor, which connects to the sitting room by large folding doors. Undoubtedly, the dining room lies beyond the sitting room, and the kitchen is farther back, probably through the door near the maid. One might fancy that this young lady has married a widower and has come to live in his house. The furnishings are inexpensive for the most part, nearly all dating from the 1880's or before; the French Antique side-

**127**

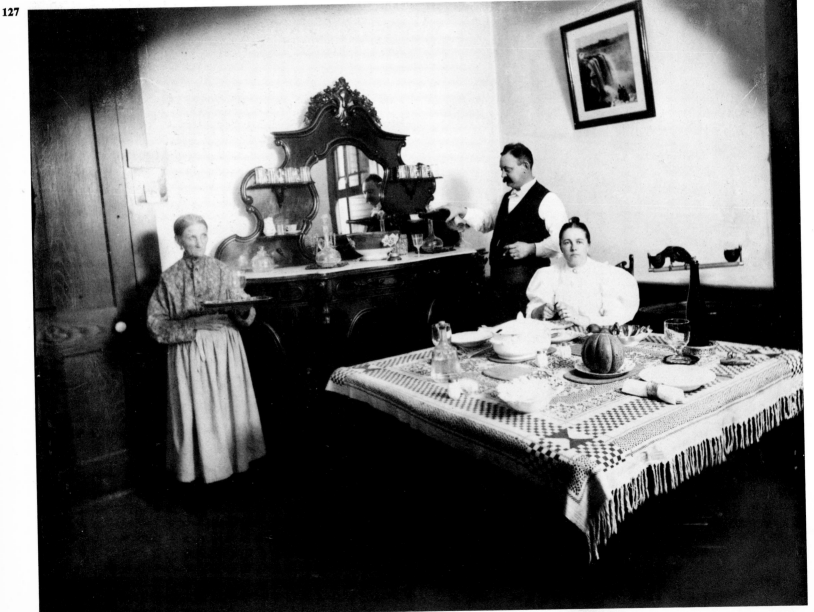

board and Grecian table in the dining room had once been very fine and might well be the products of New Orleans factories of the 1840's and 1850's. Ideas of the 1890's are evident in the sitting room. There is a conscious effort to appear relaxed in the informal arrangement of furniture and the comfortable chairs; some of the clutter has apparently been removed from the art shelves over the mantel. The drabness of the rooms is set off by a scattering of personal belongings—cigarettes, books, pictures, pet turtle and parrot, and keepsakes of several kinds. Art units do not really exist here, except in the slight suggestion of arrangement over the mantel. Objects are spread out, and fewer in number than would have been the case here five years before.

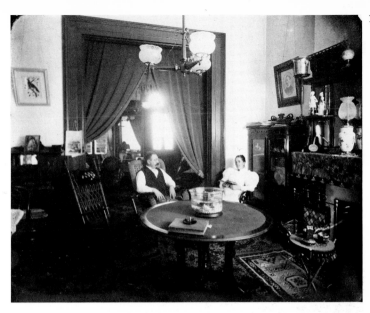

128

## 129. Library, Upstate New York, ca. 1895

The room is obviously new, reflecting the Arts and Crafts movement of the time, but, on a more popular level, this would have been considered a colonial library. Built-in bookcases and waiscoting form a shoulder-high band of varying textures around the walls, while the surface above might be canvas or burlap, painted and with a stenciled border. The tea table, perhaps a permanent setting beside the fireplace, is an inheritance from the Anglo-Japanese taste of the two previous decades. Few rooms better illustrate the forces at work in domestic design in the 1890's than this one: against the hand-crafted architecture of the room, a colonial revival gasolier, brackets, and lamp complement colonial revival furniture; over the mantel is a classical frieze, echoing a national craze for fine art and architecture that gained popular support through the Columbian Exposition at Chicago in 1893. And the three figures in the firelight, recalling a similar photograph of Woodrow Wilson and his daughters, express so well the "home spirit amongst us" that Gustav Stickley would soon write about in his essays on the Craftsman way of living.

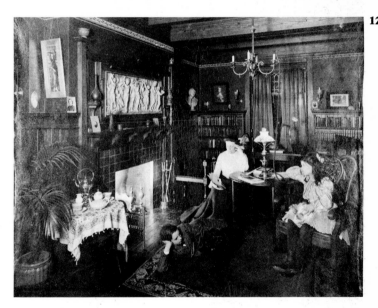

129

**130. Sitting Room, Boston, ca. 1895**

The personal use of a room determines a great deal about its organization. This sitting room, although anonymous, tells many stories. Obviously the lady is a semi-invalid, and has gathered around her a range of transient objects which she needs during the day. Sewing, books, papers, and blotter are neatly arranged on the cheap little folding table; on the dresser are her lace-covered pincushion, family pictures, books, and hand mirror. Her day bed, or perhaps it is even her bed, is against the fireplace, the opening of which has been curtained, while personal memorabilia and necessities of the bedside, like her shoehorn, are nearby. The washstand is set up as had been done since she was a girl; a splash back made of cloth is hung on the wall to protect the wallpaper. Only a plain shade serves the window in this room, which, through objects, paints for us an intimate portrait of a lady of advanced years.

**131. Parlor, House of Delight Kelley Cummings, Bad Axe, Michigan, 1895**

Everything in this parlor is mass-manufactured, from the

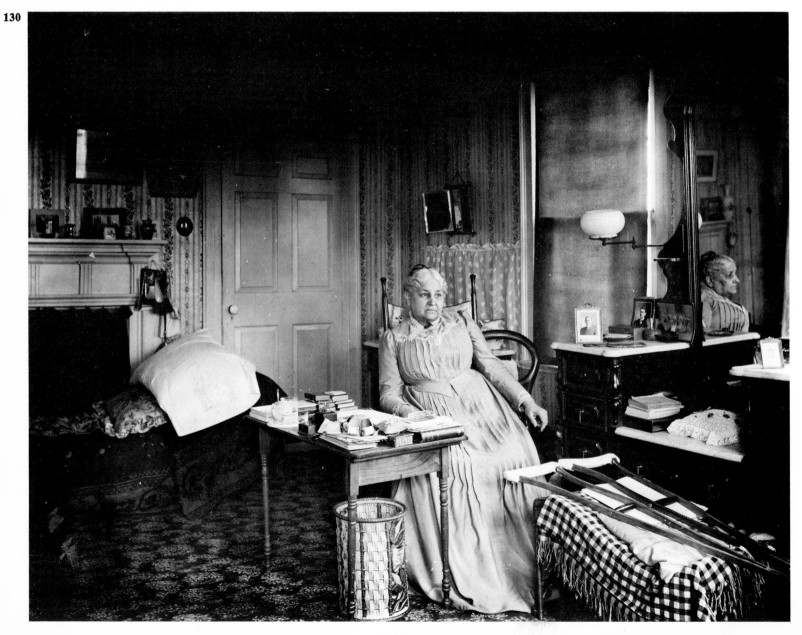

130

rose-covered carpeting to the parlor organ, the wallpaper, and the simple chairs, used in many other places as porch chairs. The organ represents the largest investment perhaps in the entire house; the room is otherwise plain, for nothing else cost much over about $3. Yet Mrs. Cummings has made it her own place, filling the bay window with potted plants and lavishly draping the opening in some white material. A whatnot shelf holds her prized books and a few family pictures, and is surmounted by a cluster of ostrich plumes tied with a bow, doubtless a French affectation and typical of the 1890's.

The Indian rug is a characteristic expression of the fascination with western decorative accessories that grew out of the Arts and Crafts movement.

**131**

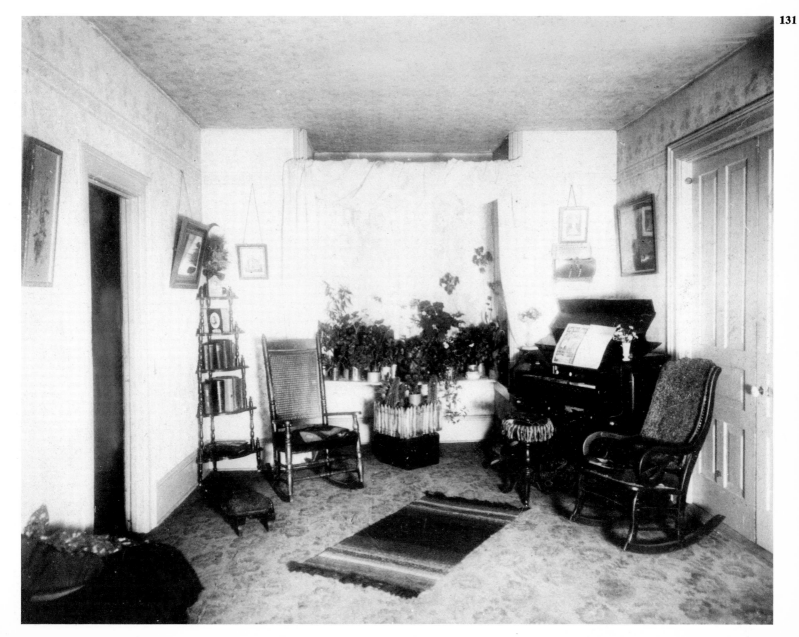

**Taberhurst, Bank Village, New Hampshire, 1897**

While not actually a hotel, this large red-brick farmhouse accommodated at least one paying family in the summertime. The Hale family of North Andover, Massachusetts, visited Taberhurst for many summers, and these pictures are from their family album.

**132.** The music room illustrates how freely at this time the colonial revival was associated with the classical, which, in 1897, was mounting to a new peak in American architecture. Colonial revival woodwork, polished floor and oriental-style rug, a plant stand patterned

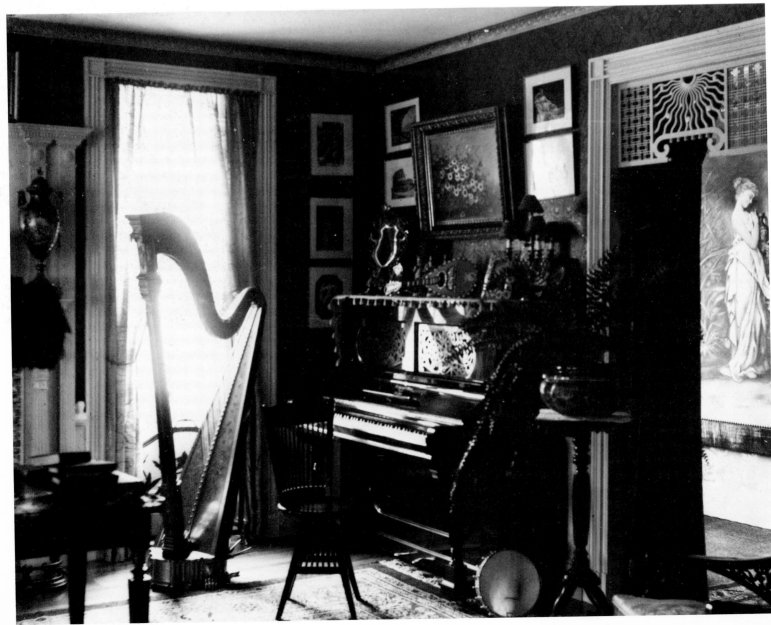

132

on an old candle stand, a Windsor piano stool, and an old side table used as a center table complete the colonial decorations. On the walls beside the piano, photographs of classical sculpture and classical-style sculpture of the early nineteenth century are deemed appropriate, as is the example of parlor art, perhaps a school project of recent date, in the hallway beyond the spindlework archway. A new urn on a colonial revival mantel, still draped, confirms the easy association the era made between the classical and the colonial.

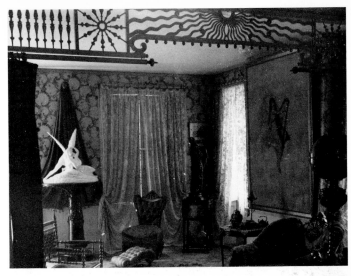

**133.** The parlor reflects the owner's awareness of the current cosmopolitan alternative to the colonial, even though the image seems vague in his mind. The room would undoubtedly have been considered French. Overstuffed furniture was usually considered Turkish, but this, with its gilded gesso ornaments, was Fancy-shaped French, and could have been quite new when this picture was taken, as was the banquet lamp in the foreground. Lace curtains, which would not diminish in popularity for another thirty years, were characteristically tied back in this very contrived manner, to give the patterned effect of light through lace without losing the animation of drapery folds. One statue is given a background drape, while the other, apparently a nude, is draped for modesty's sake. To the right is a little French table, surely a recent purchase, and on the left a spool chair, obviously descended from mid-century Elizabethan models but here probably known as colonial. Surveyed by a celestial harpist, which one of the family probably painted, the Taberhurst parlor lacks the clutter, but retains the sense of object groupings, of earlier times.

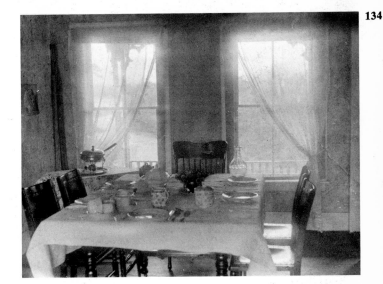

**134.** The dining room contains furnishings available in American catalogues from the mid-1880's until World War I. While it is likely that the side chairs were considered colonial, they are closely allied to much earlier creative revival types that came from the Grecian style. The end chair is colonial revival, and of a creative revival type popular in every part of the United States, costing seldom more than $1.50. White woodwork, painted floor, simple muslin curtains with lace borders, and a side table covered in a printed material and holding the chafing dish complete, with unframed art pictures: this was a very typical middle-class dining room of the period.

**135. Kitchen, Broad Channel, New York, 1898**
This plain kitchen, single-walled and utilitarian, dates from an era when even kitchens in great houses were not decorative. The anonymous couple has painted a dado, perhaps in dark green; linoleum covers the floor, and the relatively new dining table is protected by commercial oilcloth. Enamelware bowls, spoons, and kettles, all quite modern in the 1890's, become decorative to our eyes. They, and numerous little gadgets, ornament the board walls in happy disarray.

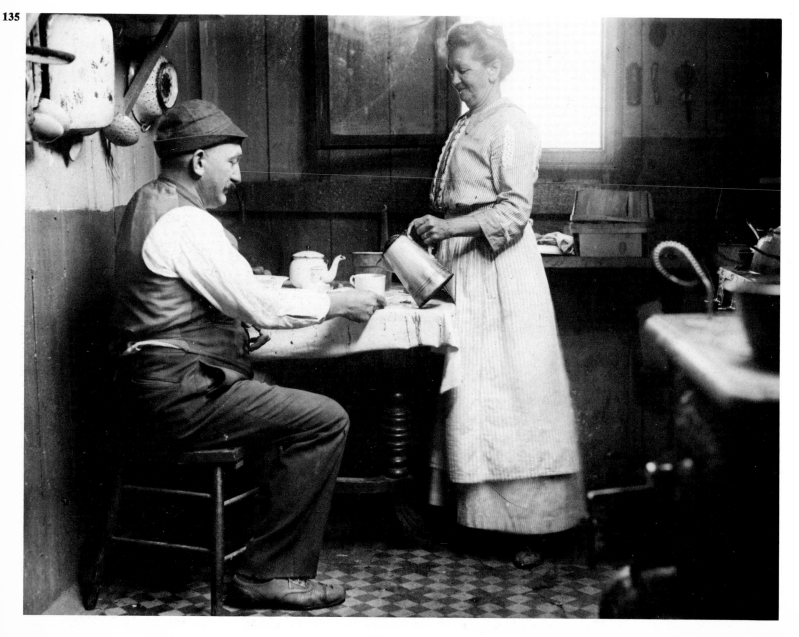

135

## 136. Dining Room, Hampton Institute, Hampton, Virginia, 1899

Apparently on a summer day, with the walls freshly whitewashed and the stove taken down, this graduate of Hampton Institute and his wife and family have begun their noon meal in a dining room which would have been quite as typically middle-class in the 1870's as it was in the 1890's. Linoleum floor covering and lambrequin-covered shelf decorate, in small and practical ways, a modestly finished room. Stain and varnish have been applied to the woodwork and the car-siding wainscoting.

Several art prints are tilted at angles from high places on the walls. The dining table, a belated creative revival piece which might, like the chairs, have been considered colonial, was advertised in Richmond in the 1890's as costing $3.50. Against the rear wall is what appears to be a sofa, not a surprising feature of a dining room even at this date.

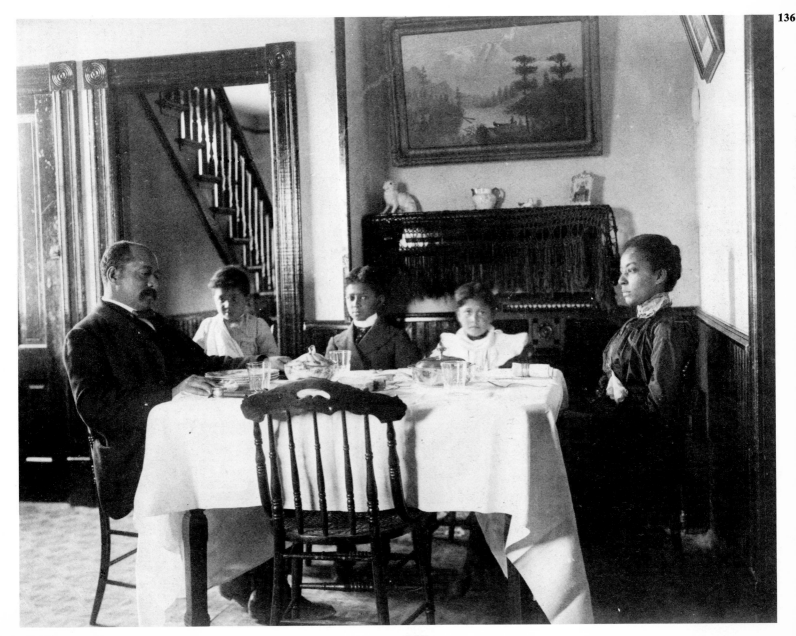

136

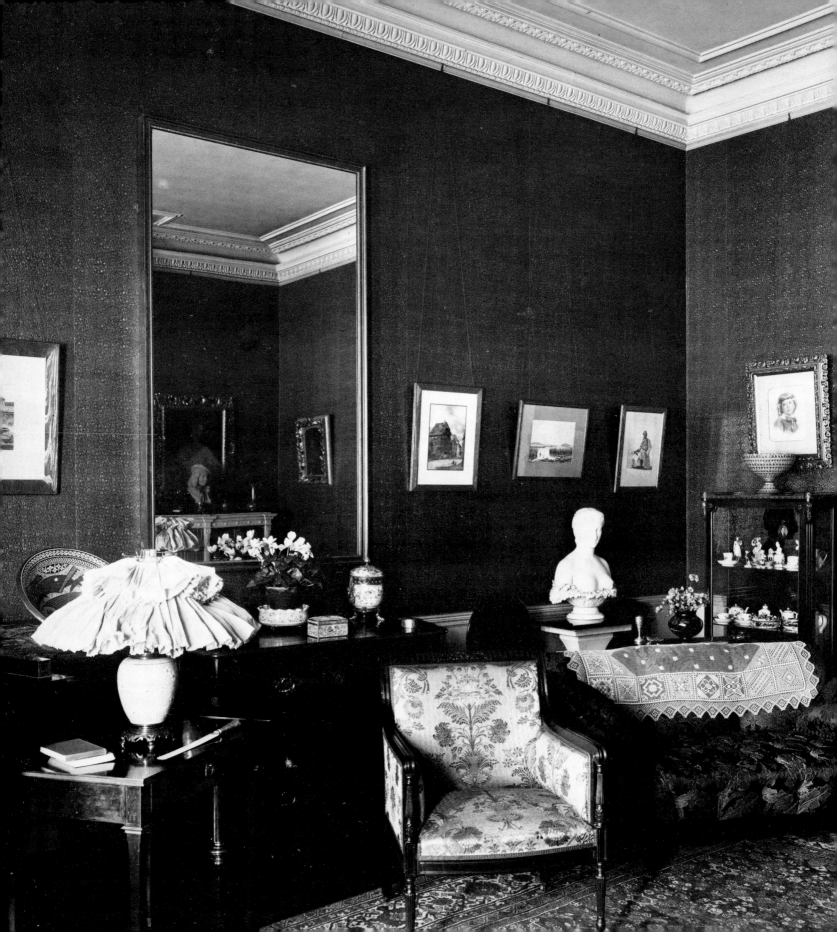

## 137. Sitting Room, House of Mrs. Edward J. Lowell, 40 Commonwealth Avenue, Boston, Massachusetts, 1897

While this room has not been decorated by an interior decorator, some of the latest concepts of the decade have influenced it, particularly in the use of reproduction furniture. The Sheraton chair in the center of the picture was available in sets; that is, a sofa and two chairs, making a threesome that would set the theme for a colonial parlor. Cosmopolitan French-style furniture, also reproduced by better manufacturers in the 1890's, here symbolizes the international affectations endorsed by Edith Wharton and Ogden Codman, Jr., in their book *The Decoration of Houses,* published in the year this photograph was taken. The ruffled shade on the vase lamp was a type very popular in the 1890's, but it was the sort of decoration Wharton and Codman denounced in favor of "restraint" and "good taste." On the tables and the French chest, a few objects have been carefully distributed; the family called the chest "the elephant." Most of the objects have been relegated to the French-style curio cabinet, while *Persephone* by Hiram Powers remains from an earlier era, spared exile to the garden and eventual ruin, the sad fate of many such nineteenth-century sculptures. The overstuffed sofa, its obvious source a familiar Grecian type of the 1840's, is leading, we can be sure, a precarious existence in such an up-to-date Boston interior.

## 138. Hallway, Bowie's Ranch House, Chugwater, Wyoming, 1897

The new restraint in interior decoration continued until well into the twentieth century. This hallway far more truly represents middle-class American taste of the late 1890's than does Mrs. Lowell's sitting room *(137).* The wide spread of French decoration in the late 1890's, translated into popular usage, engendered a new attitude toward quantities of objects, ushering in a new version of personalized decoration which contrasted with the simplicity of the rising Arts and Crafts modes. We have already had a taste of the new treatment of masses of objects in Robert Todd Lincoln's house in Georgetown *(196, 197).* This new approach was not like the restrained art grouping and the careful organization of units of objects that dominated in the 1870's and for most of the 1880's; here was a conscious effort to be stuffy and formal, an echo, in some respects, of the French Antique interiors of

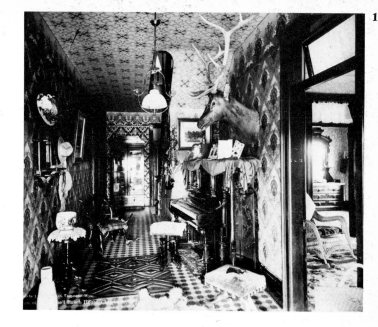

138

the 1850's. The Bowies have laid their hall with practical linoleum in imitation of tiles. Different patterns of wallpapers, dark-stained woodwork, and deliberately unmatched furniture provide the background for a range of transient objects, some personal and some not. A little music area is made of the back hall with a collection of objects, used less for their own sakes than architecturally, to define the space.

137

157

**139. Parlor, Apartment of Mr. and Mrs. Reginald de Koven, 85 Irving Place, New York, New York, 1897**
French Empire furniture of recent date dominates this parlor, decorated to look urbane and French. Against the right-hand wall a cozy arrangement of bear fur, cushions, plants, and oriental rug has been elevated upon a dais. Against the dark wallcovering, a portrait has been set in a galaxy of china plates that depict scenes in France. Opposite this luxurious couch, the mantel has been obliterated by velvet swags and curtains which cover not only the chimney opening but fall from the top

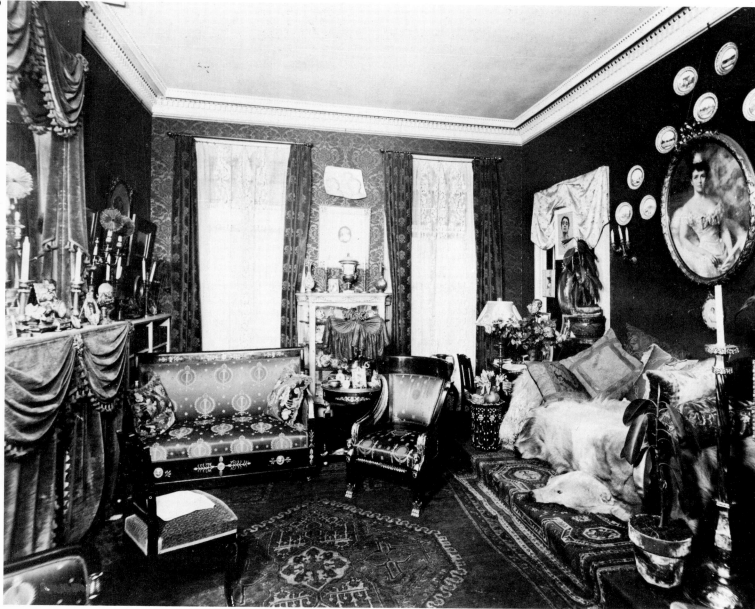

139

part of the mantel mirror. Gas "candles" are surmounted by silk shades, the oil piano lamp by a paper Empire shade, and a ruffled fabric shade covers still another oil lamp. Furniture and curios are here gathered into a conscious whole, serving en masse the purpose of architectural enrichment. The de Koven's parlor is a telling example of how popular taste dominated even the settings of sophisticated city life.

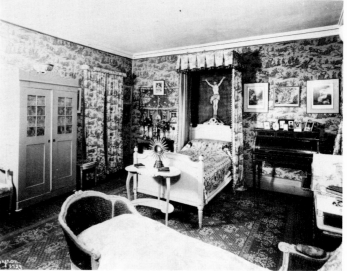

### 140. Bedroom, Apartment of Elizabeth Marbury, 122 East 17th Street, New York, New York, 1898

In contrast to the de Koven's version of the French mode *(139)*, Miss Marbury, a theatrical agent, had an apartment decorated in the sophisticated Louis Seize revival style. She probably assembled this bedroom herself, following current ideas that favored period European settings. In New York, such interiors as this were becoming well-established late in the 1890's; the diminutive furniture was light and could be moved easily from apartment to apartment, and it had a theatrical elegance that made it fit well nearly anyplace. Toile wallcovering, curtains, cornice, upholstery, and bedspread are unified *en suite,* and the toile has been used to cover a letterbox and, one can suppose, a wastebasket as well. The enameled Louis Seize furniture is quite new and quite historical, following actual antique models in most cases, but especially in the instance of the roll-top desk against the wall. Here the desired effect is to suggest a room in an ancient French house, one filled with time-worn objects and renewed from generation to generation with fabric and paint. A wardrobe of about 1875–80 has been painted to match the expensive French-style furniture, and glass has been added to its doors; Miss Marbury doubtless called it an armoire. Beside the bed, a little altar has been erected, and perhaps the roses on it are artificial.

**141. Library, House of Mr. and Mrs. Theodore Sutro, New York, New York, 1896**

Its walls stacked with paintings, its floors painted, varnished, and covered in a few small oriental rugs, the Sutro library approaches the middle-class ideal of a tasteful room. A collection of pictures here takes the dominant and architectural role in the scheme. More often than not such collections as this were really accumulations, lacking either the character or balance essential to please a connoisseur. But the spirit of collection nevertheless became an important aspect of interior decoration for nearly all classes from about 1893 until World War I. With varying degrees of success, collecting fulfilled a wish to gather and exhibit the good and the worthwhile, not merely to possess quantities of things. Ten years earlier, this room would have been full of movable objects, its floors deep in carpeting. It might have been the same in 1896 had not the crowded French look been paralleled by a new sparseness which characterized both the historical revival and the experimental Arts and Crafts settings of the decade. That sparseness is very much in evidence in the Sutro library.

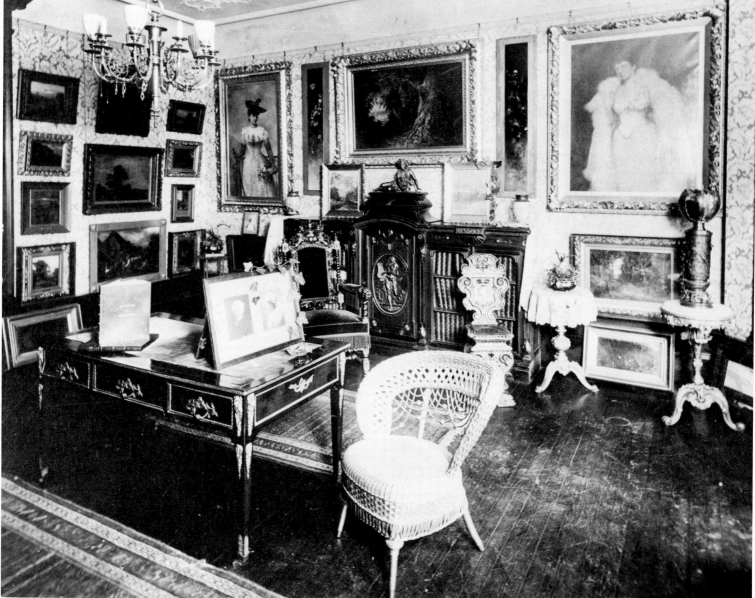

141

**142, 143. Drawing Room and Dining Room, House of Edward Lauterbach, 2 East 78th Street, New York, New York, 1899**

Historical period interiors became very popular for pretentious houses in the 1890's, and the trend was to last, to a degree, on all levels for more than a half century. The owner here was a partner in the law firm of Hoadly, Lauterbach, and Johnson; his sumptuous Manhattan house, obviously the work of an interior decorator, carried all the trappings of business success. His French parlor, furnished entirely in new period sets, has tile flooring

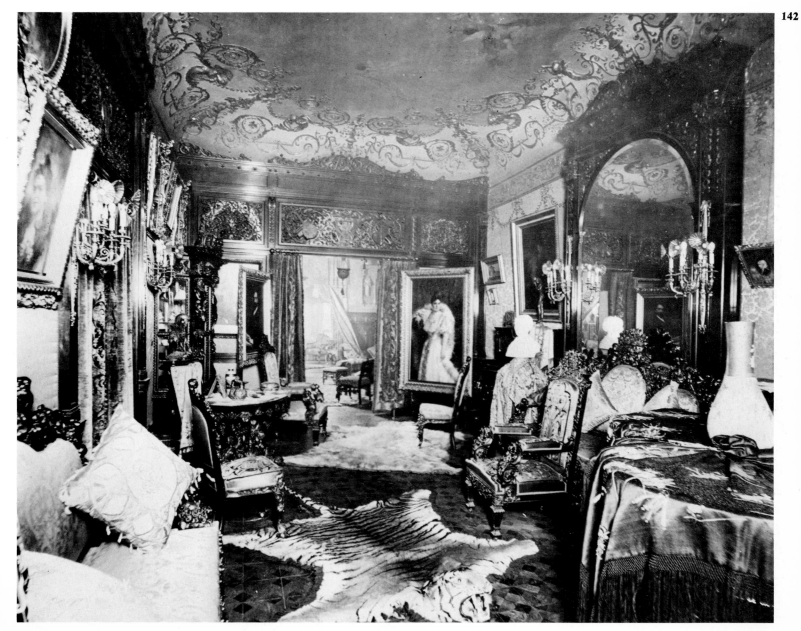

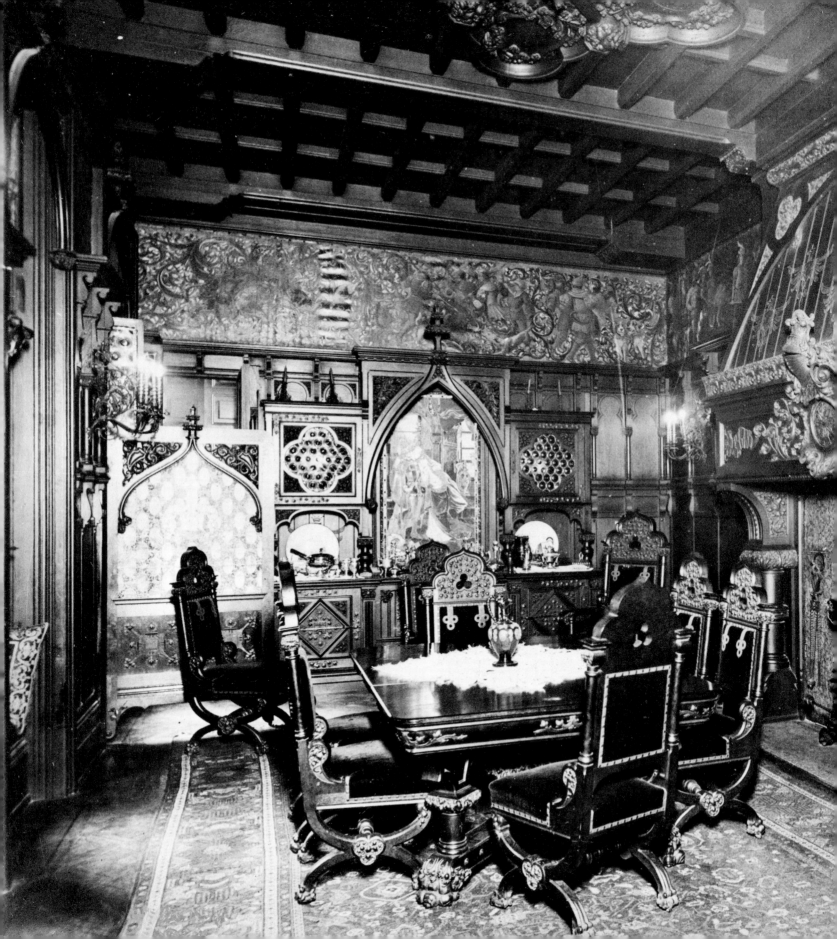

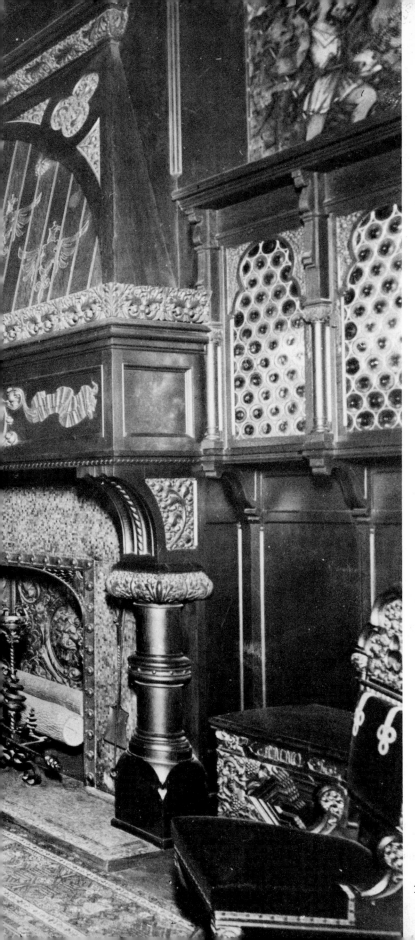

and rich architectural embellishments in gilded plaster and wood, which itself might actually have been grained plaster. The ornate furniture has clear sources in the French Antique style of the mid-nineteenth century, but is of a kind made in the 1890's, and up to the 1920's, in many classes and at many prices. While that ubiquitous French prop, the "crystal" chandelier, is here absent, the ceiling is adorned with a painted scene of cherubs and clouds. Electric and gas wall brackets—by now again called sconces—are equipped with reflectors, and the brilliance of the electric bulbs can be seen in the dining room, where they are lighted. On the grand piano, the silk cover has been gathered into a rosette, its fringed edge thus falling ray-like, in folds; silk damask covers the walls, and satins and damasks on the furniture accentuate the shiny and smooth texture that is a unifying theme of the parlor. In contrast to the banks of furniture along the walls, the bareness of the floor is pointed up by the tiger and bear skins. A Moorish room lies beyond the filigreed archway.

Elsewhere in the house is the medieval dining room, a fine example of an 1890's period ensemble executed by an interior decorator. With electric lighting, stained glass could be effective anywhere. It is woven like a tapestry into the architectural fabric of the sideboard, which is creative revival, and, in the form of antique bull's-eye glass, simulates high casements beside the fireplace. A painted border of medieval hunting scenes bands the room beneath a heavy paneled and beamed ceiling. Probably the fireplace did not really burn wood, but served as a register for the steam heating system. Both the drawing room and the dining room of the Lauterbach house, each furnished in sets, each expressing period themes conveyed through careful planning, are expensive and modern settings for big-city life at the close of the century.

**143**

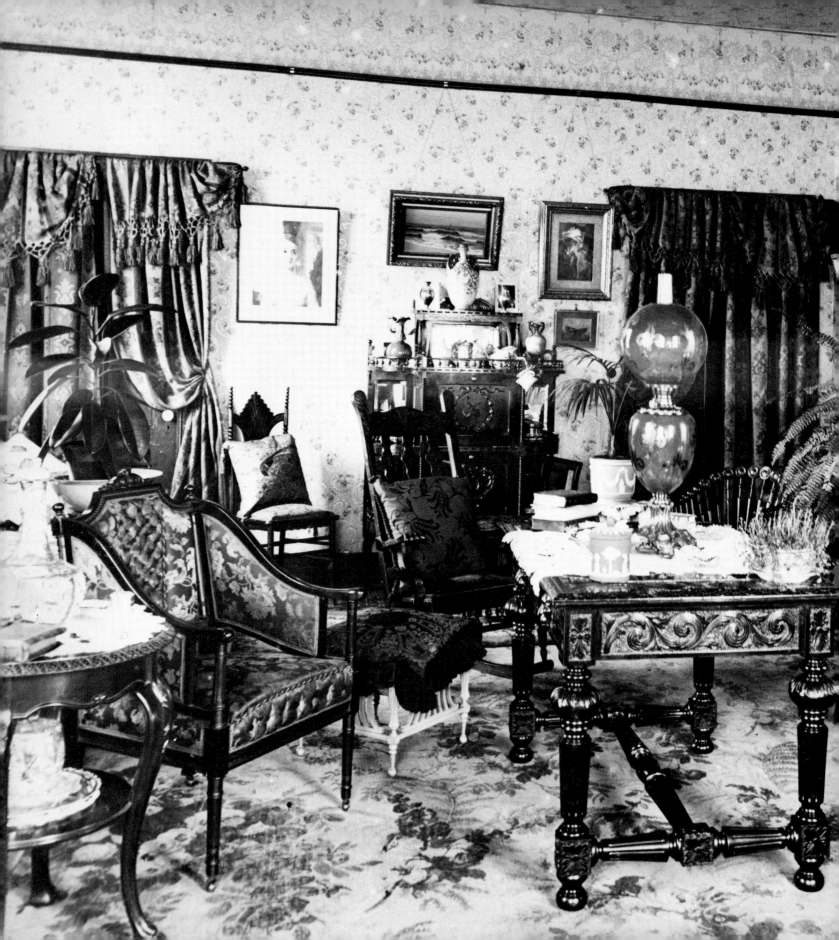

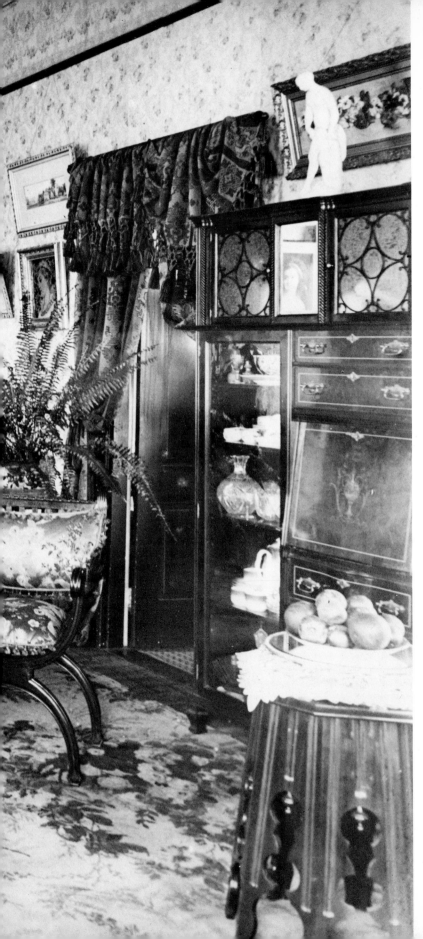

## 144, 145. Parlor, Apartment of Captain E. O. Patterson, Broad Street, Charleston, South Carolina, December, 1899

These two views of the same parlor show an American room as it stood in the last days of the nineteenth century. The furniture is all new and medium-priced. Patterson was captain of a dredge, and had moved into this apartment within the past year. The setting is generally 1890's French, yet the room's contents present a wide sampling of the historical and period furnishings available on the market at the time, and most of them are more English than French. A Sheraton-style backless windowseat and upholstered armchair illustrate the interest in the English antique styles which would supersede the French modes by the time of World War I. First known as an aspect of the so-called, and often unclear, English Quaint, the English revivals ran through several more accurate phases, including Chippendale, Hepplewhite, Tudor, and Jacobean—which were often the same —and Queen Anne, a reproduction which should in no way be confused with the creative forms that carried that name in the 1870's and 1880's. In America, the spread of the English styles was hurried by the popular glorification of Anglo-Saxon heritage. While the center, or library, table of Captain Patterson was probably considered Renaissance, Chippendale or perhaps Queen Anne was the name applied to the round table with the lower shelf containing bottles and vases. The mahogany desk and attached side cabinet, a type available back in the 1880's and still popular well into the twentieth century, is creative revival, and would have been called colonial —also believed to be pure Anglo-Saxon—without a moment's hesitation. Near the bay window can be seen part of the sofa, the only French-style piece of furniture in the parlor. The arrangement of the room is French, and the theme is carried farther in the pale wallpaper and the probable pastels of the carpeting, which is laid over matting. Fancy draperies ornament the doors, but there is light and airy lace netting at the shuttered windows. The use of so many objects here is not for an art effect; instead it is to achieve a continuity of spatial richness which gives the room a single, rather than a varied, impact.

Parlor, Apartment of Captain E. O. Patterson,
Broad Street, Charleston, South Carolina,
December, 1899

145

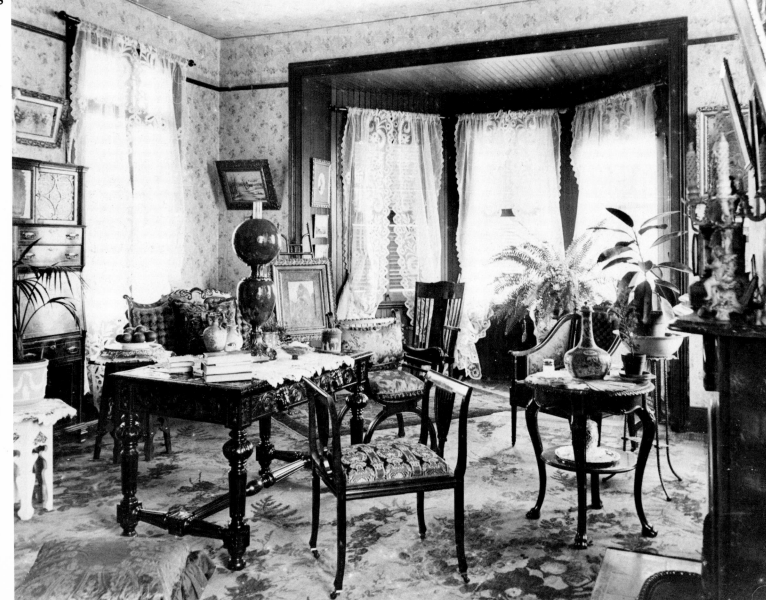

**146. Parlor, House of Gabriel E. Manigault, 6 Gibbes Street, Charleston, South Carolina, December, 1899**

Professor Manigault's parlor contrasts with that of Captain Patterson (144,145) in that there are only a few new things here—perhaps the bentwood chair and the vase on the center table. Heir of an old Charleston family, Manigault was surrounded by inherited furniture both antique and just out of date. To thus enclose one's daily life in certain kinds of old things became a local style in Charleston as in a number of other cities across the United States; people even collected such relics as these in an effort to achieve an ambience of enduring aristocracy and lost fortunes. With the exception of the two Hepplewhite-style chairs and portraits, nearly everything in this room was common to antique shops along the East Coast. The arrangement of the furniture, however, is up to date. Absent are the personalizing features of the past twenty-five years; the rich architectural elements of the early nineteenth century have been covered for the most part with objects, creating almost a new architecture for the room. A window is erased by paintings, and the octagonal wall is smoothed out by hanging other paintings over the corners. The most forceful architectural quality left in the room is in the two remaining windows, so they have been flattened out by fringed window shades with borders. Room and contents here become one, quite as effectively as in Captain Patterson's far more stylish and costly new parlor.

**147, 148. Parlor and Dining Room, House of Phoebe Apperson Hearst, New Hampshire Avenue between 20th and O Streets, Washington, D.C., 1899**

This house of the newspaper magnate's charitable mother was remodeled in the 1890's by the firm of Hornblower and Marshall, Architects. These two very different interiors show the contrasting preferences in stylish taste at the close of the nineteenth century as interpreted by interior decorating companies. Sparse and expensive-looking, the French, or Louis Seize, salon contains not a single antique; its furniture is American, the latest continental style, gilded and upholstered in embroidered white satin. Louis Seize ornamentation, adapted but not distorted, adorns the overmantel, panels, and ceiling, in various textures. The faded Aubusson might be an old one, although it is more likely a copy, perhaps made especially for this room. What appear to

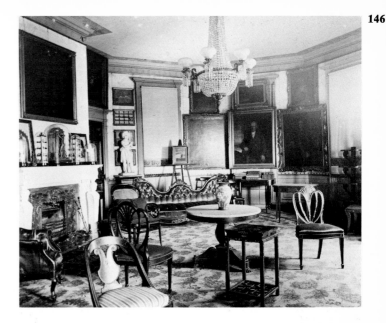
146

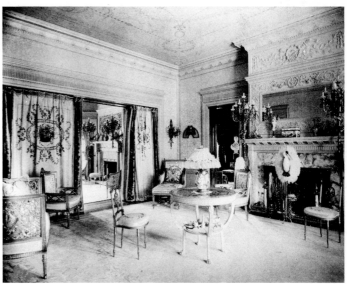
147

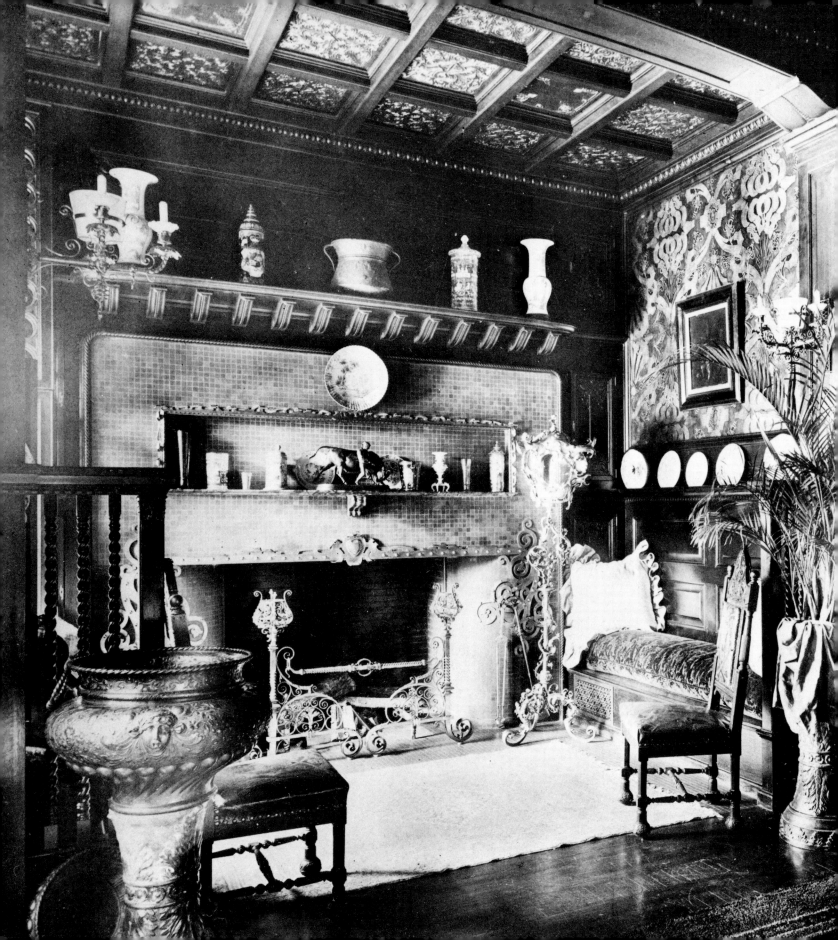

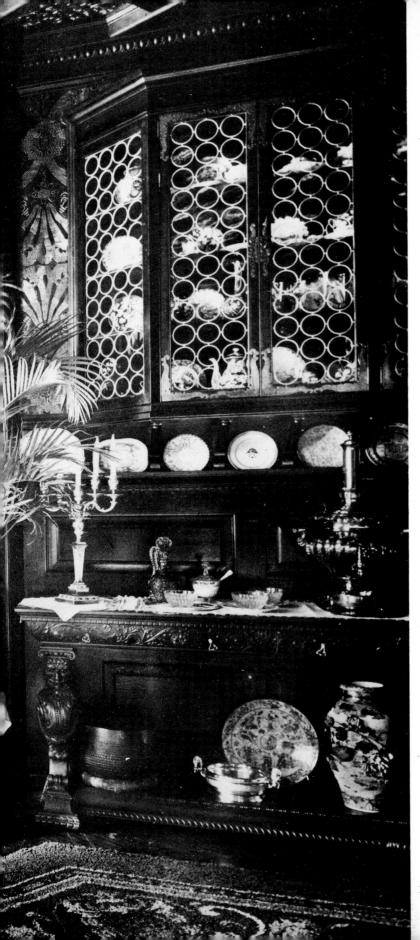

be embroidered silk portieres bordered in heavy velvet are hung in the great opening. The walls are papered in a dim figured pattern set in gilded picture molding, leaving a border of painted wall around each section, which further accentuates the richness of the neoclassical door facings and cornices, and heightens the extreme orderliness of the room ensemble. A stuffed heron, mounted in a tortured sunburst made from its own wings, serves as a fire screen.

This very fashionable setting was counterbalanced in another part of the house by the inglenook in the dining room. Fireside nooks epitomized homeyness; cozy and intimate, they were retreats for winter evenings and after-dinner conversations. In this ambitious inglenook dark-stained walnut wainscoting, with a plate rail, gives strength to the side walls which might otherwise appear weak next to the overpowering fireplace. Overhead a grid of walnut beams frames several patterns of arabesques, all matching the shiny covering of the upper parts of the walls, doubtless in deep reds and greens, with gilding. The fireplace is faced with ceramic tiles. They form a glistening border for fires, and make of the firebox a cool chasm in the summer. Pots and porcelains, with the polished floors, the gold and dark colors of the walls, the woodwork and the tiles, pick up the flickering light and further enhance the enchantment of the nook. A French parlor, with its formal mood of urbane sophistication, and a nook, informal and romantic, were not uncommon together in houses of the 1890's.

### 149. Parlor, Boston Suburb, 1900

While only the chair in the center of the room is actually colonial revival, this parlor would have been considered colonial. The house is obviously colonial revival, with its columned doorway and mantel and with its Georgian woodwork and grand staircase painted a high-gloss white, an effect possible, without the application of varnish, for about twenty years. The striped wallpaper was familiar to both colonial and French rooms. A more sophisticated colonial room would have had, by this time, a symmetrical picture arrangement, perhaps without the exposed wires. This room, however, was not planned by an interior decorator but put together with odds and ends. The sofa and center sword chair are new, and the Turkish chair beside the fireplace may be new, but is probably of the late 1880's and was modified when re-upholstered in silk damask. The little side chair could be as early as the 1870's, its creative revival styling now somewhat disordered by the bright chintz upholstery. American orientals cover most of the floors, leaving only the polished wood showing at the edges. Art units and personalizing effects are gone from this room. With electricity, the changing quality of light is now minimized; dark corners are swept clean, and colors are brightened. Bareness and restraint are slowly being accepted by the middle class.

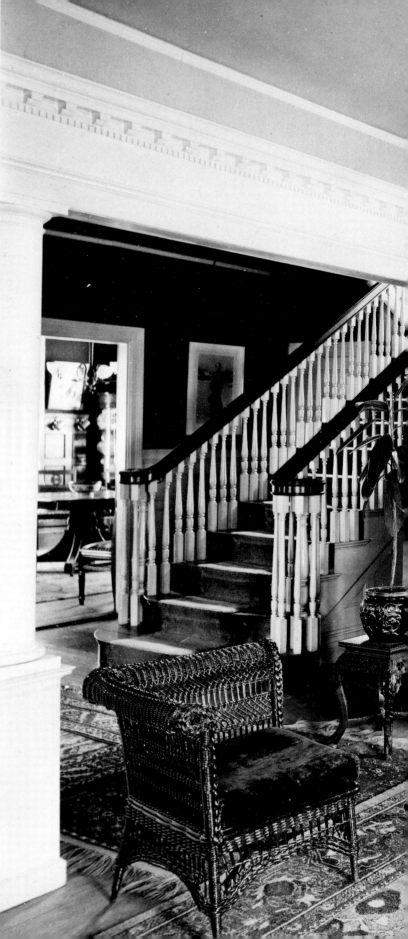

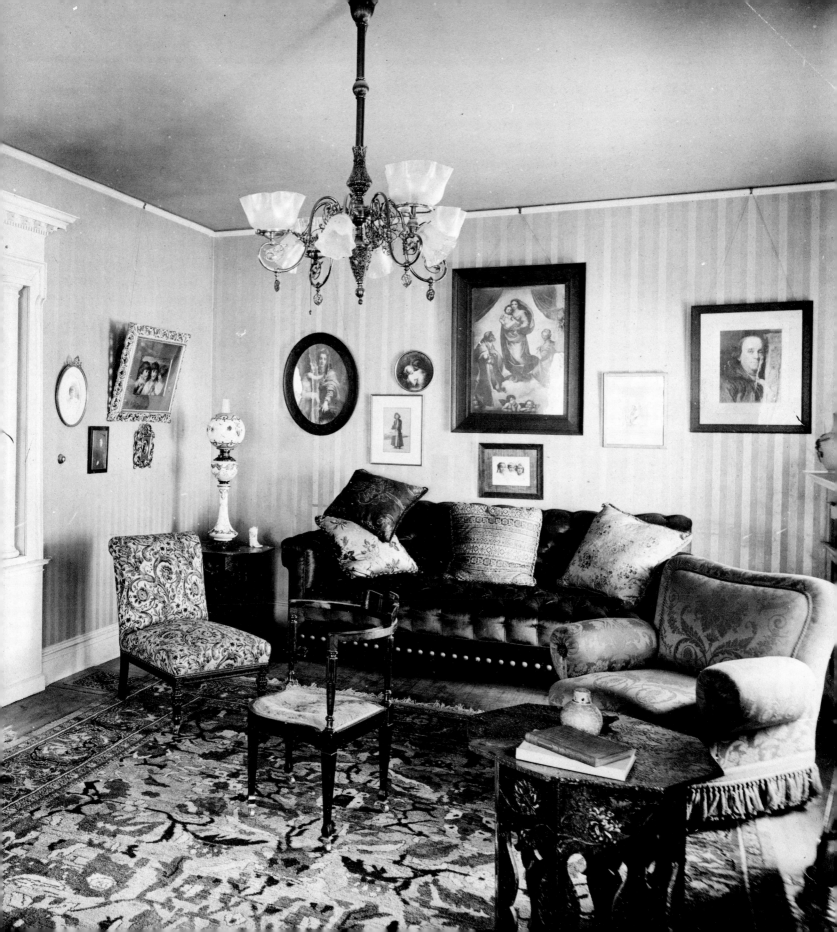

## 150, 151. Library and Bedroom, House of E. L. Flaherty, 113 Broadway, Helena, Montana, 1900

E. L. Flaherty was an undertaker who lived in a house in the Queen Anne style. His library is furnished in new Golden Oak, as he would have called it, in a variety of styles. Most of these furnishings are examples of the massive mode, which preceded and rivaled the Arts and Crafts furniture style, represented here by the bookcase in the corner. The desk is colonial revival, a title nearer the truth in this case; but the object is still creative revival in fact. In the bay window, the Morris chair, a recliner named for the English progenitor of the Arts and Crafts movement, makes the massive-mode effort to look rich and heavy, in a historical way. Probably the colonial white of the woodwork is very recent. The massive-mode platform rocker is a kind turned out by Midwestern factories in vast quantities. They were cheap to make, requiring only a minimal frame and springs and abundant stuffing and upholstery, all assembled by immigrant labor; poor workmanship could be hidden in the deep tufting and pleating. The large and individualistic furniture makes a relatively sparse room of the library, even though

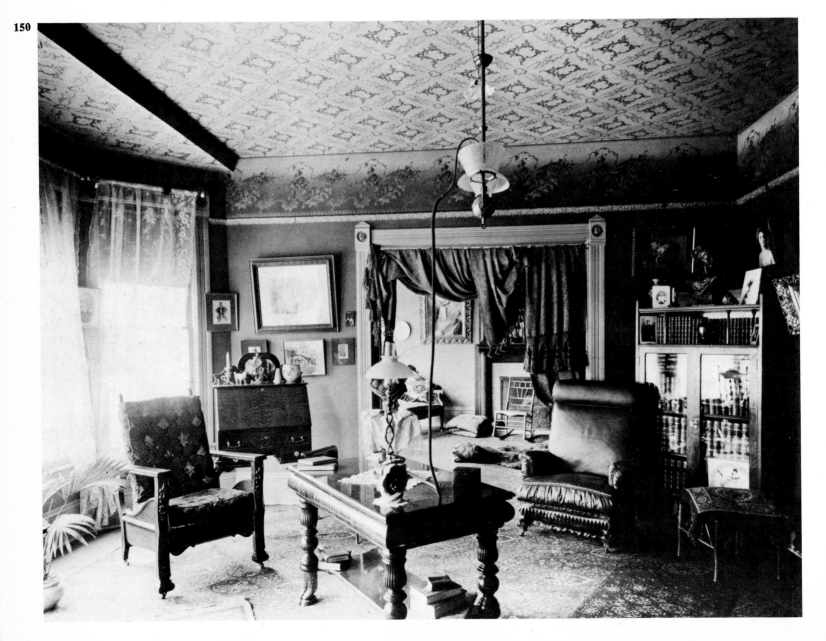

150

the areas around the desk and bookcase form subdued versions of art units, linked by curtains in the opening.

Flaherty's daughter May, on the other hand, felt free to personalize her bedroom in an elaborate scheme. In addition to her matching Golden Oak French bureau and dressing table, she has backed her brass bed with a cloud of photographs rising to the deep foliated border and dipping down to a polite little Turkish cozy corner full of cushions. From the gilded picture molding hang various prints, all new in the late 1880's, including one of cherubs kissing—a popular motif of the French craze.

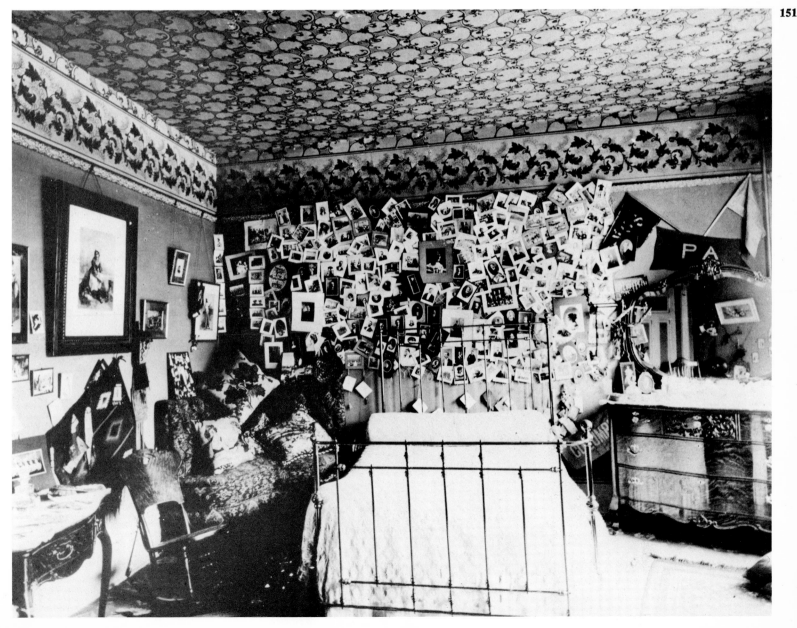

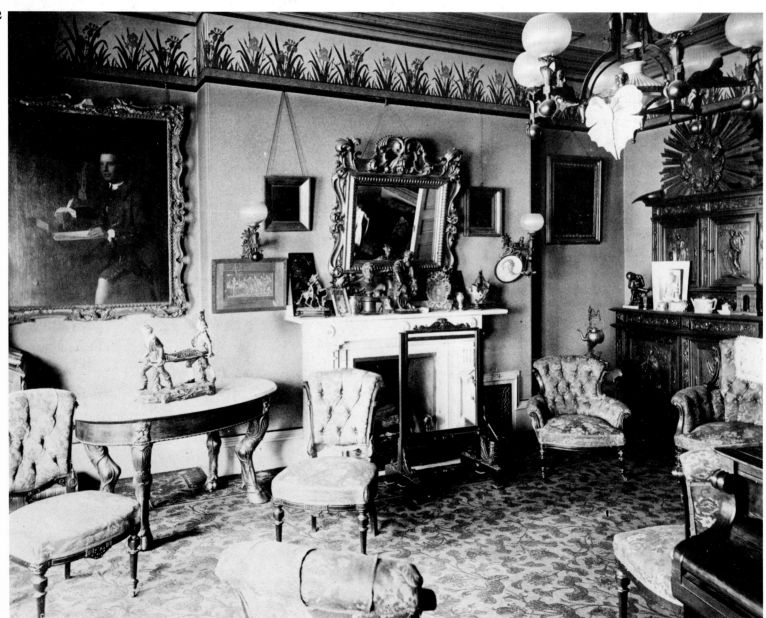

## 152. Parlor, House of Julia Ward Howe, 241 Beacon Street, Boston, Massachusetts, 1900

Mrs. Howe occupied this Boston house for many years, and was eighty-one when this photograph was taken. Thirty-eight years had passed since her *Battle Hymn of the Republic* had first appeared in the *Atlantic Monthly,* but in spite of the passage of time and her preoccupation with her literary work, she kept the Beacon Street parlor relatively up to date. The room has been newly wall-papered with a lively border of irises and a popular foliated pattern in a faint color, probably silver-gray or the yellowish color called oatmeal. Photographs, statuettes, and a painting with a dragonfly and flowers fill the mantel, and the seemingly informal massing is carried out into the walls on either side with pictures. A tea set and trophies from travels abroad are arranged on the cupboard, which is also probably an acquisition from European travels. The New Grecian parlor set of about 1875, re-upholstered in damask, is scattered informally in small French conversational groupings. A former center table, in this case the ancestor of Flaherty's library table *(150),* now becomes a side table between two chairs. A paper butterfly has alighted casually on the serious old gasolier; already at the turn of the century people were showing contempt for such Gilded Age flamboyance as Egyptian light fixtures.

## House of William B. Church, 1000 Corona, Denver, Colorado, 1900

William Church, vice-president of a Denver brickyard, built his house in the late 1890's; so it was rather new when these views were taken by members of his family.

**153.** Through a velvet-hung opening is the dining room, furnished in the English style. Golden Oak has been used here in an adaptation of Sheraton-style furniture. Over the table an electrolier hangs from the wall-papered ceiling, which has a centerpiece. Beneath the table is a foot bell which rang in the kitchen. This room expresses the gradual popularization of the period ideal already well-established in England. The day would soon come when furniture of this type would flood from American factories.

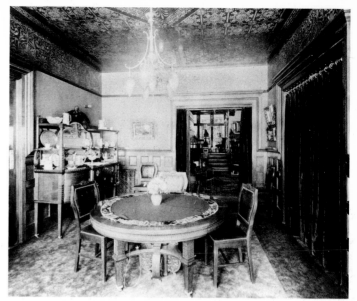

153

**154.** The living hall is richly executed in the so-called Richardsonian Romanesque, a monumental style by then familiar in American houses and public buildings and named for the architect Henry Hobson Richardson. Woodwork of this kind was purchased ready-made at millwork factories nearly everywhere in the United States, and it could also be ordered through catalogues. The rambling staircase girdles the hallway and carries the eye up to distant spaces and nooks, here punctuated with selected objects of porcelain and sculpture. By and large the hall is, like Jefferson's at Monticello, a museum to house a collection. Church was a collector of minerals, and open shelves filled with his specimens line the walls of the landing.

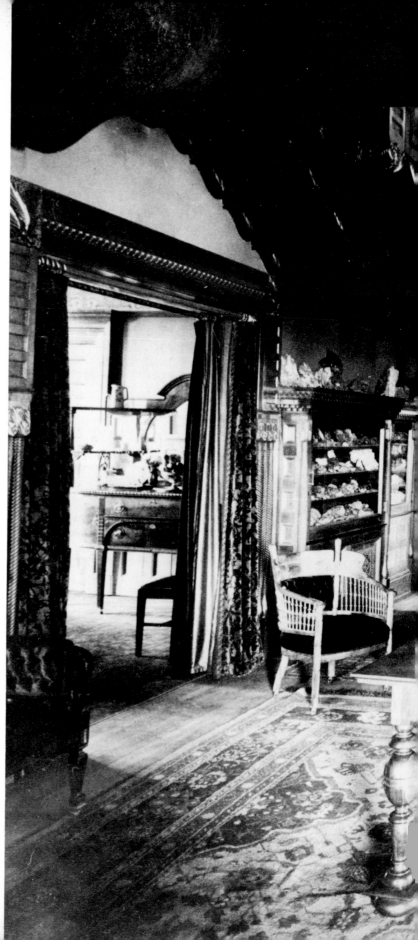

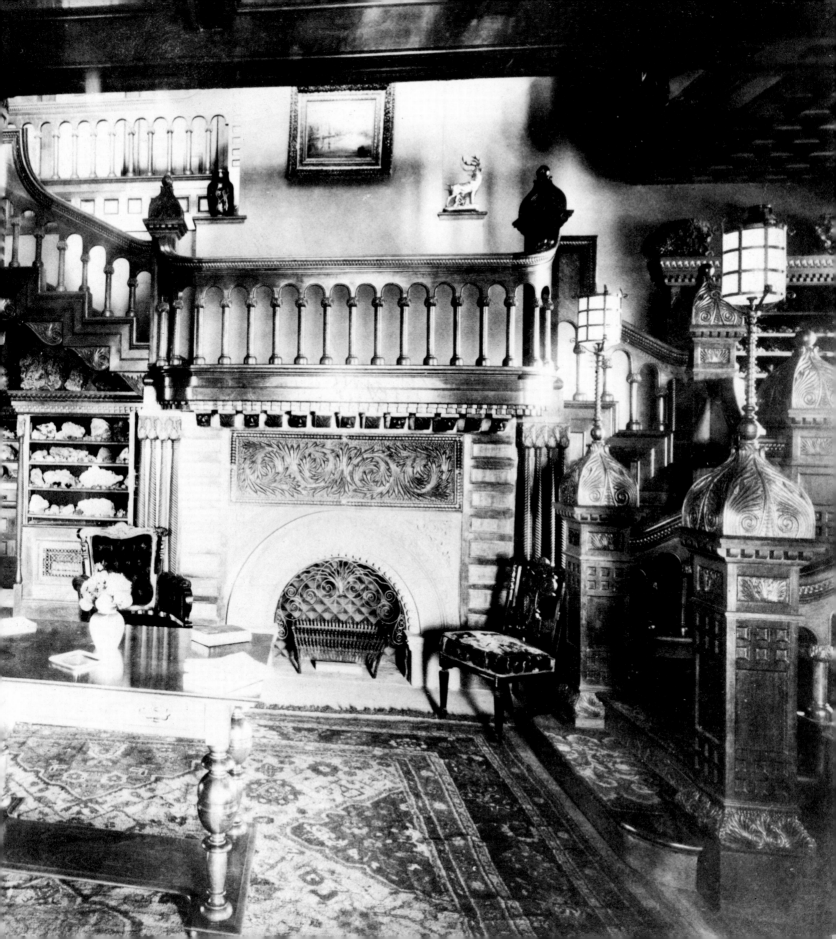

**155.** Matching wallpaper border and fabric swags are the principal decorations of the sewing room. The taste for matching materials, such as paper and cloth, had begun on a small scale in the late 1880's, but by the twentieth century, it was rather common. These classical hangings were in the English taste, and probably were made from patterns purchased at the store. Inexpensive wicker furniture, straw matting, and white batiste curtains are more in the spirit of sun-room decorations than those of sewing rooms, which once were simple affairs for mundane purposes. Light bulbs, still awkward and new in American rooms, poke out from brass pipes; elsewhere in the Church's house they are screwed into receptacles sunk into the walls and left uncovered.

**156. Parlor, House of William B. Chisholm, 68 Meeting Street, Charleston, South Carolina, 1900**

The architectural elements of this room might have been called Free Classic by the original designer, but were undoubtedly believed by the owner to be colonial. Painted colonial white and set off by the subtle tones of the filigreed wallpaper, the woodwork has traces of gilding and

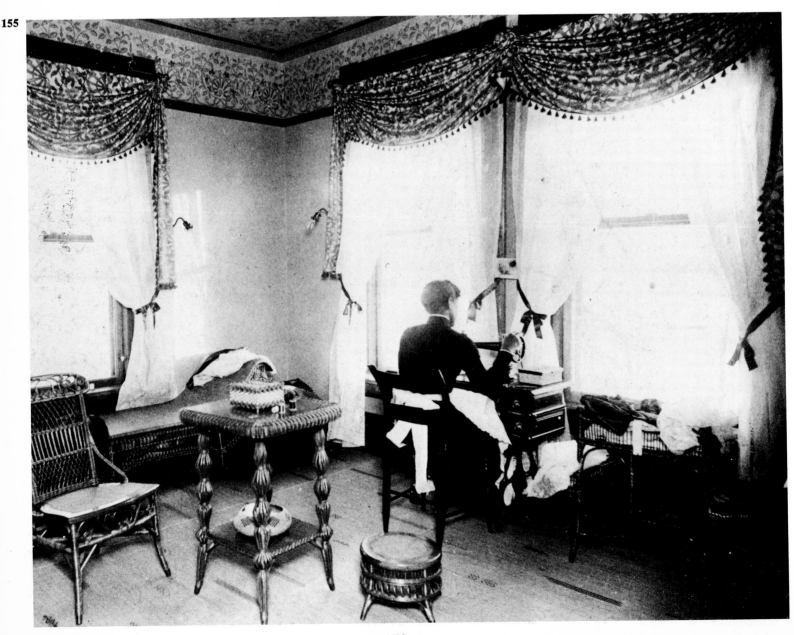

forms ceremonial transitions between the rooms in the open plan. The Art furniture dates from the 1870's, and is ebonized with incised ornamentation which has been gilded. The source for this creative revival furniture seems to be the historical Louis Seize revival that immediately preceded it. Near the curtained doorway to the right is a pair of chairs in the English style. They were probably considered Sheraton, if not merely English, or Quaint. Chisholm has made no effort to personalize his parlor. His French arrangement is composed of furniture well out of style, yet the ensemble is quite up to date.

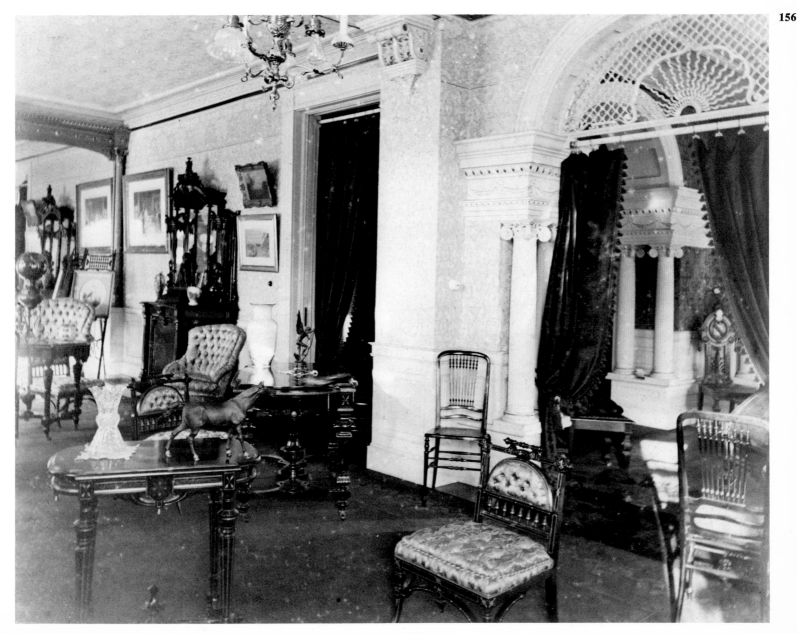

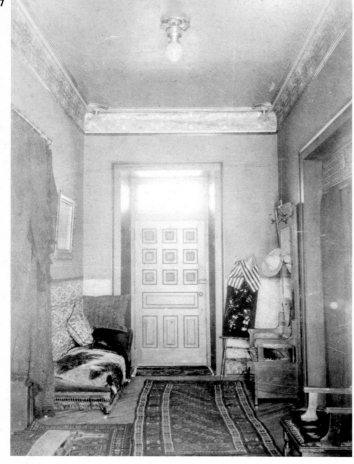

**157, 158. Hallway and Parlor, House of Eugene A. Fiske, Santa Fe, New Mexico, May, 1900**

The Fiske house, which we saw earlier *(98–101)* was redecorated in 1899. These two views show the extent to which provincial taste changed in the 1890's. In the hallway, the cove is wallpapered, and light bulbs dot the ceiling. Pillows and a fur throw decorate the chaise longue in the corner. Wallpaper or linoleum has been used as a decorative wainscoting. Oriental rugs are used as runners on hardwood floors which have been laid on the diagonal.

The simple parlor with its tailored curtains and Queen Anne mantel has been revised into being a room of some monumentality. A ponderous Romanesque style chimneypiece of glazed brick crosses the corner and provides several stages for the display of picket-like rows of porcelains. Strapwork, probably in plaster, covers the ceiling, and from the center of a great circle an electric lamp illuminates the parlor; possibly the rosettes in the center of each square contain—or were meant by the manufacturer to contain—receptacles for light bulbs. A rich plaster cove frames the ceiling. Except for the wicker chair, none of the furniture is new, and the carpeting is the same that was in place before. The window has been rebuilt as a bay, over which lace curtains are crisscrossed and tied back high. A classical swag hides the rod and rings, in imitation of early nineteenth-century window treatments. Both rooms as redecorated demonstrate the increasing awareness of materials, particularly masonry and wood, which had begun to affect houses as a partial result of the Arts and Crafts movement. Objects are used, in a sense, as architecture, and seem to exist as part of the whole.

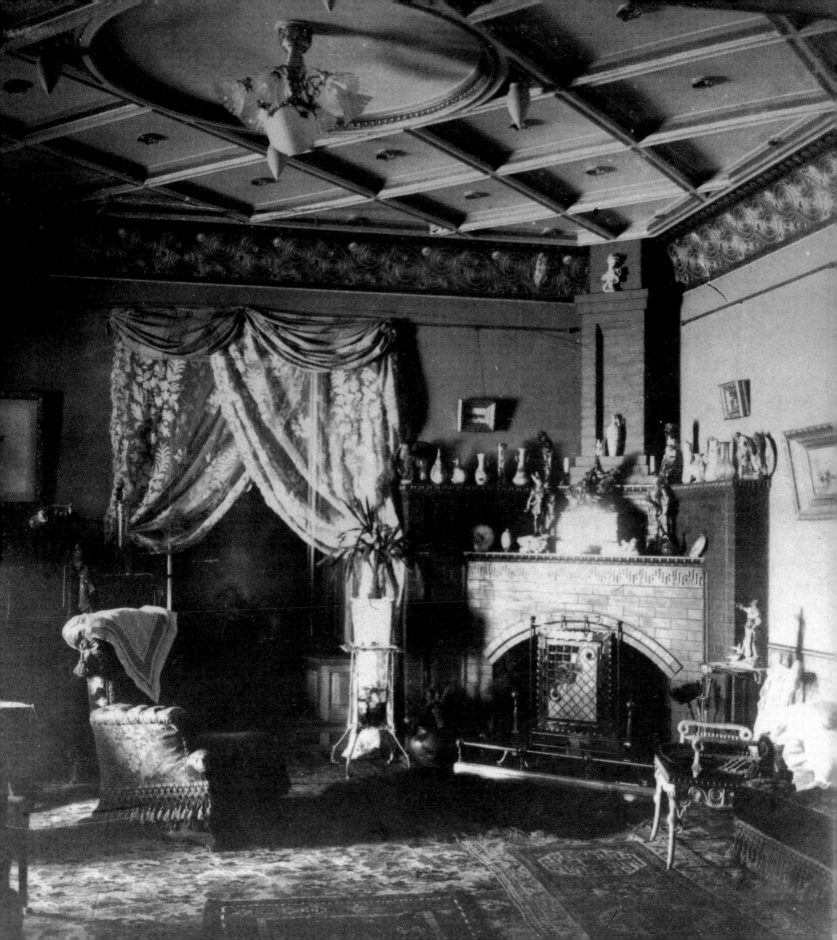

**159. Parlor, Boston, Massachusetts, 1900**

This anonymous colonial revival parlor has been furnished in the English style of the late 1890's and early 1900's. Sheraton-style furniture of the late eighteenth century was the inspiration for this adaptation; but this could not really be considered creative revival, because it remains more or less close to the original idea of the Sheraton style, even though great freedom has been taken. None of the upholstery matches, a further denunciation of the appearance of being a set. Curios on the mantel include a compote, photographs, and plates, one

of which depicts Napoleon I, a historical motif echoed in the lamp shade. This is an excellent example of a consciously period parlor of a middle-class family.

**160. Bedroom, Boston, Massachusetts, 1900**

The house was undoubtedly built in the 1870's or 1880's; perhaps all of its rooms have been redecorated like this one, to minimize the architectural nature of the interior and create a modern setting. All of the woodwork has been painted to match, perhaps over the heavy varnish applied in the past, and the color might be green or gray.

159

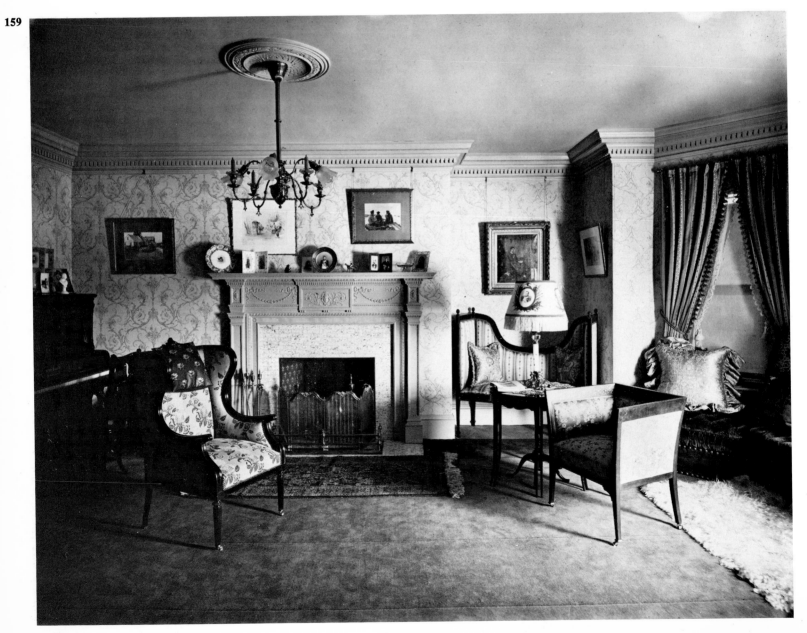

Wallpaper with leaves and flowers sets the colonial mood, while a chintz slipcover on a wing chair is the major object. On the mantel are photographs, and above, new prints showing historical scenes. In the bay a cozy grouping of chaise longue and chairs has two tables, one covered with an embroidered shawl, and the other, a little wicker one, for books. Unity of color and pattern were considered an effective means of simplifying immovable decorations in rooms of a generation before.

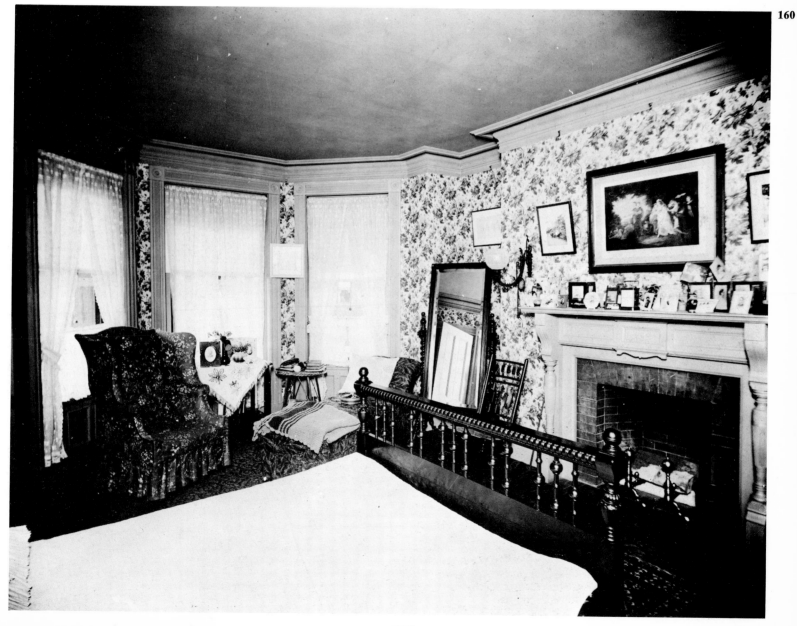

160

**161. Smoking Room, House of J. A. St. John, 149 Milk Street, Boston, Massachusetts, 1900**

Strong patterns in wallpaper, fabric, and imitation oriental carpeting bind this room into that rich but plain sort of an ensemble beloved by people in the 1890's. The objects and furnishings are of recent date and are very inexpensive, from the cheap prints to the plaster monkey placed on the radiator. Inconsequential parts are lost in the oriental designs that dominate the whole. Every effort has been made to convey the impression of this as a man's room. In the 1890's gender became an important element in the decoration of rooms and has remained a nearly endless vocabulary. French furniture was believed appropriate to women's uses, while the more sober revivals and nearly all the modern styles were believed suitable for masculine purposes.

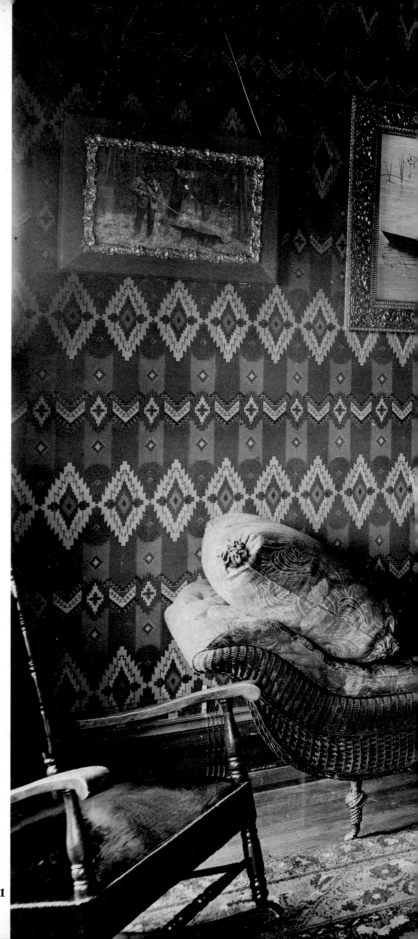

161

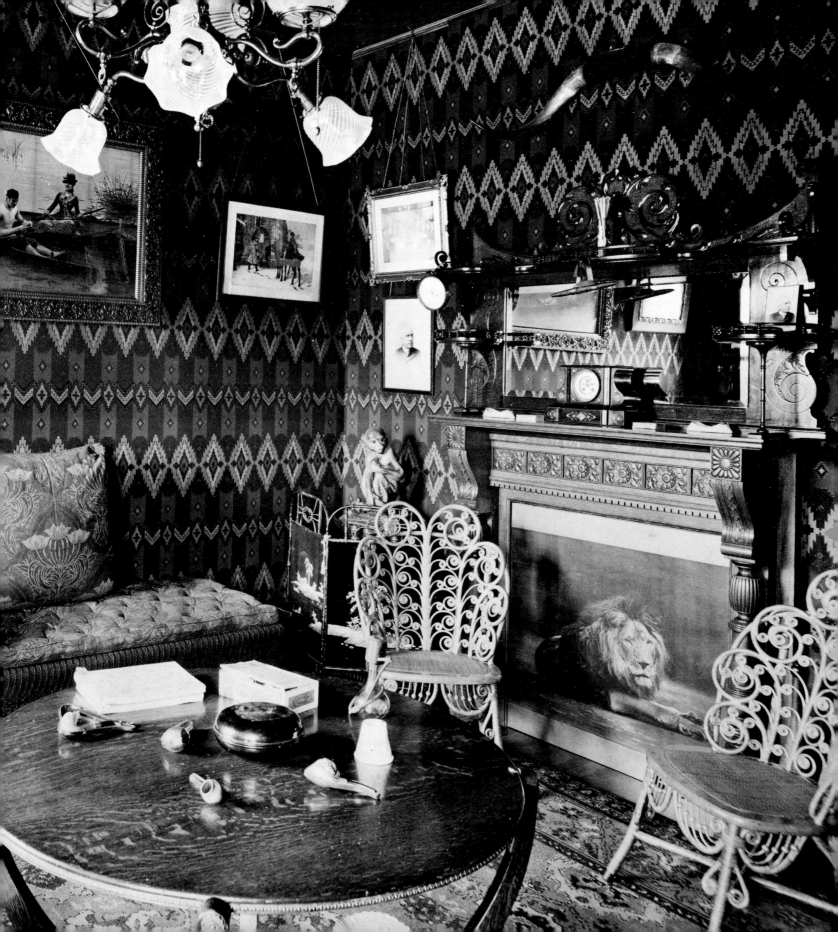

**162.  Bedroom, House of Stephan L. Littler, 707 North Klein Street, Springfield, Illinois, 1902**

Wallpapered in an English pattern which might, in sophisticated circles, have been called Adam, this bedroom has colonial revival cabinet pieces and a brass and onyx bed. Nearly everything here is new. The colonial bureau and dresser are not creative revival; they depart considerably from anything eighteenth-century—freely mixing in aspects of Grecian design—but there is no mistaking their intent to look colonial. In all probability the room arrangement is seasonal; maybe now it is summer. Until

the end of the first quarter of the twentieth century, it was customary to revise furniture placement especially in bedrooms and sitting rooms, to accommodate the climate.

**163. Study Corner, House of the Robinson Family, Adams Street, Dorchester, Massachusetts, 1902**

Antiques from many periods have here been grouped into a colonial setting, clearly representing the mood of the past which was popular particularly in New England, the heartland of the colonial revival. Although the furni-

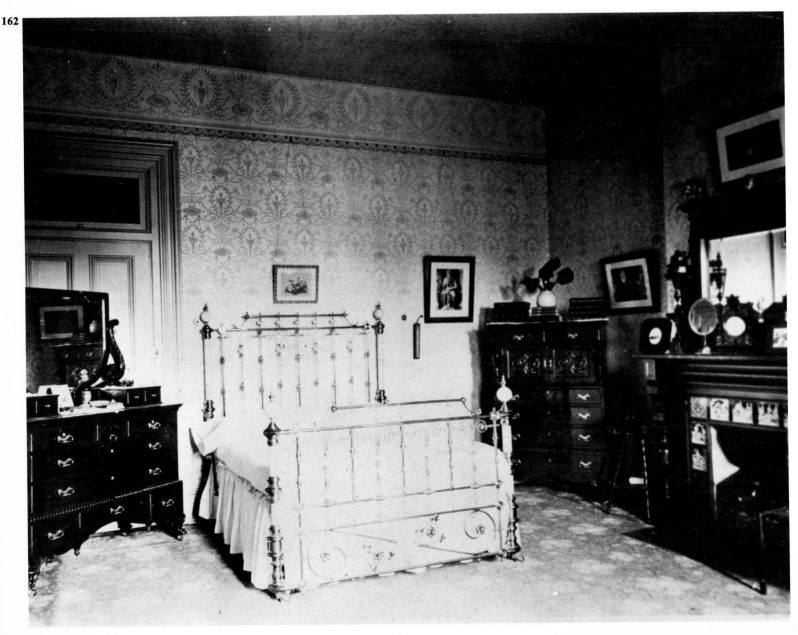

162

ture here varies, from the Grecian stool of about 1850 to the eighteenth-century desk and French Antique easy chair of about 1870, the ensemble is not far removed from the careful period settings already established in some places and still popular in the United States today. The curtains tied back, the desk left open and filled with little things, the bonnet, hung in the corner seemingly by chance, and the comfortable and time-worn look of the whole, are indelible characteristics of antiquarian taste in the early twentieth century.

163

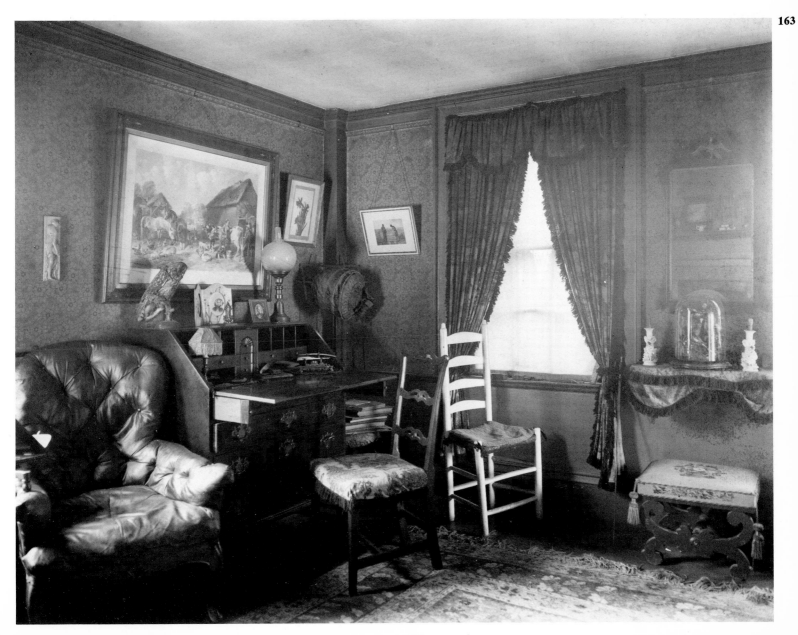

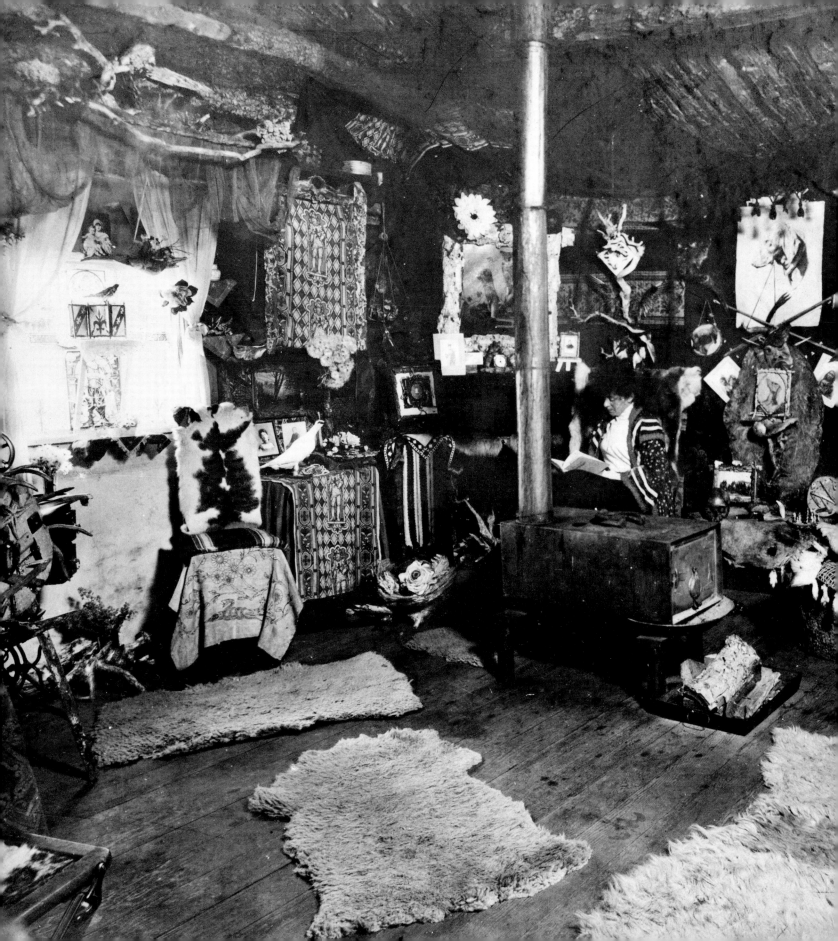

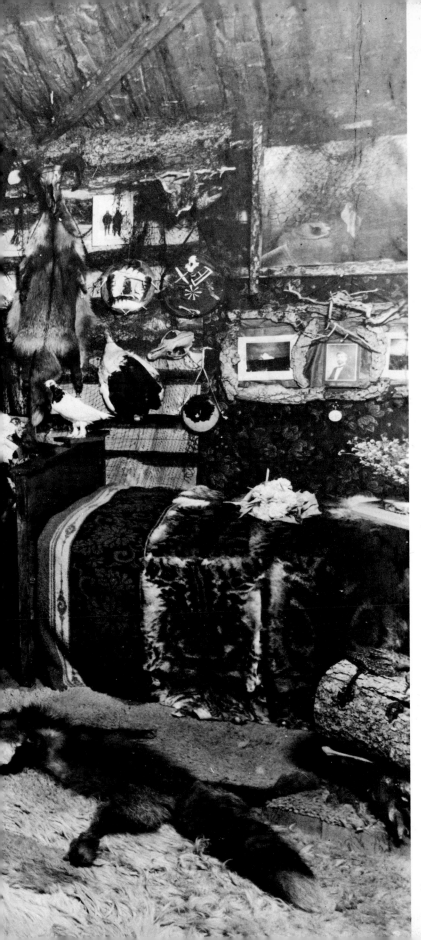

### 164. Cabin, Alaska Territory, 1903

The new sparseness was by no means the rule. This photograph is labeled, "What artistic taste and refinement can do in an Alaskan cabin." It might well have been written in 1880, but the room's decoration is no reflection of the home art of that time. It is quite modern. There are no art units nor art corners; objects here are architectural, supplementing the raw simplicity of the cabin. The female figure, doubtless the author of this transformation, sits in the midst of it all, as a physical part of her grand conception. She has, in a most unusual way, captured the spirit of the French craze of the late 1890's. To a lesser degree, such decoration was not unfamiliar in most parts of the United States until World War I.

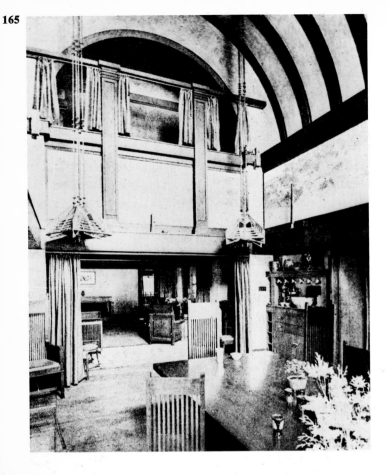

### 165. Dining Room, House of Susan Laurence Dana, East Laurence Avenue and 4th Street, Springfield, Illinois, 1903

The widow of Edwin W. Dana, who inherited from her father a fortune in western mining interests, commissioned Frank Lloyd Wright to expand and remodel her Springfield house and permitted him also to design all its furniture. In an age struggling to blend house and contents as one, Wright was given the opportunity of being the lone creative hand. The finished house presented a series of large interlocking spaces, the most dramatic of which was this full two-story dining room with its barrel-vaulted ceiling. Like the monumental living halls which had been features of houses since the 1870's, this space, although well-defined, offers views beyond its confines into other parts of the house somewhat in the romantic manner of the Queen Anne. The furniture is well within the current Arts and Crafts style, but has the delicacy so popular in the various Quaint modes. Its forms echo the lines of the room; architecture and furniture support and complement one another. Architectural details replace the usual wallpapers and auxiliary objects. Against the rich and varied background of the house, the furniture is sparse and simple in the same sense as were some of the creative revival furnishings of forty years before. This furniture, although not mass-produced, has in common with catalogue styles the look of infinite duplication.

### 166, 167. Living Hall and Sitting Room, House of Charles S. Hills, 5065 Lindell Boulevard, St. Louis, Missouri, 1904

The desire to blend the house and its contents was most prevalent in the so-called Beaux-Arts taste that began to be popular in the mid-1890's and spread intermittently over the nation in public buildings and costly mansions such as this. Very few, of course, were planned by men actually trained at the Ecole des Beaux-Arts in Paris; but neither was the particular American adoption of this philosophy of historical revivalism always like that of the Beaux-Arts. Designed by the St. Louis firm of Barnett, Haynes, and Barnett in 1899, Charles Hills's house was decorated by professionals who sought to achieve in it the perfect blending of house and furniture. Design was their index, quite in the same way that design served the Arts and Crafts. The entrance hall goes far beyond the tradition of the living hall in being the most luxurious and formal room in the house; from its ornate walls, the eye could wander through openings and up along the stair to distant vignettes and plays of light. New furniture in the Renaissance style is invitingly grouped in some areas, and in others it is lined against the walls. At night, the opaque globes of the electrolier cast soft light onto tapestry, needlepoint, ornate plaster, deep carpeting, and brass gas and electric sconces. The sitting room on the second floor is in the Grecian style of the day, and architecture and furniture together carry the theme. Poplar groves and romantic forests are painted on the walls, while white benches and chairs with cushioned seats adorn the room, its painted surfaces shiny like polished marble. There is a little fountain in the center of the floor, and an abundance of potted plants. The house is as self-consciously perfect as modern designers and machines can make it. There is really no effort here to be antique; the historical themes are merely decorative devices for a house whose main appeal is its utter devotion to its own time. Coziness and manufactured momentality are strange companions in such a businessman's mansion, but the effect is typical. Well-constructed and filled

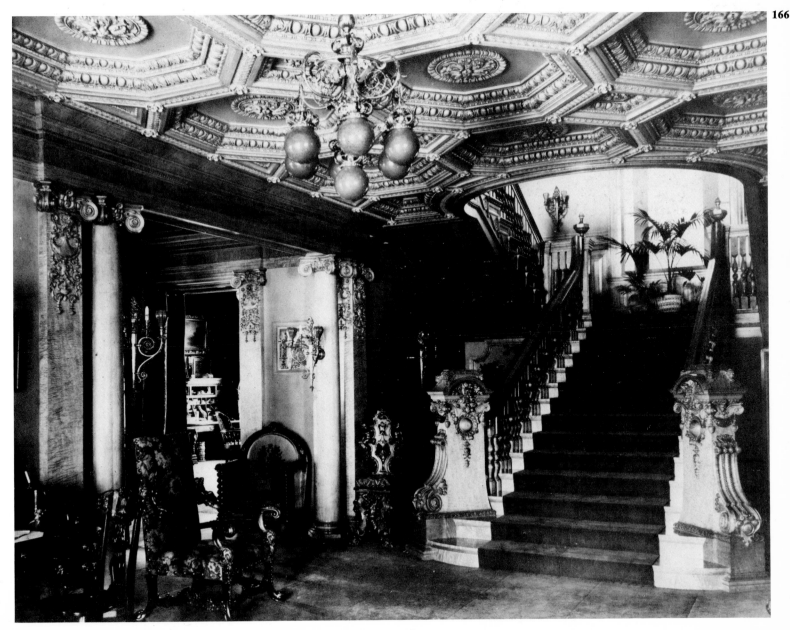

with conveniences, a house of this kind with perhaps twelve or fifteen rooms might cost, in 1903, about $130,000 complete.

## 168. Parlor and Dining Room, Apartment of William S. Murray, 408 East Main Street, Richmond, Virginia, 1904

Murray, a salesman, occupied at least a portion of one of the houses built by the Haxall family in the early 1830's. Many of these old residences in the downtown area had been abandoned or subdivided, and the more desirable new houses were built in the suburbs. Even as recently as the 1870's, these rooms must have been furnished in stylish sets, going by the apparent high quality of the ceiling fresco and stenciled cove. The wallpaper is new; the grained woodwork, badly worn, has merely been cleaned, while the floors are stained dark, after having doubtless spent most of their careers under the cover of matting or carpeting. Murray's biggest investments are in his two upright pianos. Except for the two old Marie Antoinette chairs—of the kind which were then appearing in junk shops—the rooms are furnished inexpensively

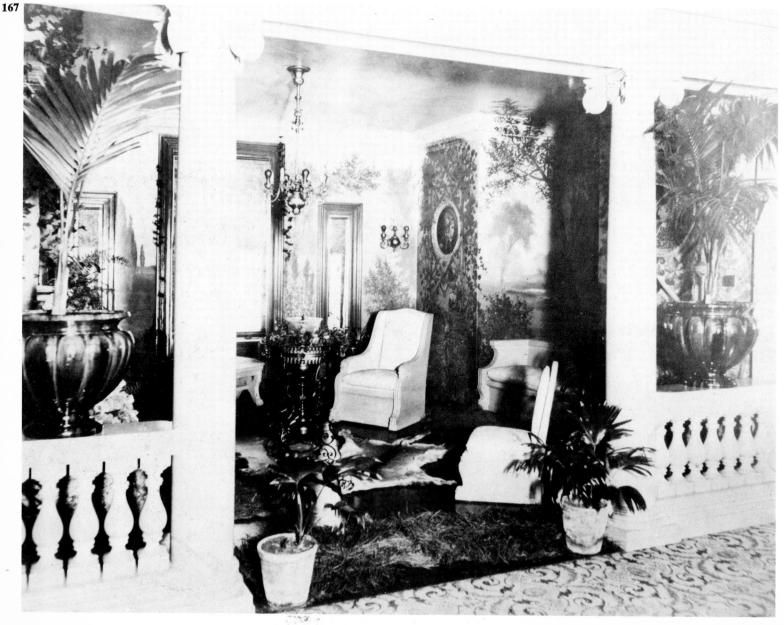
167

in new colonial revival wooden, and fancy wicker, rocking chairs. Many of the pictures seem to have been painted at home, perhaps by Mrs. Murray; they show nymphs, bunches of roses, and some pastoral scenes, arranged asymmetrically with oriental scrolls and other art objects in an attempt to reduce the scale of the room.

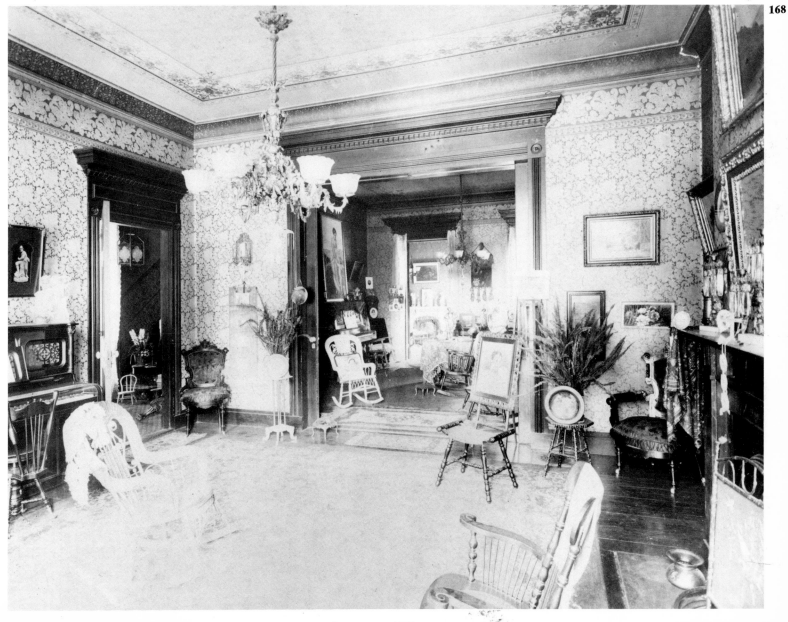

168

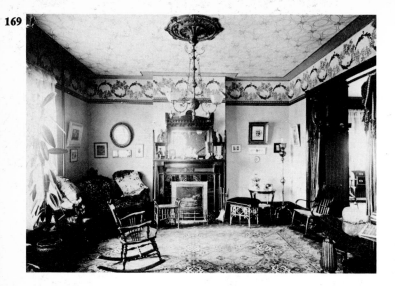

**169. Parlor, House of Alexander P. Thatcher, 912 Dearborn Avenue, Helena, Montana, 1905**

Thatcher was assistant secretary of the Missouri River Power Company. His coat of arms hangs on the wall of the parlor, which his young wife Ella has decorated. It is not a new house; the New Grecian mantel must date from the 1880's, and the Renaissance revival rosette in the ceiling might even be older. An old Louis Seize revival sofa, covered in cut velvet, assumes the attitude of a cozy corner with its big pillows. Delicate little clusters of framed pictures form a line at eye level around the room. Above that, a wallpaper depicting intertwining ropes of leaves and flowers, borders the wall above the picture molding, and the ceiling is covered in a pattern that suggests a web, framed at the outer edges by a plain border and gilded molding. The parlor has two colonial revival rocking chairs, a small French parlor table, an English library table, and other objects which could have been ordered through mail-order catalogues or bought in one of Helena's five furniture stores. Sparse without being barren, the Thatchers' parlor is the beau ideal of a middle-class parlor of the early twentieth century.

**170. Dining Room, House of Eugene B. Braden, East Helena, Montana, 1905**

Electric light bulbs came into the world naked and the question of how to cover them, or whether to cover them at all, produced many kinds of answers. The dining room of the manager of the American Smelting and Refining Company is furnished in Golden Oak of the massive mode. Not as austere as it might have been, this manufactured set has panels of pressed work that simulate carving. The dining table with three leaves, four or six colonial chairs, and the mirrored sideboard—with French-style hardware—could be bought as a set for about $18–25. These pieces were well-made, their natural wood-graining bright and showy beneath several heavy coats of varnish. A painted table, undoubtedly homemade, serves this set as a side table. The room is painted white on plaster, with the woodwork in two tones perhaps of gray or green. An oriental rug on the floor and matching white scarves for the furniture complete the very typical scene. Silverplate, which knew a certain renaissance in America beginning in the Gilded Age, is exhibited on the sideboard and the table, which is set for a meal.

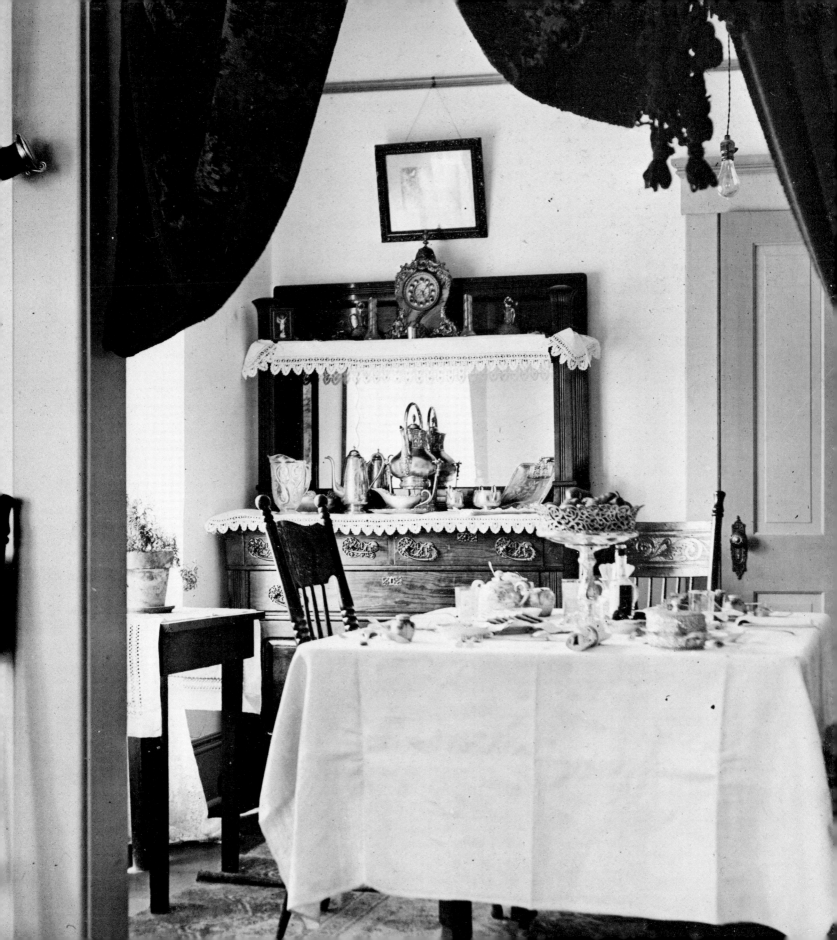

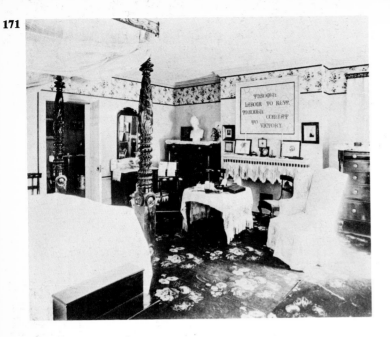

## 171. Bedroom, Chalkley Hall, House of the Weatherill Family, Frankford Junction, Pennsylvania, 1905

A short train ride from Philadelphia, this suburban estate, purchased apparently for its interest as an old house, was restored according to the antiquarian ideas of the day. While the large Weatherill family bought the house in the 1890's, they tried to give it the look of an old and established household. The Sheraton bed might have had its posts carved recently, a rather common practice during the craze for featherwork and American Empire furniture. A tester has been made from old gilded curtain cornices of the mid-nineteenth century and hung with gauze. Old Brussels carpeting, patched and worn, has been left. A pair of chests flank the chimney and may be new American Empire reproductions. Children's pictures, a framed pocket watch, a crocheted and beribboned lambrequin, and the inevitable colonial touch, candles, ornament the mantel, while on the wall above it a marbled panel has been inscribed with a maxim. Floral wallpaper has been applied in a band around the upper wall. Washstand, tables, and other surfaces are fastidiously supplied with human conveniences like hand towels, soap, writing paper, and books. These comforts and various other personal accessories were essential features of sophisticated decorating in the early twentieth century.

## 172, 173, 174. Parlor, Eureka, California, 1906

At first glance, this parlor seems to date from the late 1880's, and certainly no later than about 1895. Yet the copyright dates on some of the art pictures confirm that the room cannot be prior to 1906. Here is art clutter, carefully divided into units and kept to the walls, instead of in the center of the room. The taste is decidedly out of date by twenty or more years, but it is still vibrant and lively. Whoever created this setting must have spent considerable time primping the sideboard tableau and refreshing the floral arrangements, some of which harken to the 1860's in style. The hand that took one panel of lace on each window and looped it up over the valance was truly dedicated to home art, and not at all in step with the new sparseness and love of creature comforts.

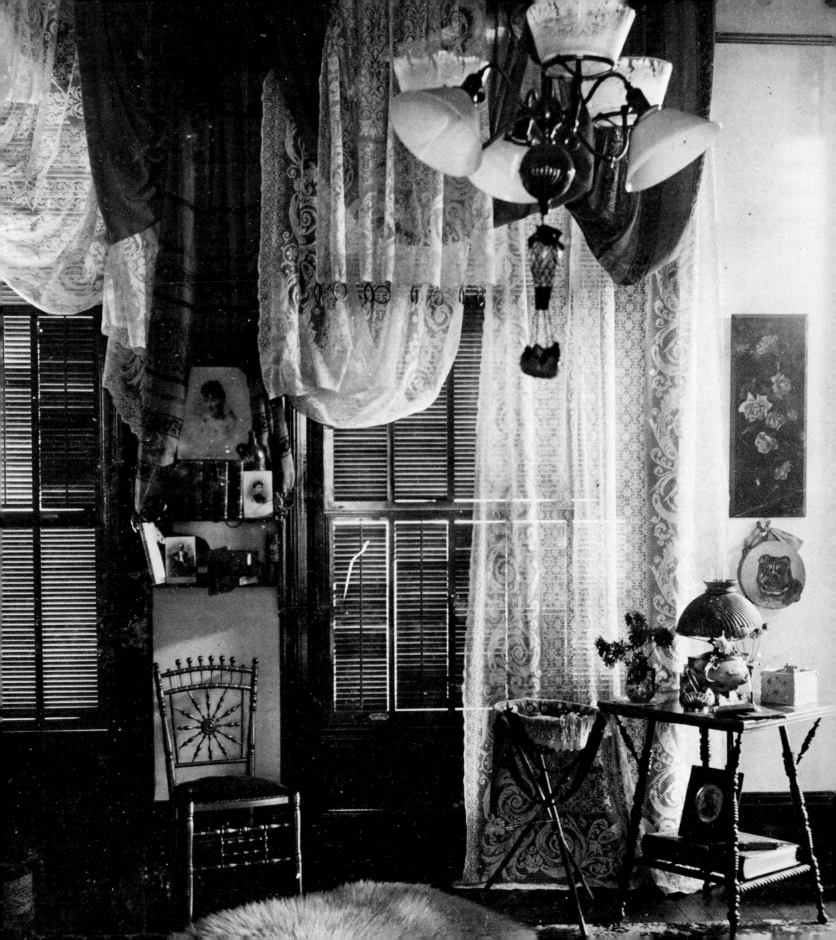

Nor were the chaste ideals of the Beaux-Arts present in this creative act. Most of the furniture seen in this parlor was, by 1906, long familiar in furniture catalogues of the inexpensive manufacturers. The tieing of bow ribbons on the backs of chairs had about died out. Nevertheless, a strong will assembled and arranged this room; and the influences that played upon that unknown person might have built up over two or three decades, to find consummation at last in this parlor in Eureka, California.

173

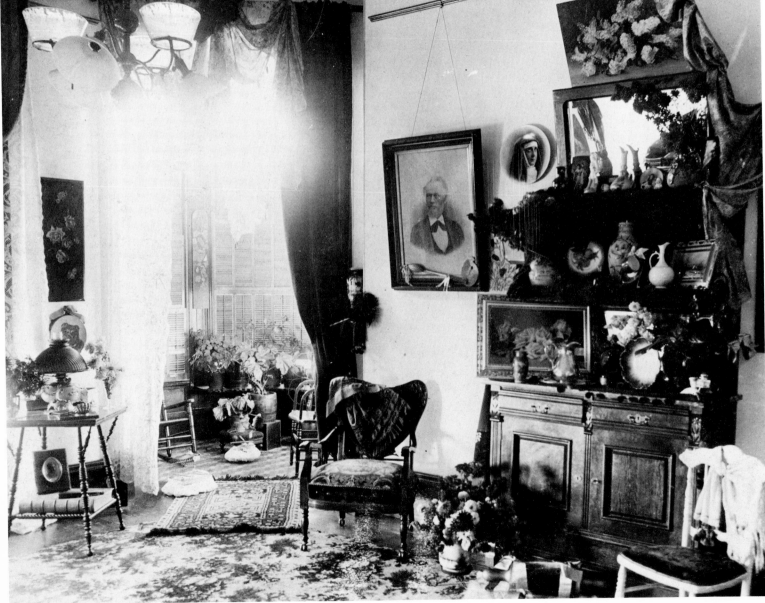

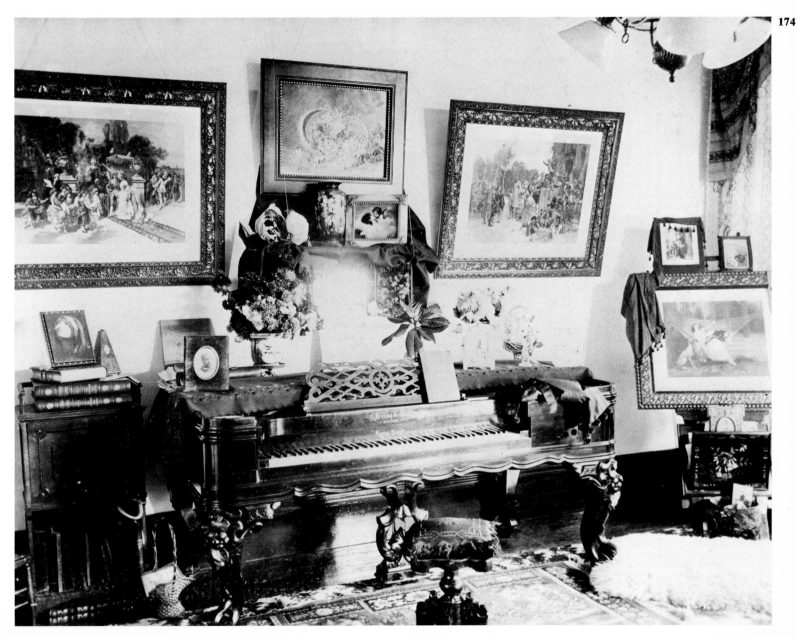

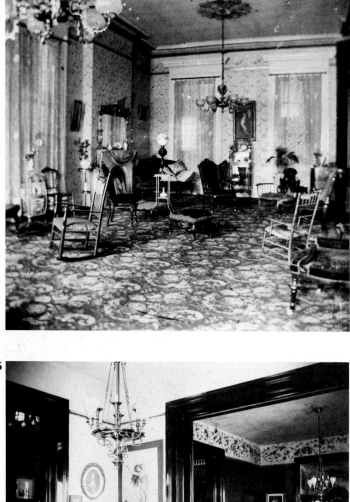

### 175. Parlor, Mobile, Alabama, 1906

In a house of the mid-nineteenth century, an up-to-date French parlor has been created, which is vaguely reminiscent of French Antique settings of the 1850's, except that the individual objects are light in weight, and the room is airy. A Louis Seize revival parlor set is mixed with new rocking chairs, French tables in brass and wood, vases, plants, and cushions. It is a comfortable room with its cool white woodwork and lacy wallpaper, and long panels of white lace at the windows. The colors in the crown molding may linger from earlier times, as probably does the gilding on the rosettes from which the French Antique gasoliers hang.

### 176. Library, House of C. T. Herrin, 1056 Government Street, Mobile, Alabama, 1906

While the catalogues often had conflicting descriptions, most of the furniture here was probably called Chippendale or perhaps just English. The library table in the foreground, with its cabriole legs and palmettes, might even have been considered Louis Quinze. Tables like it were available gilded, and some had French scenes painted on them. The woodwork is stained mahogany color and gleams under a high varnish. White walls in one room contrast with dark walls in the next. Monumentality was sought in the decoration of the dining room. China and glassware are kept in china closets, not on display as they would have been ten years before, and the table is bare, except for a doily in the center. Hardwood floors, left uncovered except by little rugs, add another dimension with their glossy surfaces. A great stair hall lies outside the library; baronial stairways, such as this appears to be, were essential features even in some rather small houses of the early 1900's. They could be ordered in parts through the mail, or made to order by carpenters on the spot, using newel posts and spindles from manufacturers' catalogues. The Herrin house could have been nearly anywhere in the United States, the only slight difference being perhaps in the high quality of its woodwork, as Mobile was in an area of prosperous sawmills.

**177. Parlor, House of Betty Brown, 2328 Broadway, Galveston, Texas, 1907**

Built by her father in 1858–59, Betty Brown's Italianate mansion faced Galveston's palm-lined boulevard. Throughout the late nineteenth century Miss Brown had been sent abroad and to the East to study in art schools. Returning home, she was inspired to bring style and taste to her parent's old-fashioned house. Under her direction, the French Antique parlor of the 1850's was converted into a French room to more properly satisfy the European appetite of the early 1900's. She painted the old parlor set white and frosted it in gilt; imitation Aubusson upholstery and shimmering silk damasks of the sort endorsed by Edith Wharton and Ogden Codman, Jr., replaced what had been there before. The gasolier was painted white and gold. Miss Brown's own canvasses of cherubs and floral cartouches enlivened the plain white walls. New French tables and curio cabinets were added. Even the Gothic chair to the rear got a coat of white and gold, and the room was named the Gold Drawing Room.

177

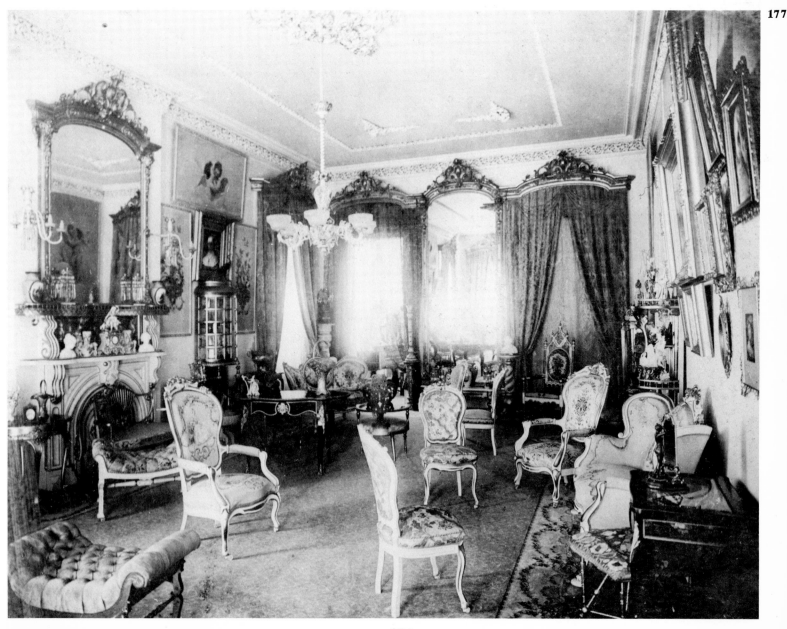

**178, 179. Living Hall and Dining Room, House of Thomas Harmer, North 30th Street, Tacoma, Washington, 1908**

Thomas and Deborah Harmer were married in 1900 and moved from Grand Rapids, Michigan, to the West Coast. In 1903, they moved into this new bungalow overlooking Tacoma Harbor. The bungalows extolled by the Arts and Crafts movement were quite expensive, but builder bungalows like this one were mass-produced and not costly. Bungalow plans were similar everywhere: usually there was a living hall with a dining room, and some-times a second living room, immediately behind it and often a bay window in the dining room, as here. Bed-rooms were ranged one behind the other along the oppo-site side of the house. Usually there were at least two bedrooms and a sewing room, and there was very often a bathroom. The roofs were steep and the eaves deep. Later on, the attic, reached by a stair, could be finished for purposes other than storage.

These two views in the Harmer house show the liv-ing hall and dining room. Illuminated by abundant win-dows and electroliers, the rooms are cozy and comfort-

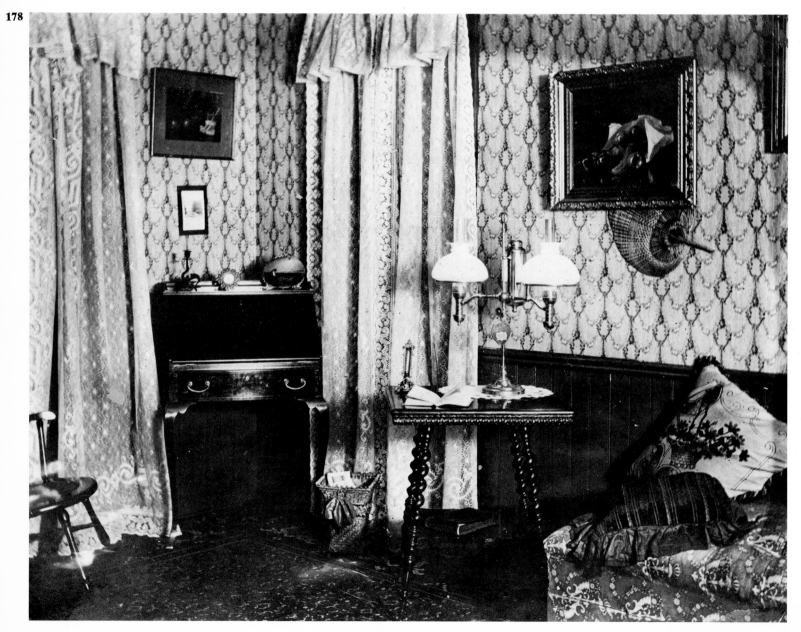

178

able. Lace curtains in the parlor are used with a popular French wallpaper pattern, and a wainscoting made of car siding and probably painted brown. The Quaint parlor table, student lamp, and colonial revival rocking chair might be local purchases. Mrs. Harmer was given the Queen Anne desk for Christmas in 1899, and it was made at one of the factories in Grand Rapids. The dining room contains a built-in sideboard; sometimes these had doors in the rear that opened from the kitchen for convenience, and sometimes there was a screen made of wire that slid down from above to protect food left on the

sideboard. A spindlework archway defines the broad opening from the second sitting room, which lies between the living hall and the dining room. Dark woodwork and wallpapers with borders are in proper accord with the bungalow style. Plants are massed on a homemade table, and beyond the lace curtains can be seen a sailing ship in the harbor. Such bungalows as this, more a part of the American dream than mansions like that of Charles Hills in St. Louis *(166, 167)*, stem from old traditions of American housebuilding.

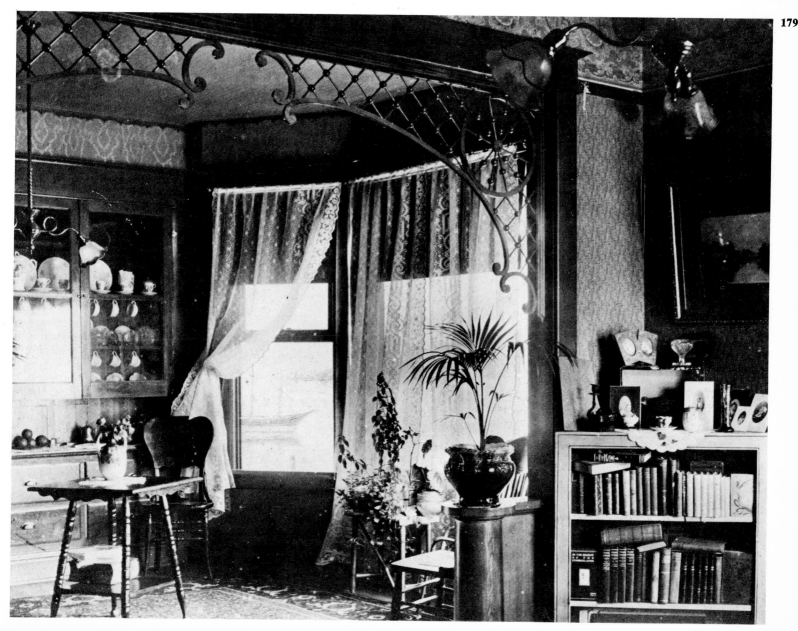

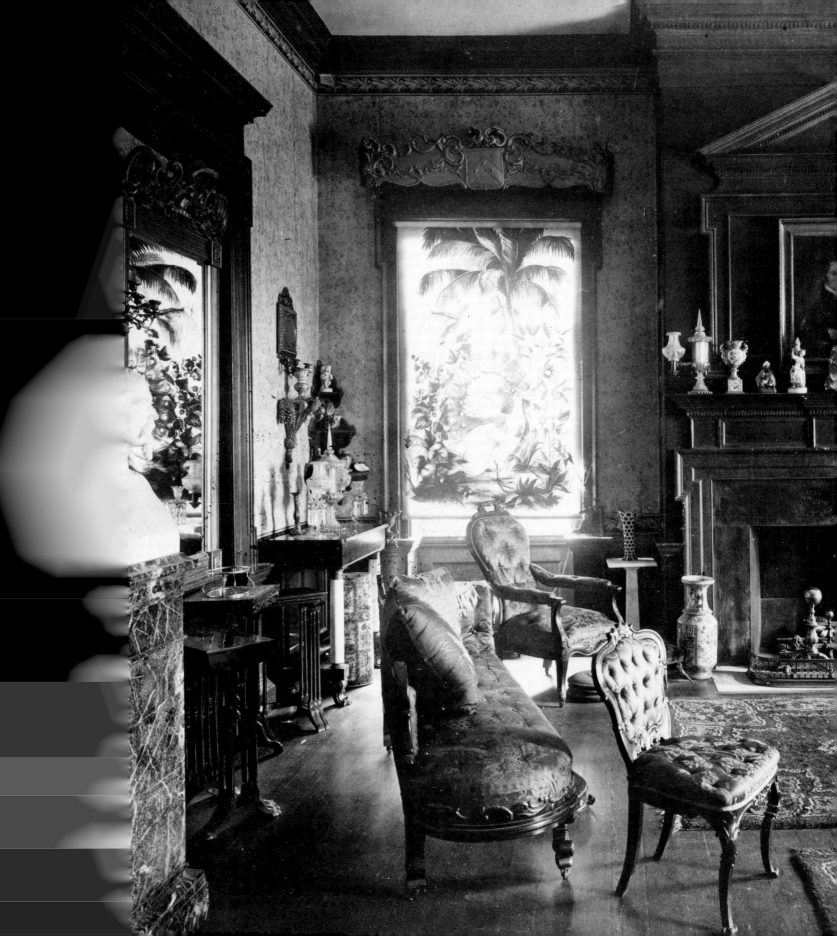

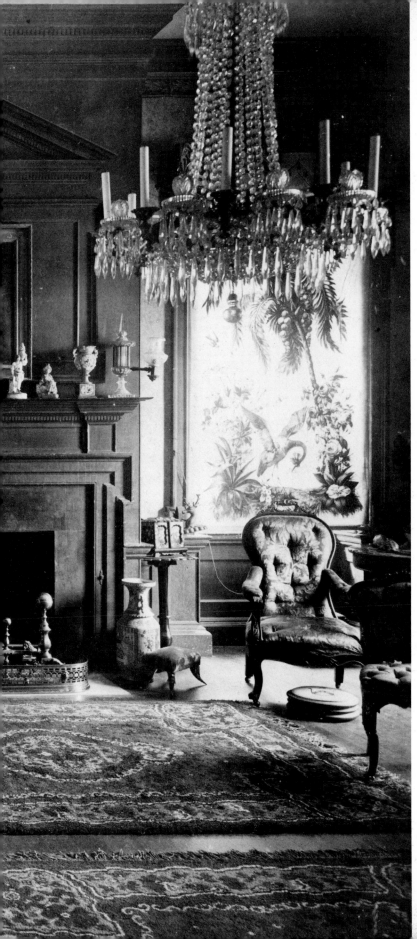

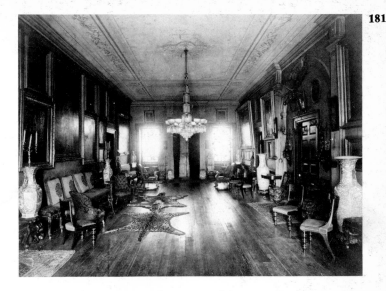

**180, 181.  Parlor and Hall, Hampton, Baltimore County, Maryland, 1908**

Built 1783–90 for the Ridgley family, the rooms of Hampton came as close as any in eighteenth century America to approaching the palatial scale of those in English country houses. It served the Ridgleys for 150 years before becoming part of a national park. Hampton has an exterior design appropriate to an academy, courthouse, or even a cottage, which makes its immense scale even more surprising. In 1908, as the continuing home of one family, it had undergone some modernizing. Most of the furnishings of the hall and parlor are nineteenth-century family possessions; to these, other objects have been added through the years. The setting is essentially that of 1908, showing the interest of the age in palatial effects and grandeur. All the wall-to-wall carpeting has been removed and the floors are heavily waxed—a sure sign of the times. Leopard and tiger skins are placed in the hall, and there are new imitation oriental rugs in the parlor. The large accumulation of furniture, some Grecian some French Antique, becomes architectural in its massing, being banked almost to invisibility against the cluttered walls, so as to play up the classical qualities and big spaces of the house and minimize the outdatedness of individual pieces. More recent accessories—horseshoe, horn stools, porcelain vases—together with the particular disposition of the many chairs and tables, convey an impression of comfort and daily use. There are, curiously enough, no colonial affectations here.

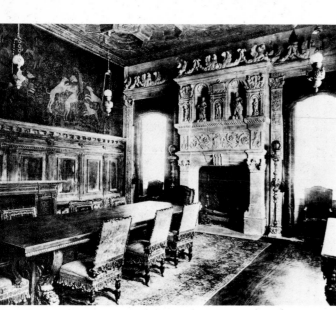

**182**

**183**

## House of Payne Whitney, 972 Fifth Avenue, New York, New York, 1909

Designed in the cinquecento style, this Manhattan *palazzo,* by the architectural firm McKim, Mead, and White, was begun in 1906 and occupied three years later. The design was directed by Stanford White, who planned its interiors prior to his death in the year the building commenced. Here architecture and furnishings are one in the sense of design and historical association. No house in the United States surpassed this one as a representative of high-style Beaux-Arts classicism, although there were houses far grander. Only two years after its completion, the magazine *Town & Country* wrote that the Whitney house was "a triumphant blending of decorative art old and new, a marvelous assembling within this century's walls of pictures, tapestries, velvets, and wood carvings which seem veritable voices of that ancient Italy of Leonardo da Vinci, of Benvenuto Cellini and others of the Cinquecento." These three photographic views were taken for the architectural firm immediately after the house was completed; entrance hall, dining room, and drawing room, showing few traces of human habitation, comprise three of the most important rooms of their time in the United States.

**182.** The cold marble of the entrance hall is purposely warmed in the slightest manner by the stair carpet, animal skins, and the ring of plants around the fountain. Richness here is kept at bay in a largely architectural treatment, which provides a more leisurely experience with high classicism than the façade on the busy street could possibly do. This room serves in a sense as a second façade to be experienced unhurriedly, setting the tone for the other parts of the house.

**183.** The monumental dining room is without flowers, linens, and table service, and looks vacant and barren. It was not meant to be seen this way. Aged wainscoting and the weathered stone mantelpiece convey the Renaissance mood of the house. A part of the effect was to appear ancient, for Stanford White's wish, as for those many others of the American Renaissance, was to capture the flavor and texture of age, as well as to achieve the appearance of a certain style of architecture.

**184.** This comes across much better in the drawing room, where faded velvet has been stretched over the walls to set off an intensely detailed ceiling and doorways which contain mirrored panels and heavy portieres. Upholstery here is made to look worn, and the wood is waxed and has been given the patina of age. Old palace candlesticks are converted into floor lamps with fringed shades. Some designers preferred to use old parchment pages for shades, or old colored prints instead of silk. Porcelains, historical sculpture, and paintings, and contrasting patterns of fabrics are carefully juxtaposed to give just the right animation to the room. The furniture is brought away from the walls into a circle between the center table and the fireplace. There is no center light fixture, nor are there many objects. Architecture and furniture are kept in careful balance and form a unified whole, expressing the ideal of the era.

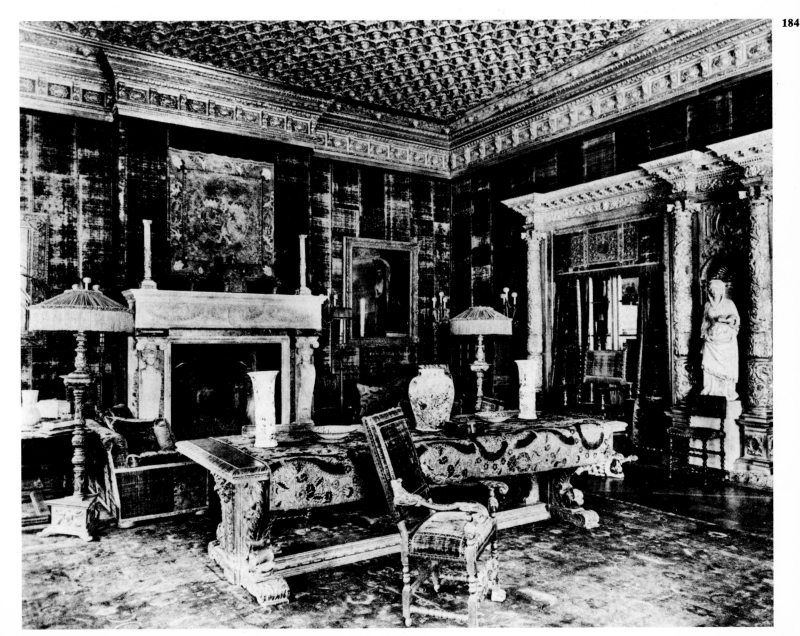

184

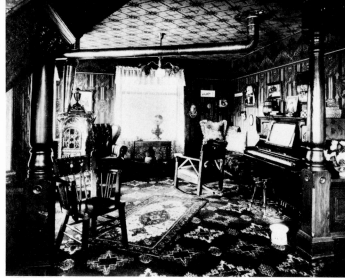

185

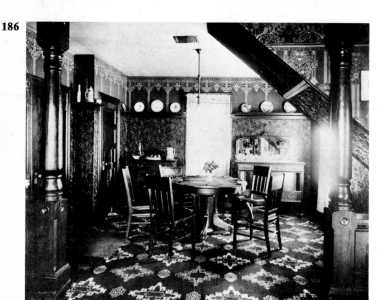

186

## 185, 186. Parlor and Dining Room, House of A. S. Oliver, Nome, Alaska Territory, 1909

This Alaska bungalow is furnished nearly entirely in manufactured products. These are views taken in two directions in a double room. Oriental-patterned carpeting covers the floors, with smaller rugs scattered about where there is heavy traffic. Arts and Crafts dining-room chairs and the sideboard to the right are mixed with slightly more decorative furniture designed in the massive mode. A Craftsman-type rocking chair and armchair are in the parlor. The overstuffed platform rocker and the chaise longue in the corner offer the only comfort in either room. Walls, border, and ceiling are papered in different patterns in both parlor and dining room. Only in the parlor has there been any effort to use similar patterns. The stove, an "art garland" of about 1905, heated these two rooms probably adequately. A similar stove was undoubtedly in some similar location in the second story. Pattern here is used as a substitute for architectural features, and its effect is strengthened by objects on the wall that nearly clash, like the china plates in the dining room and the small pictures in the parlor. In the front window a vase lamp decorated with roses has been given a place of honor.

## 187. Dining Room, Omaha, Nebraska, ca. 1910

Set rather curiously for a meal, this dining room was like many others in every part of the United States. The Junior Oak stove is flued into a brick chimney which, as they often did, rises from a high place on the walls, with no foundation except the studding. Cheap wallpaper and border, pasted onto the plaster walls, are above a wainscoting of car siding. The Golden Oak sideboard is decorated with a display of glasses, pitchers, and painted china. On the wall to the left is a telephone, but there seem to be no electric lights. Calendar and cut-out pictures decorate the walls. The room is clean and utterly simple; its only style is catalogue style, its taste born of simple uses.

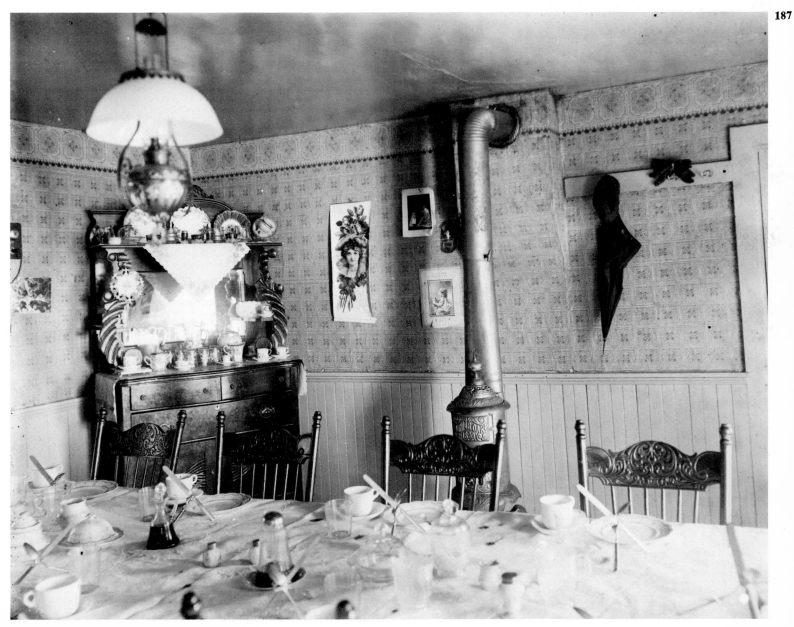

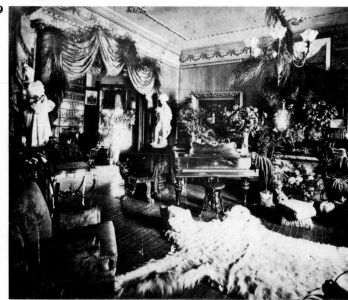

189

## House of James Joseph Brown, 1340 Pennsylvania Street, Denver, Colorado, 1910

Brown's wife Margaret—the unsinkable Molly of subsequent *Titanic* fame—bought this house in 1894 and moved to it from the mining town of Leadville. The house was photographed at about the time Molly Brown was beginning her world travels; she had been scorned by local Denver society. Her large Queen Anne cottage, perched high on its lot, overlooked the best residential street in Denver.

**188.** From a deep porch filled with plants, the front door opened into the living room with an inglenook which she turned into a Turkish cozy. Its walls are covered with papier mâché in imitation of morocco, and the woodwork is Golden Oak. Swags in Moorish stripes cascade over the little corner sofa with its matching ruffle and cushions. Blackamoors hold a card tray and torch. The little fireplace is set in glazed tiles.

**189.** To the immediate right of this room was a relatively small parlor which is shown decorated for a party. The floors are bare, except for the polar bear fur rug; when the Browns bought the house, the austere interiors had wall-to-wall carpeting. The fashion-conscious Molly pulled them up and waxed her hardwood floors. Fancy French trim has been added to the cornice and ceiling, and the striped wallcovering is in imitation of silk. Flowers, greens, and feather boas garland the massed banks of furniture and the openings. The statues of the boy and girl were typical guardians at such double-parlor doors, and the Browns have given the girl some real flowers to mix with her marble ones.

**190.** Behind the parlor, the library was the family sitting room, where there was a sunny bay and walls of Globe-Wernicke modular bookcases with glass doors. Upholstered platform rockers and that particular kind of bookcase were standard in middle-class libraries and sitting rooms, as well as offices.

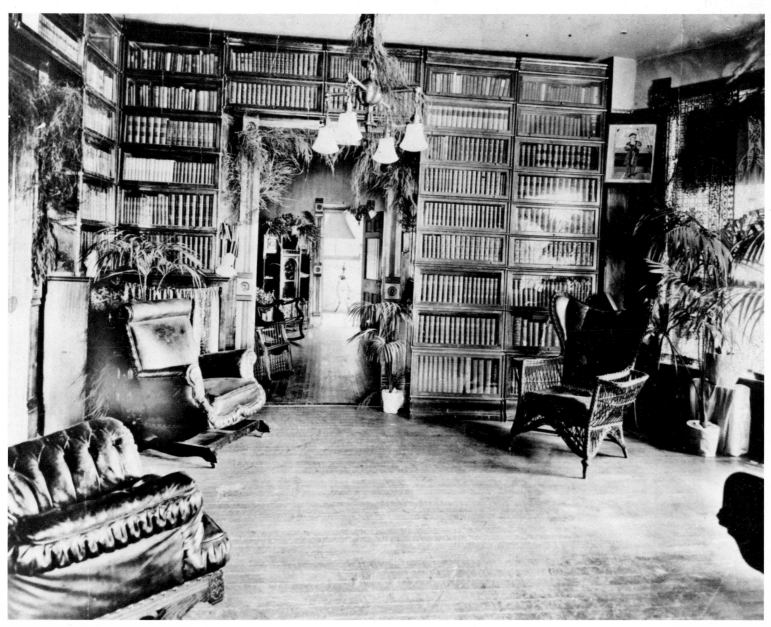

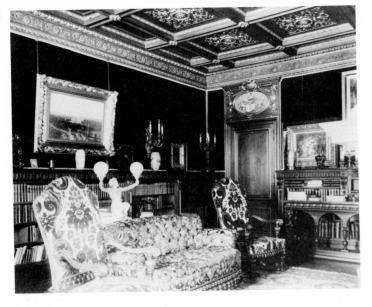

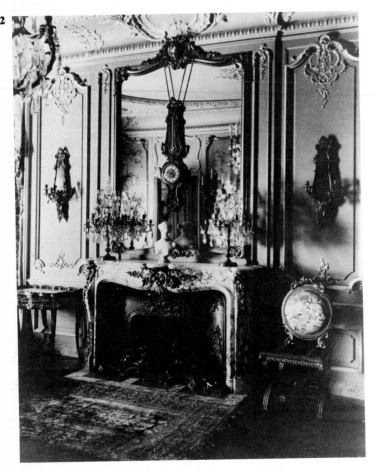

## House, William G. Roelker, 66 Cooke Street, Providence, Rhode Island, 1910

**191.** Roelker's library was in the Venetian style, its walls covered in velvet and its ceiling paneled and richly carved, perhaps in plaster grained to resemble wood. Low bookcases, of which the late nineteenth century was extremely fond, band the room, their tops suitable for the display of ornaments and the walls above them places to display pictures. In the bookcases are sets of books both old and new, forming a wainscoting of rich leather textures and color. A Turkish sofa and baronial chairs face the fireplace; an exotic figure holds electric torches for the convenience of readers. Adjacent to the period drawing room, this library is a retreat for comfort and family life.

**192.** This drawing room, executed in the Louis Quinze style, was in the best European or cosmopolitan taste of early twentieth-century America. Painted in contrasting pale tones, this wealthy man's salon conveys the richness of eighteenth-century court decoration in France; none of it, of course, is French, but the work of city decorating firms which turned out such interiors for hotel suites and mansions alike. This room is French Antique a half century after the peak of its first movement. Unlike the predecessor, however, a principal concern here is to be authentic to French models.

**193.** Although the dining room, with its *boiserie* and damask wall covering is French in style, the furniture is English style and reproduction. The dining-room table, with its dolphins, was considered Regency, a new and rather snobbish revival of the earliest English Grecian forms of the nineteenth century; the chairs are essentially colonial revival and would have been called Chippendale. Adorned with three giant platters on easels, the mahogany sideboard is English and would have been called Regency. Glass candelabra and silver pitchers are arranged with silver goblets behind the big platters. Electric sconces, hung high on the wall, have light bulbs shaped in imitation of flames, an innovation of about 1910.

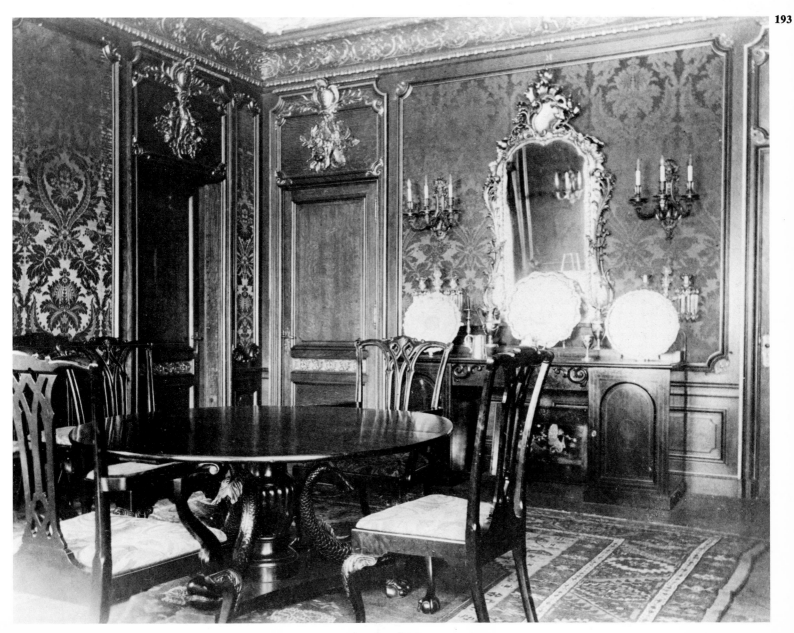

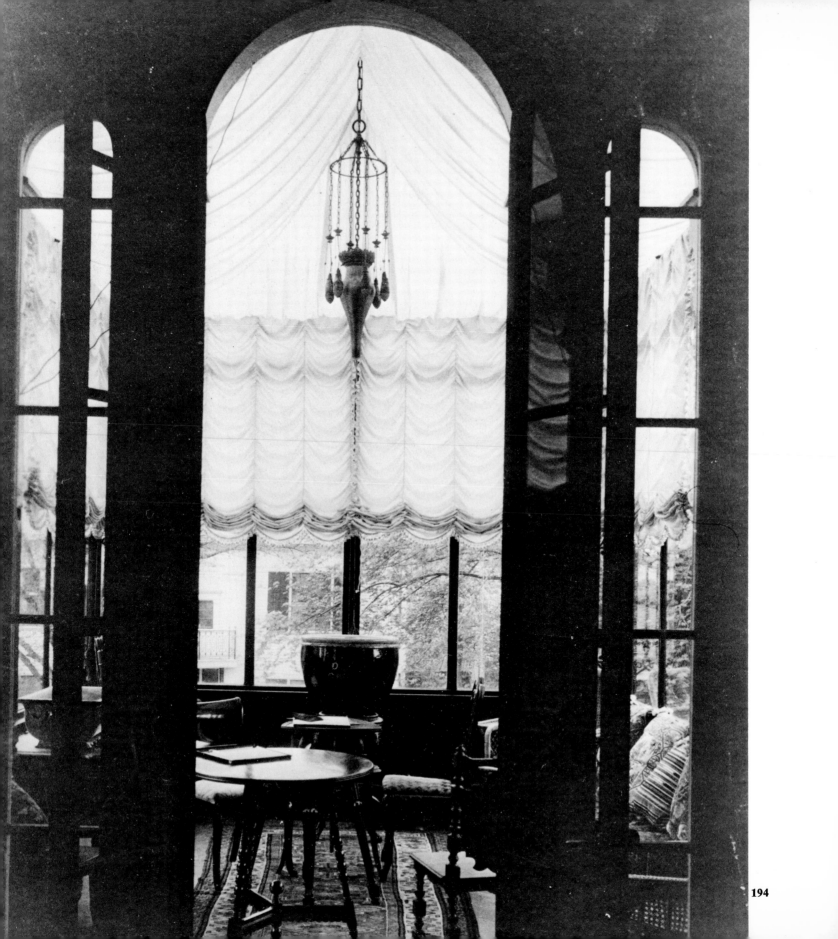

**194.** The second floor conservatory is tented with fabric, and its windows are curtained with Austrian shades. Current English-style revival furniture of a rather common sort on the American market is scattered through the glazed room, and a large pottery bowl awaits the potted plants it doubtless normally contains. Heavy drapery of this sort was endorsed by the community of interior decorators in the East, establishing a custom which prevails today. Whether such curtains actually enhanced a room or merely covered up architecture as a means of freeing the decorator to use whatever furniture and accessories he wished was debated at the time. Interior decorators were, after all, businessmen; and a large part of the profit was from expensive fabrics and the making of curtains. If curtains could provide architectural definitions of space, there was all the more excuse for curtains.

### 195. Bedroom, Boston, Massachusetts, ca. 1910

Quaint, or colonial, this room was up to date in manufactured furniture for its time. The Quaint dresser might have been called Fancy-shaped, or French. It was a highly popular and widely mass-produced design; one can suppose the dressing table, barely visible in the lower lefthand corner, was of the same character, as is the little chair beside the bed. In the center of the picture, the colonial revival Windsor chair has been painted white and covered with decals of French decorative motifs. Behind it is a colonial revival desk, probably Queen Anne. A simple and whimsical pansy wallpaper, a kind increasingly popular, covers the walls up to a thin picture mold set at the ceiling. The woodwork is probably ivory or light green.

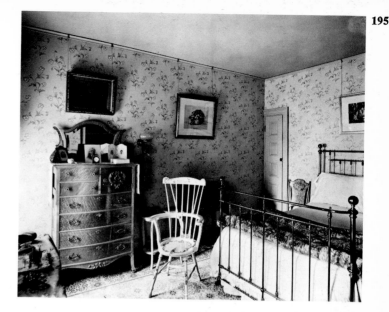

## 196, 197. Dining Room and Parlor, House of Robert Todd Lincoln, Washington, D.C., 1910–13

President Abraham Lincoln's son had a mansion in Georgetown that was probably decorated professionally in the 1880's by its previous owners. By 1910, the Anglo-Japanese restraint the rooms might once have had seems to have been nearly obliterated by the addition of new objects. The dining-room furniture is Renaissance revival of a moderately priced type produced in the 1870's and still being made in the 1880's. One of the hanging shelves matches the furniture, but the rest are oriental in style. Porcelains and silver become part of the architectural whole; even the sideboard's lower part has had the doors removed to permit further space for display. Objects in these rooms are backgrounds for the uncluttered seating areas. In the parlor, some of the light chairs from the 1880's have been allowed to remain, while little pictures and statues, manila shawls, and paintings cover nearly every surface near the walls in a carefully planned state of imbalance. Instead of massive pieces of furniture, as in the dining room, the groupings in the parlor are comprised of small things—myriad objects banked against the walls almost as though they were carved in the material itself. The feeling here is one of informality, in contrast to the past days of the formal art units and the oriental stiffness of arrangement that had accompanied the creative revivals of the 1880's.

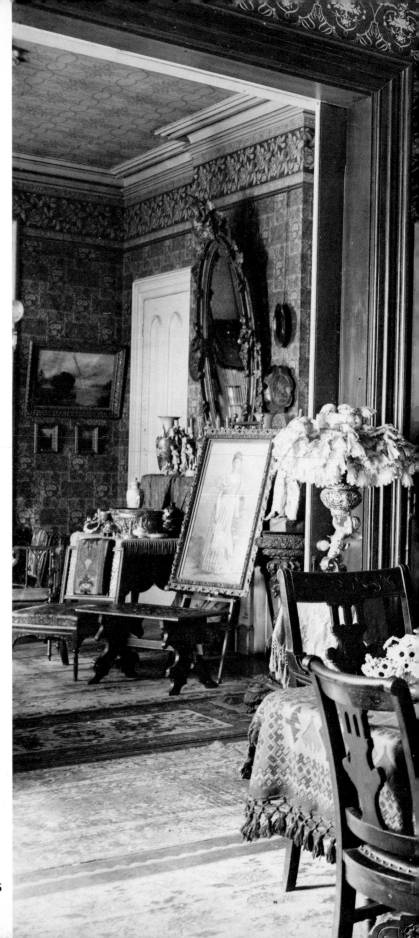

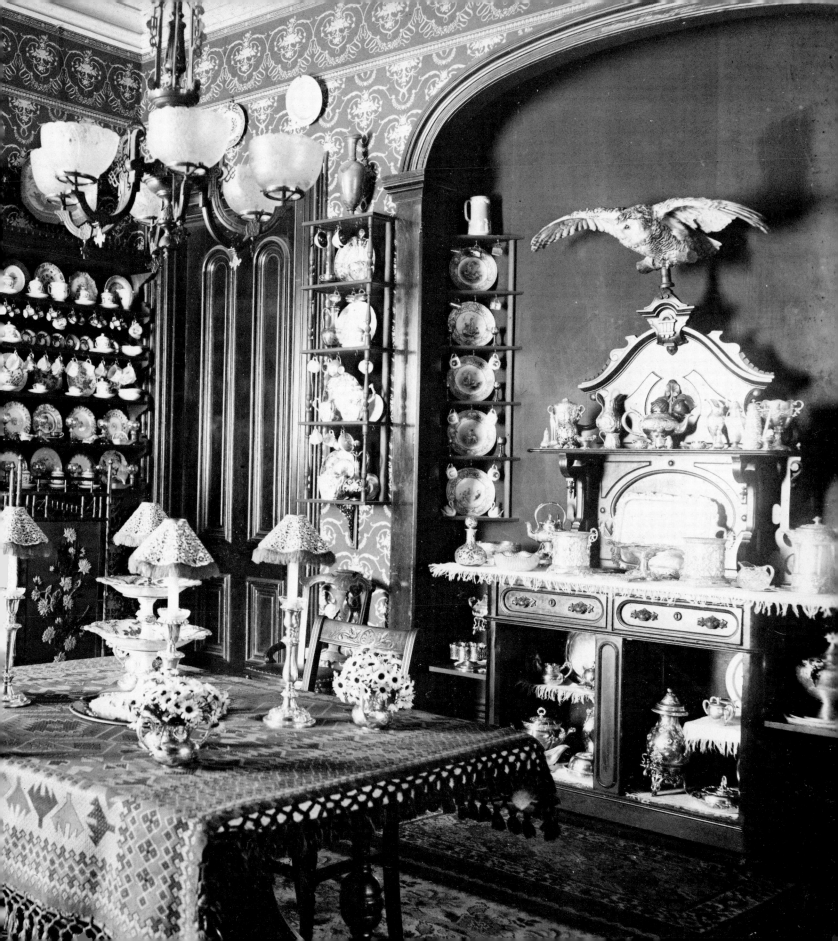

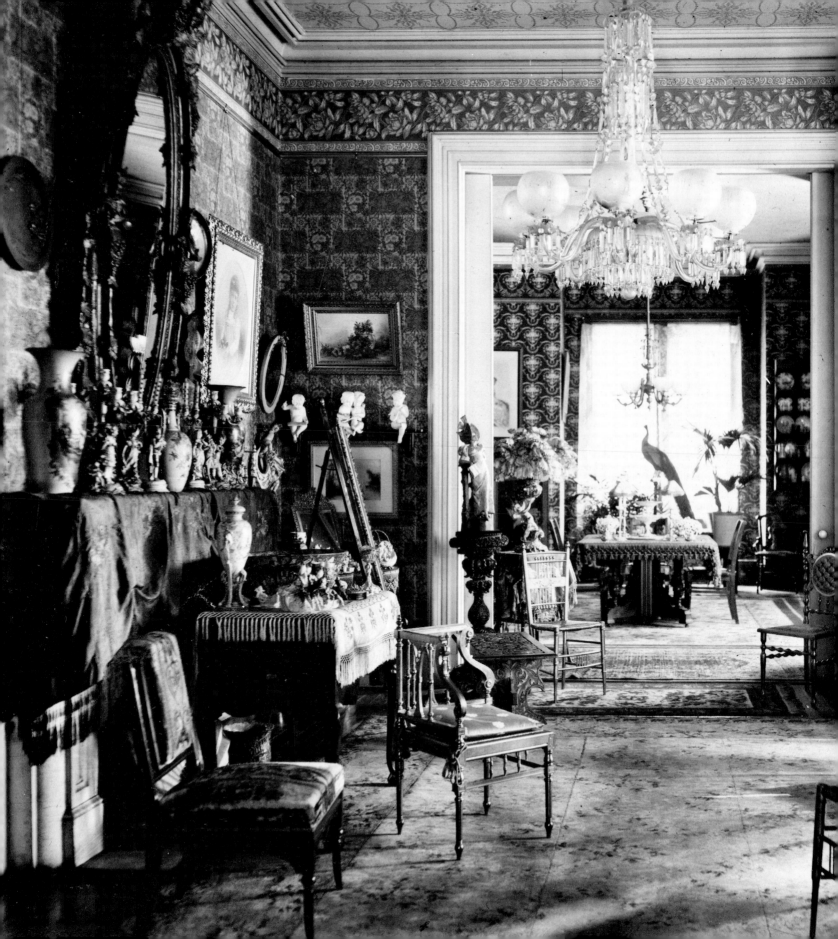

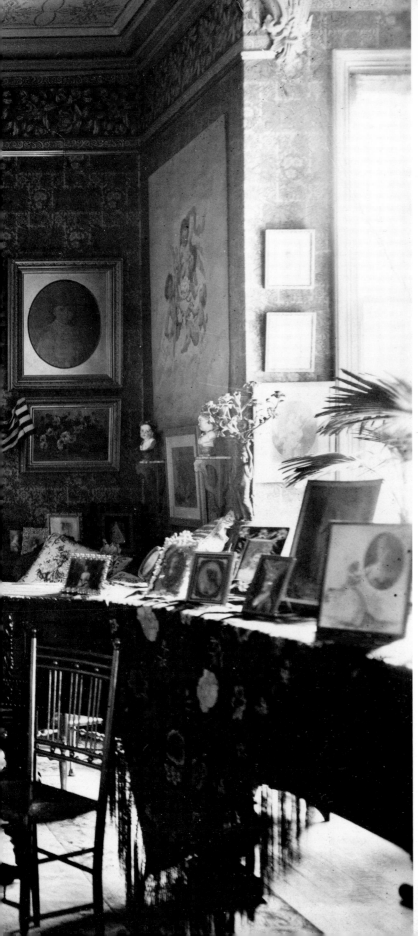

**Dining Room and Parlor, House of Robert Todd Lincoln, Washington, D.C., 1910–13**

**Hall, Dining Room, and Drawing Room, House of Frederick Leopold William Richardson, Charles River, Massachusetts, 1911**

In 1902, after studies at Harvard and at the Massachusetts Institute of Technology, H. H. Richardson's son and his wealthy bride, Anne Blake, moved to Paris, where he enrolled in architecture at the Ecole des Beaux-Arts. He was following in the footsteps of the legendary father he could not remember; but while their paths were somewhat the same, the mode of travel for the second generation was more comfortable. The young Richardsons oc-

cupied a luxurious apartment, and snapshots in their scrapbook chronicle the leisurely holidays and tours that were mingled with his hard work in the *atelier*. Back in the United States, they acquired a 120-acre farm near the village of Charles River, and in 1910–11 completed Laneside, a house in many respects far in advance of its time. These three views show the sort of interior design which expressed, as one of their sons later said, "my father's particular point of view about how one should live."

**198.** The rooms of the lower floor were few and

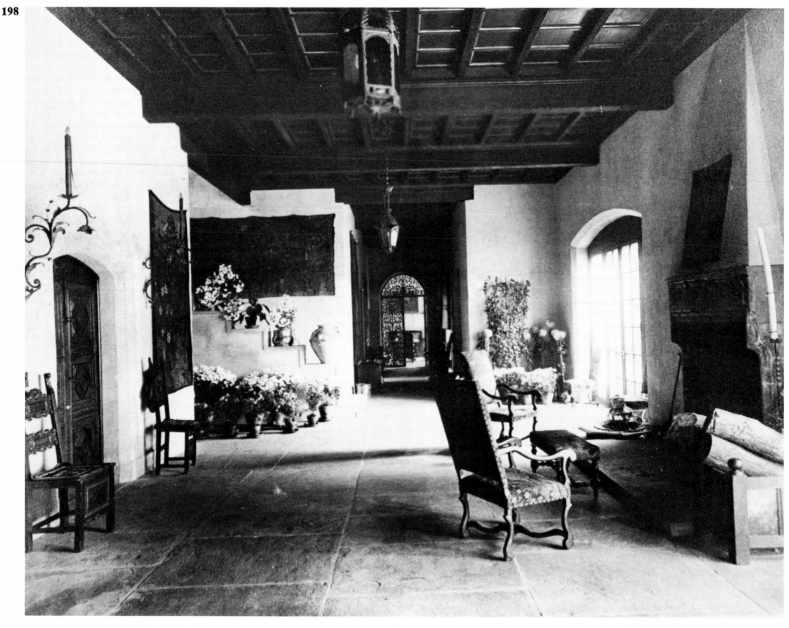

very large, and connected by this lofty, sun-lit hall, an American meditation on the provincial Louis Treize interiors the Richardsons had admired in rural châteaux abroad. In style, the furniture, tapestries, sconces, and lanterns are late seventeenth-century French. All of them were bought as antiques, but the important concern is that each object, new or old, was selected by the same hand. To add anything else to this hall scene would be to intrude upon a cautious blending of stone, metal, fabric, living organic material, and wood.

**199.** The same might be said of the dining room, which more stiffly evokes the Louis Treize revival style, popular when the Richardsons arrived in France. The dining room's chill is warmed by the very modern look of the palms and oriental rug, neither of which must have been part of the designer's original plan; by now, however, they were beloved characteristics of the most expensive sort of American rooms.

**200.** Nearby lies the oval drawing room, inspired by the Louis Seize revival salon of the Richardsons' Paris apartment. The painted sofa, chair, and stool are part of a set purchased and used by them in Paris, and the upholstery is the same. Antique tables are scattered conveniently about to hold lamps, ash trays, and little objects, which, like the clutter of thirty years before, are there to attest taste, despite any apparent restraint. French themes which might otherwise have dominated this drawing room are kept at bay by the more dominant colonial revival. In such suburban settings, the Louis Quatorze, Quinze, and Seize were considered too urbane and worldly, and were usually introduced only as these are, to accent a more dominant theme. Against pale painted *boiserie,* neoclassical door facings—similar to antique ones familiar in many parts of New England— lend regional aristocratic authority of the kind which would become characteristic of interiors like these in the 1920's and 1930's. An American Empire sofa, which might have been called Regency in this case, and electrified astral lamps, together with girandole mirrors, give a strong touch of what was being called the Federal style. Notice that the American props are far more historically accurate than the French objects, which, being a full decade earlier, are adaptations of period models. The contrast between these things is a comment upon the narrowing gulf in international design between the old world and the new. Richardson's rooms present a staccato of

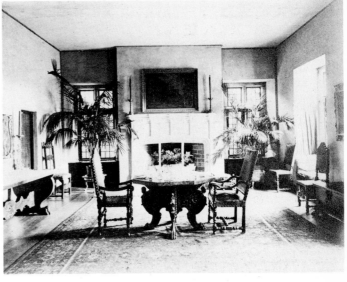

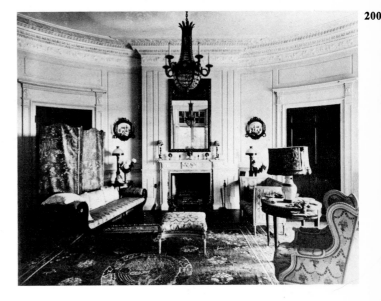

pairs, a custom in interior decoration which had risen to favor in the 1890's and continues today, in curious commemoration of the nineteenth-century fascination with duplication.

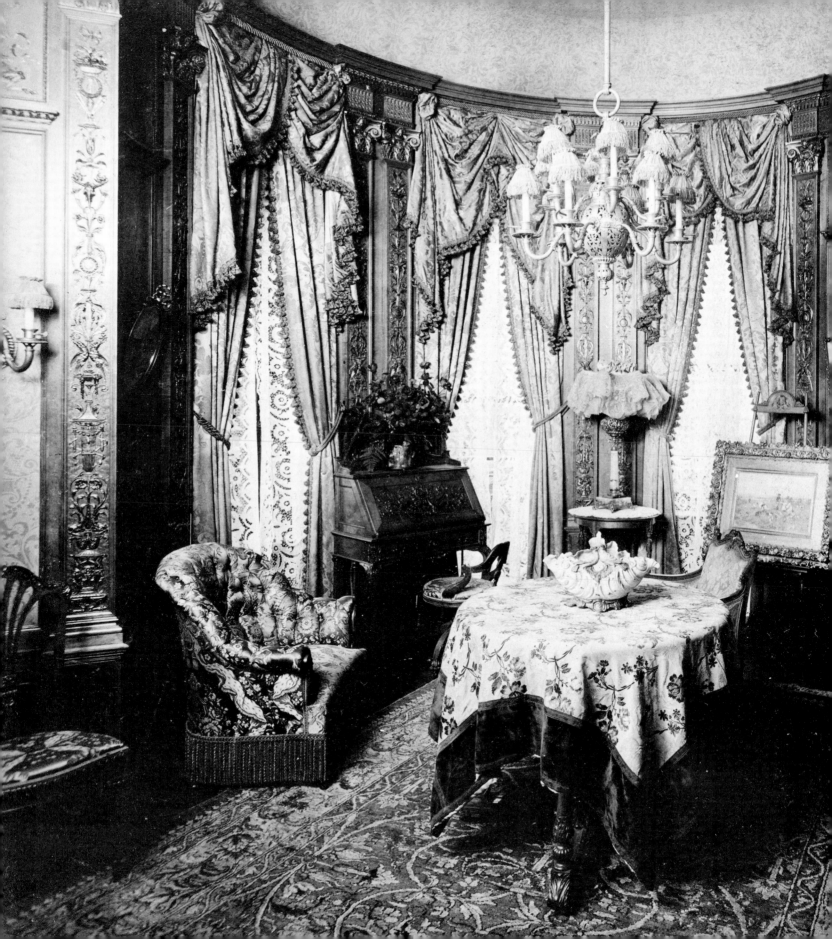

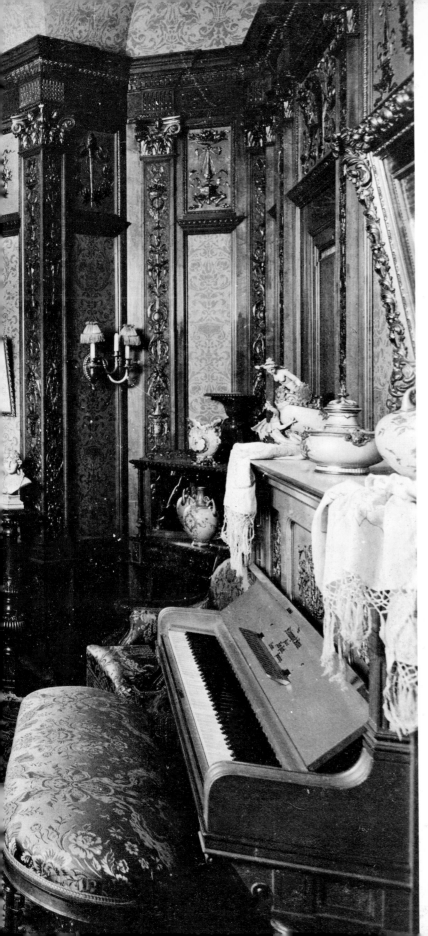

### 201. Parlor, Baltimore, Maryland, 1912

The architectural intention of this room was to be English, with the manufactured Adam woodwork and the neoclassical rounded corner. However, the treatment otherwise is in the French style of the early twentieth century, and it may well have been the work of an interior decorator or of a furniture store, with the advice of the owner. Lavishly curtained windows, more and more characteristic of the well-dressed room, contrast here with what is an essentially mediocre parlor. The center table, out of style for two decades, is here revived with a heavy cover typical of the 1890's. A colonial revival desk is in the bay, with a fancy banquet lamp and fabric shade on a table to the right. An overstuffed and fringed chair, still a common sight in the catalogues, is placed beside a reproduction Sheraton chair. The piano has been painted a light color, its carved elements picked out in gilt. Art vases and pictures, with panels of damask, complete the setting. This ensemble, which could have existed in the 1890's, represents popular decoration as it was in many a middle-class house where the owners made some pretension to being formal. A room of this kind would have been kept closed most of the time, and used only for special occasions, an old custom still in practice at the time of World War I.

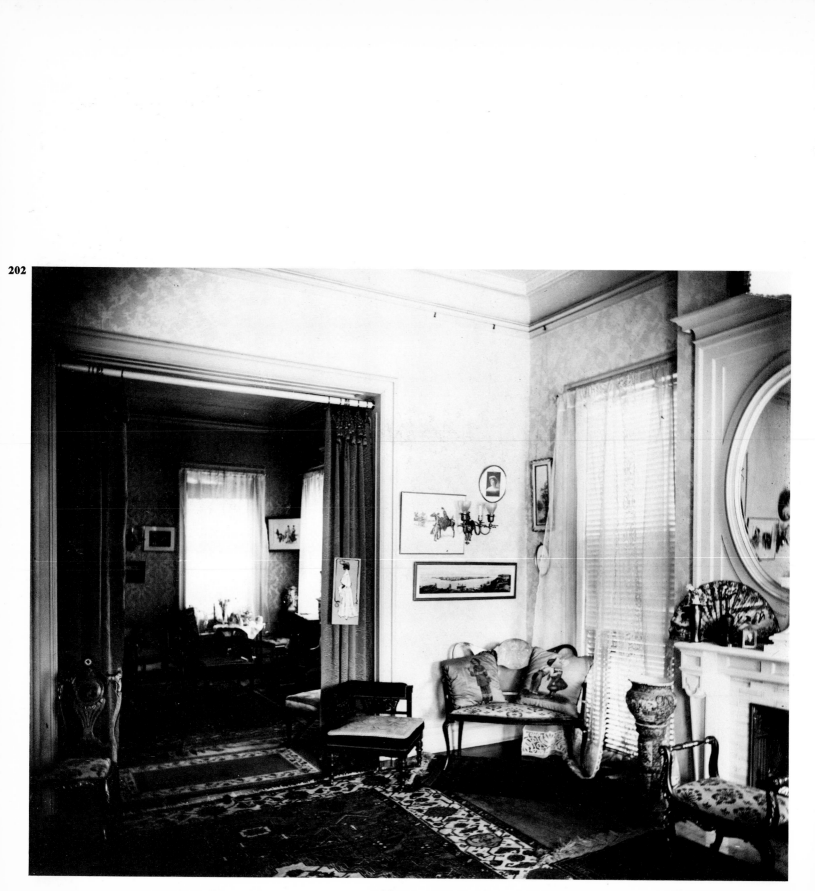

**202. Sitting Room and Parlor, House of R. H. Clark, Mobile, Alabama, 1912**

In Clark's new house the rooms lead into one another through double openings. The design is more or less colonial with white woodwork and mantels with overmantels, although here the interpretation is so free as to be nearly obscure. Venetian blinds here make a dramatic return, even before they were considered colonial beginning in the 1930's. The furniture is the so-called French of the late nineteenth and early twentieth centuries; the chair to the left is something of a combination of several eighteenth-century English styles and might even have been called Chippendale or Queen Anne, for the latter term, particularly, was tossed about recklessly. Simple curtains on rods are at the windows, while the portieres are hung from rings typically without being pleated. American orientals are carefully placed to cover nearly all but a border of polished floor. The pictures, mostly prints, are hung at random, to convey an informal look, which is accentuated by the picture casually pinned on the portiere.

**203. Dining Room, House of E. S. Smith, Illinois, 1912**

Because the censuses of 1900 and 1910 are closed, the location of Smith's house cannot be determined, although it is possible that it was in the river town of Alton. In any event, his house seems to have been somewhat larger than the average bungalow; the work on the built-in sideboard is a little finer than the average, with its carved swag glued on and its beveled mirror in the back and smaller tilted mirrors. Cabinets, doors, and windows rise to the level of the picture molding, a familiar effect in the better sort of bungalows and one of the simple but dramatic kinds of detailing characteristic of houses of the Arts and Crafts type. The dining-room set is in the massive mode; the chairs and the table could be bought singly. White walls and plain rugs play up the Spartan, though solid, effect of comfort and stability.

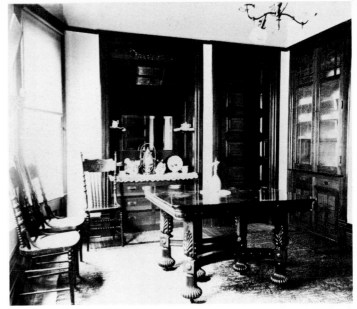

203

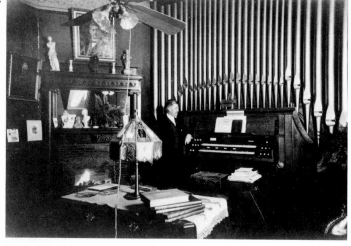

204

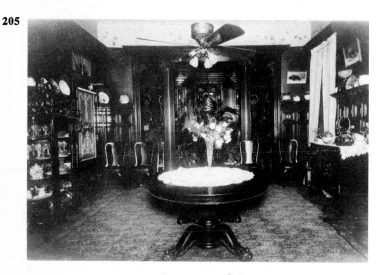

205

## House of Martin Luther Hinchee, Park Street, Beaumont, Texas, 1912

Hinchee, from the East, was organist at the Methodist Episcopal Church South in Beaumont when he met Caroline Gilbert, member of the choir and heiress of a new oil fortune. They were married, and she commissioned a local architect, H. C. Mauer to build them a new house. Mauer, a native Texan and graduate of Pratt Institute in Brooklyn, had moved to Beaumont shortly after the Spindletop oil boom, just after the turn of the century. While the Hinchees' house might be described as Free Classic, with its Palladian loggia, curving galleries and deep, sloping green-tile roofs, its owners doubtless considered it colonial. Here the Hinchees lived for the pleasant, if brief, duration of their marriage. Mrs. Hinchee died in 1912, and, not long before her death, Mr. Hinchee was photographed in his study beside the pipe organ she had had built for him.

**204.** On the center table are books and a common kind of art-glass lamp, one of the first and most effective means of ornamenting the source of electric light. Overhead, the little glass shades are not so different from those once used on gasoliers, only they are not set upright; sixty years before, gas shades of the better sort had been sometimes tinted red, pink, or blue for decoration and to soften the glare.

**205.** This dim photograph of the dining room shows the American Empire table, Queen Anne chairs, china cabinet, and sideboard, all mahogany and purchased in 1907, probably from Keith and Company of Kansas City, Missouri. The mahogany woodwork is particularly rich in this room, which terminates in a screen of Ionic columns and an apse of pale green and violet stained glass, through which could be seen the palm trees in the narrow yard outside. It is unlikely that the woodwork was made for this house; it could be bought through the catalogues of many major millwork establishments across the United States. Numerous plants, potted and elevated on stands, fill the apse. Teapots, vases, and plates, perhaps painted by Mrs. Hinchee, are lined up along the high plate rail, which surmounts the mahogany wainscoting. Above the dark wallcovering, a light floral border rises to the cove.

**206.** Immediately in front of the study and organ room was the entrance hall, its ceiling frescoed, reputedly, by Mrs. Hinchee, and its walls adorned by her paintings. Opposite the Free Classic mantel is a circular staircase. The ceiling fan, an innovation which appeared almost as early as the electric light, is here decorated with vines and Spanish moss, while light bulbs in tulip-shaped shades project spearlike from its base. Sometimes cut-glass or brass electroliers were suspended from the lower parts of ceiling fans; often the fans were nickel-plated and had polished mahogany blades. In the summertime, houses such as this on the Gulf coast were kept open, with thin curtains of muslin hung in the windows.

The combination of spinning fans, straw matting, and potted plants could produce a sumptuous effect.

**207, 208.** The parlor was decorated in a French sort of style that had been popular since the mid-1890's. Furnished in the massive mode in mahogany, the room contains a complete set, although not quite matched, with obvious ancestry in the French Antique Louis Quinze revival style of the 1850's. The center table is a variation on a French Antique type which manufacturers had been producing since mid-century. Plain but full panels of brocatel frame lace curtains which are backed

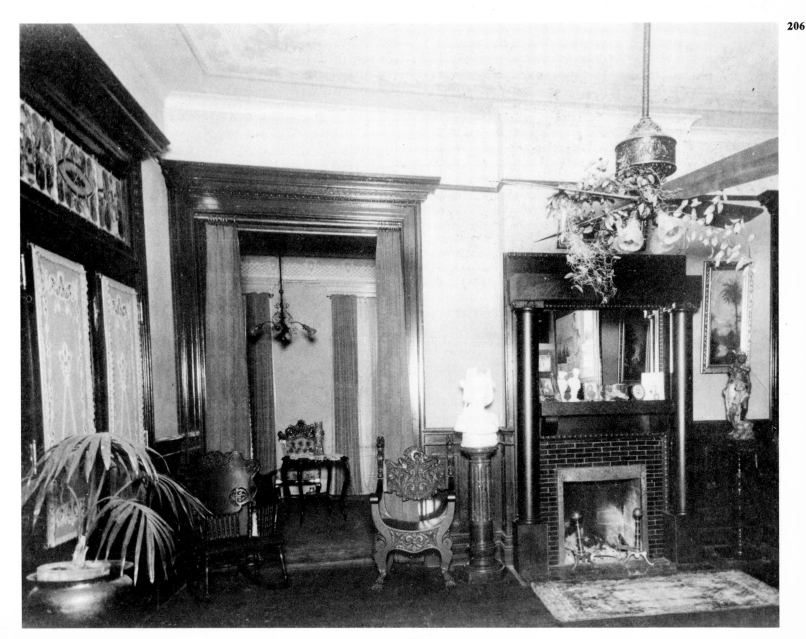

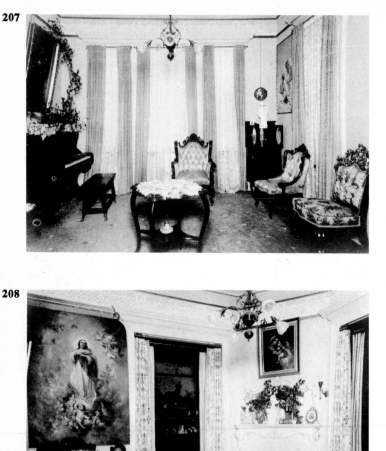

207

208

by white window shades. Ivory-colored woodwork here contrasts with dark-stained surfaces elsewhere in the house; a plaster cove and a gilded border—made with a stencil on canvas-covered plaster—heightens the delicacy of the setting. Caroline Hinchee took art lessons at the Metropolitan Museum of Art in New York, the Corcoran Gallery of Art in Washington, and at various Chautauqua assemblies in the East, according to her account book. Except for a few portraits, most of what she painted were copies of famous works, as these pictures in her parlor. Not long after her death, the house was vacated. Mr. Hinchee went to California, and the furnishings were destroyed in a warehouse fire in the 1920's.

**209. Sitting Room, House of Admiral George Dewey, 1601 K Street, N.W., Washington, D.C., 1912**
Admiral Dewey, whose naval career had begun with Admiral Farragut during the Civil War, lived out his last days in this house, a national hero, and died in 1917. When this photograph was made, he was putting the finishing touches on his autobiography. The room is filled with mementos which Admiral Dewey, at seventy-five, must have found pleasant to live with. While some of its contents are new, the room is out of style with its banks of objects and random hangings of pictures. The effect here would probably have been called Venetian, or maybe Beaux-Arts, with the mirrored door draped, the walls upholstered in damask, and the Venetian-glass chandelier hanging from a frescoed ceiling. Contemporary taste was for the open and airy; but the Admiral was an old man, and his interest in such things probably went no further than a passing acknowledgment of the interior decorator's attempt to give him a Venetian sitting room.

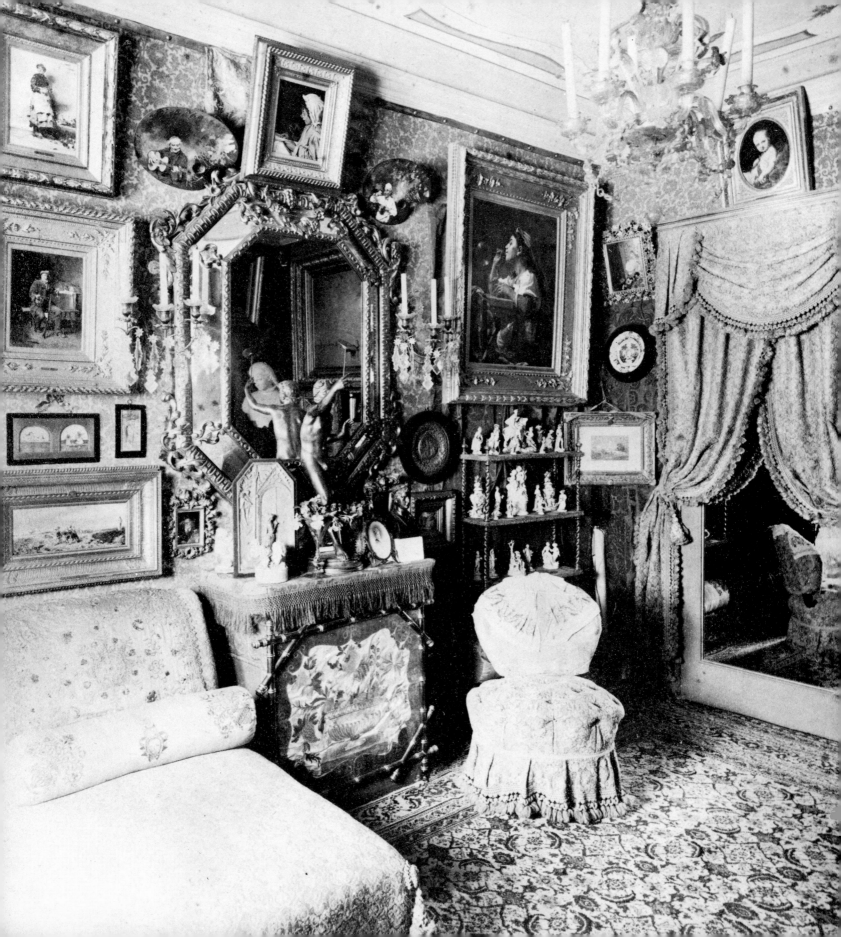

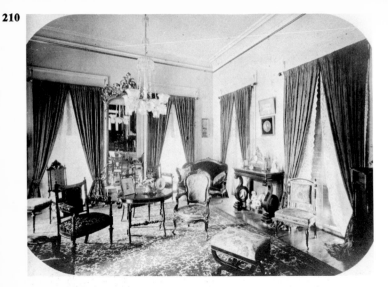

**210, 211. Parlor and Hallway, House of Adelaide Swift and James P. Kyle, Columbus, Georgia, April 19, 1913**

The parlor of this 1857 Greek revival house projected from the body of the structure and was surrounded on three sides by a Corinthian colonnade. Very little in this room is new. The furniture presents a time line of manufactured modes of the nineteenth century beginning with the Grecian pier table and footstool, then the French Antique sofa, armchair, and pier glass, and at last the several creative revivals based upon Gothic, Louis Seize, and Grecian spanning the years 1875 to about 1895 and ending with new Sheraton armchairs to the left and rear. If the furniture is an accumulation, the ensemble is, nevertheless, up to date. Gone is the massing of objects into art units; instead they are placed regularly over the foliated art carpet, follow the rhythm of the fenestration and lines of the room, and seem to emerge from its architecture. New hardwood flooring has been laid and heavily varnished. The old curtains have been removed, and are replaced by new damask ones, shirred on white and brass rods and backed by unpleated lace. While the curtains pile on the floor, they are tied back low and neatly, shaping the daylight into crisp inverted cones. This parlor bears every evidence of a recent remodeling and an awareness of current ideas about how a room should be put together.

The hallway was damaged by fire in 1898. Beutel and Company of Atlanta rebuilt it in the new classical manner, using birch stained to look like mahogany. This manner of remodeling was considered utterly appropriate for a Greek revival house. Some of the woodwork dates from the original house, but the ceiling, staircase, wainscoting, and columned archway are new, and it can be supposed they would have been considerably more curvilinear in design, had the builders not been restricted by the straight lines of the existing house. A colonial revival combination gasolier and electrolier lights the hall. Indian tablecloth and sofa throw demonstrate the fleeting fancy of the era for decorations of the Southwest and West. Quite possibly the set of furniture in the hall would have been called colonial, although neither Chippendale nor Queen Anne would have been surprising titles. The classical wallpaper was manufactured to complement such woodwork.

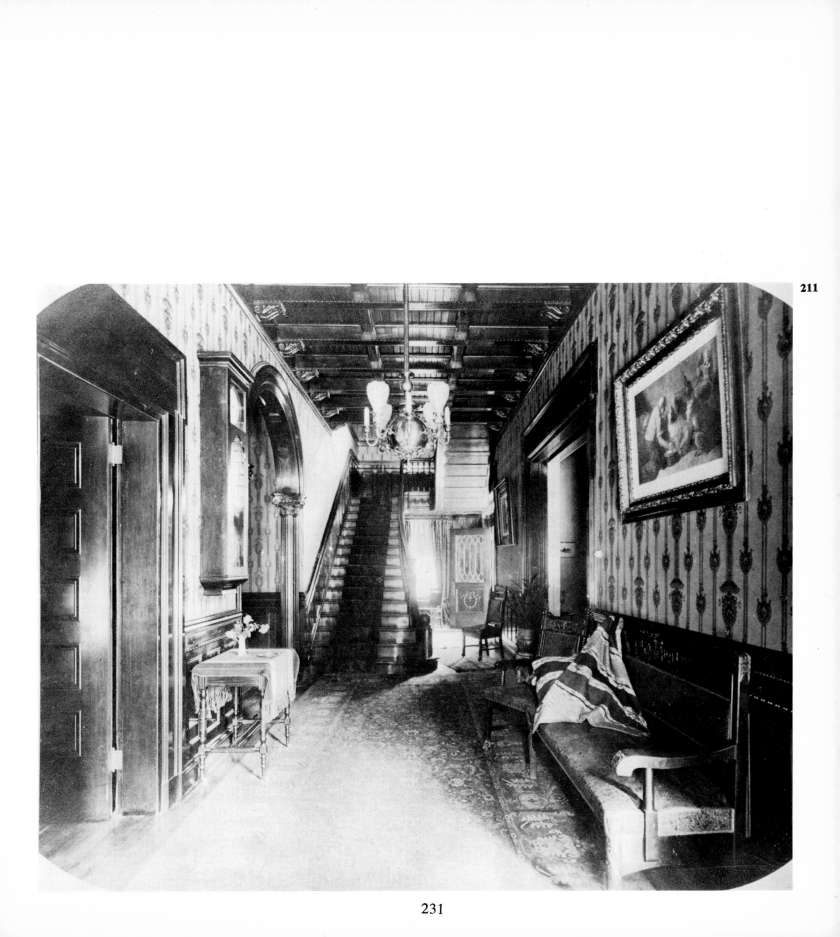

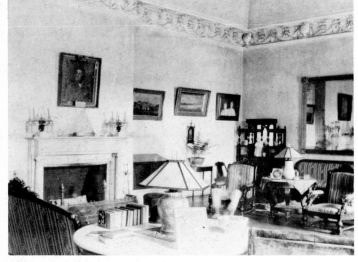

### 212. Drawing Room, Hyde Hall, House of George Hyde Clarke, Springfield Center, New York, Summer, 1913

Built between 1817 and 1835 by Clarke's grandfather, Hyde Hall passed to the grandson in 1887. The house was huge, with many of the qualities of a barn, and ancient stoves, installed in the 1830's, still comprised the principal heating. It can be plainly seen that this drawing room has been updated, but the main alteration is in the arrangement of the furniture. Original oak graining remains on the woodwork, and the raw plaster, with its troweled, marble-like finish, is untouched except by a layer of soot. Most of the contents of the drawing room have been in the family for many years: the gilded pier glass, turned now on its side, was purchased by the Clarkes from Isaac Platt of New York City in 1833; the Grecian table was purchased at about the same time from Meads and Alvord of Albany; the portrait over the mantel is the *Duke of Wellington* by John Trumbull; the marble mantel was purchased from Joseph Barnes in New York in 1833. Most of the Elizabethan furniture is upholstered *en suite*. It is drawn up into a modern conversation group around the fireplace, and old center tables now become side tables, with vase lamps, pictures, and books placed there for that look of casual convenience. It is a comfortable room in a house not yet old enough to be a real historical curiosity; it is a modern room ensemble of the early 1900's, composed of parts seventy years old.

This photograph was a long time exposure, during which the lone human subject rose from his chair, walked to the mantel, and thus evaded all but a ghost-like record of his presence.

### 213, 214. Living Hall, House of Mrs. Bosson, Boston, Massachusetts, ca. 1912

The room is finished in varnished walnut, pine car siding, and painted plaster which has been decorated while still wet by a swirling motion of the trowel. What appear to be mementos of travel to India form a sort of theme for this open area, especially around the mantel, where daggers, swords, pottery, beads, and pictures form an 1880's art unit. A plate rail caps the wainscoting, and it is filled with objects. The floor, with its islands of oriental rugs, is polished to a high gloss and relatively free of clutter. Old furniture, some re-upholstered and some left as it was, is

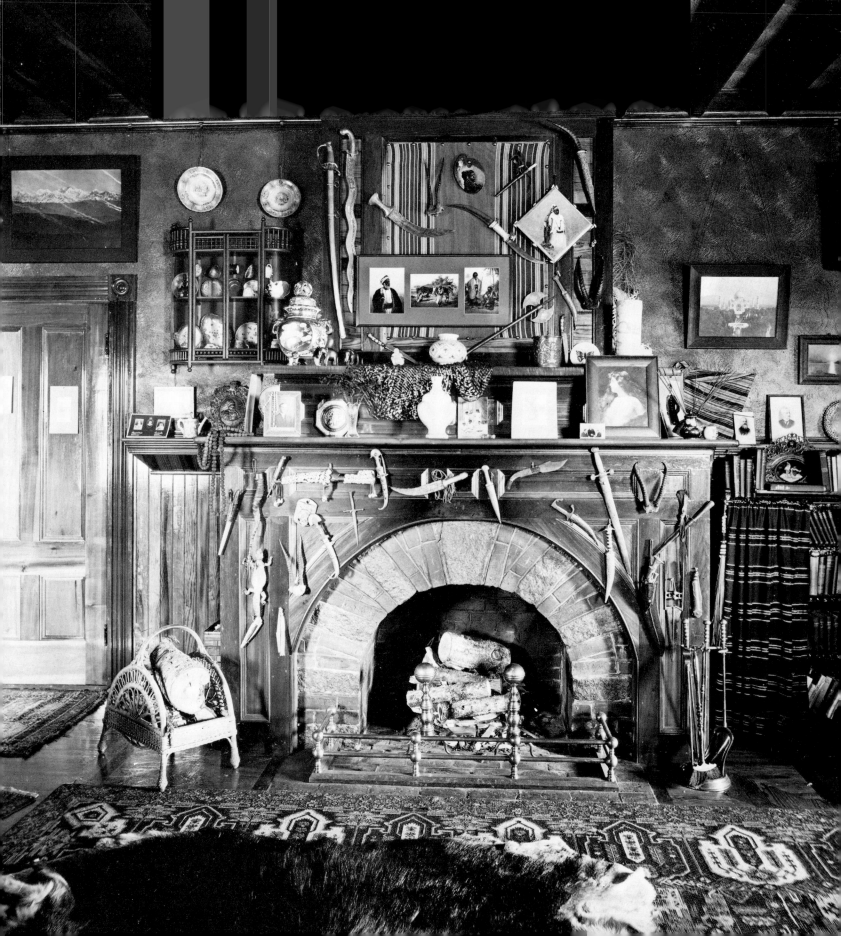

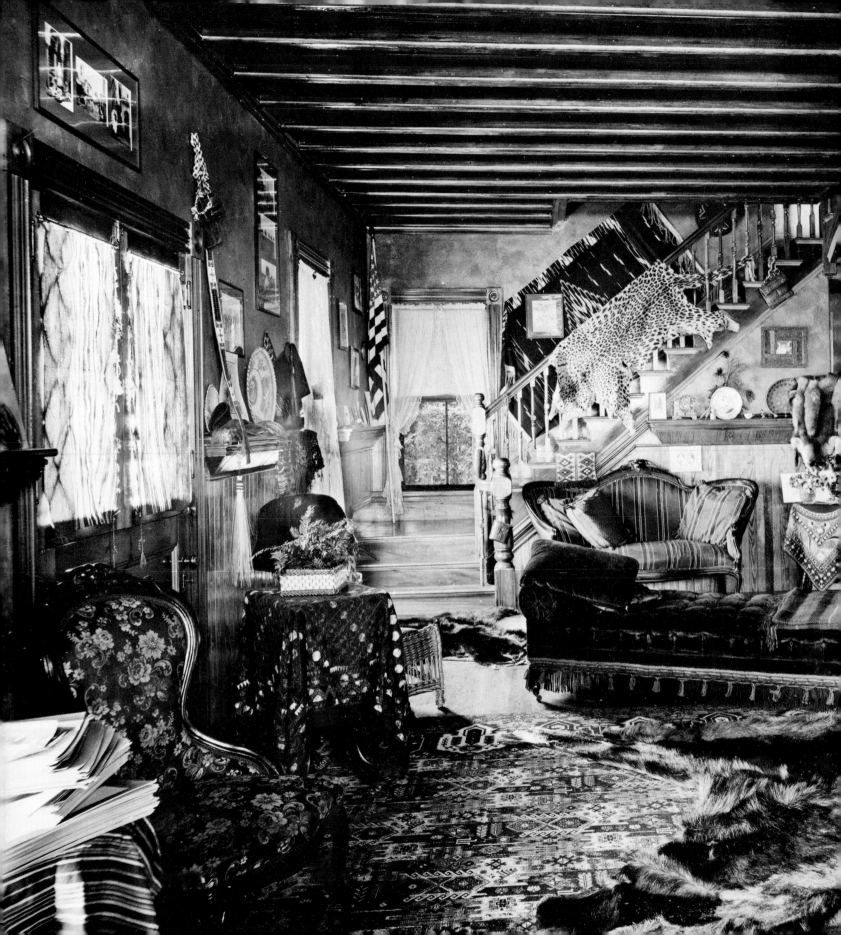

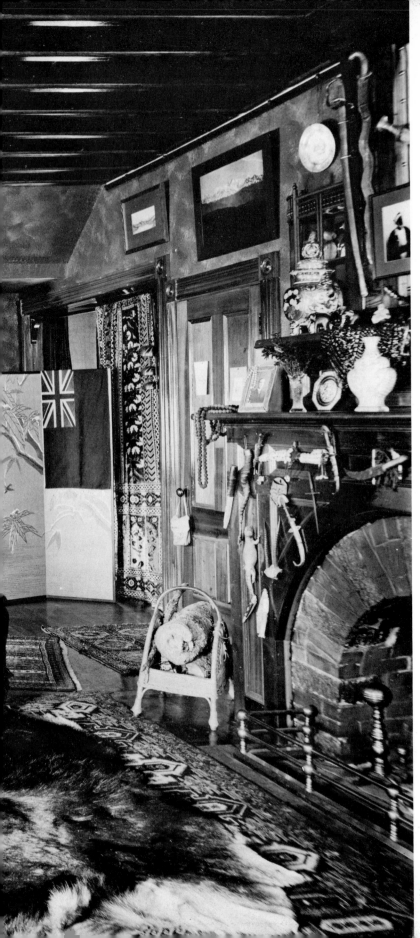

informally scattered, and can be pulled up to the fireplace, as it is needed. Books, shelved at armchair level, are protected by curtains. All is informal, if contrived to look so, almost in the sense of a summer cottage, but quite in the spirit of the second decade of the twentieth century.

## 215. Library, House of Mrs. Richard A. Townsend, 2121 Massachusetts Avenue, Washington, D.C., 1914

This mansard-roofed mansion of the 1870's was totally revised and expanded in 1899–1901 by the architectural firm Carrère and Hastings of New York into a neoclassical pavilion based upon the Petit Trianon. When this photograph was taken in the second floor library, Mrs. Townsend had not been a widow for very long. Her husband had been president of the Erie and Pittsburgh Railroad, and like many wealthy people with strong political connections, they had retired in Washington. From a broad entrance hall with rococo ornamentation in plaster, a grand staircase rose to the second level, which contained some dazzling rooms in the Louis Quinze style, and this library. For all their artificial grandeur, all the rooms had a homey quality. Downy sofas, deep cushions, convenient little tables, and cozy conversation groupings defied the best efforts of the Beaux-Arts architects to achieve ceremonial magnificence. According to current ideas of the day, the library is a particularly comfortable inviting room. Portraits, family pictures, memorabilia, and even a homemade lampshade on an emergency oil lamp compete with the rich mahogany woodwork and damask wallcovering. Even the costly Axminster carpet has been partially humanized near the fireside by a polar bear rug.

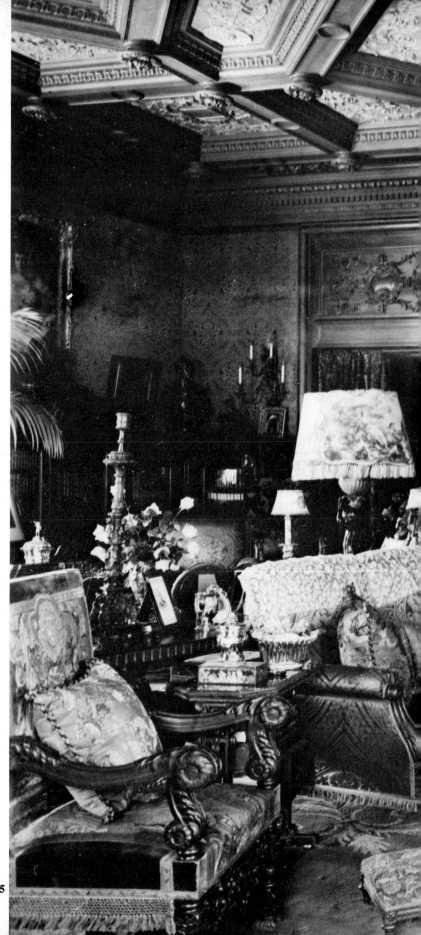

215

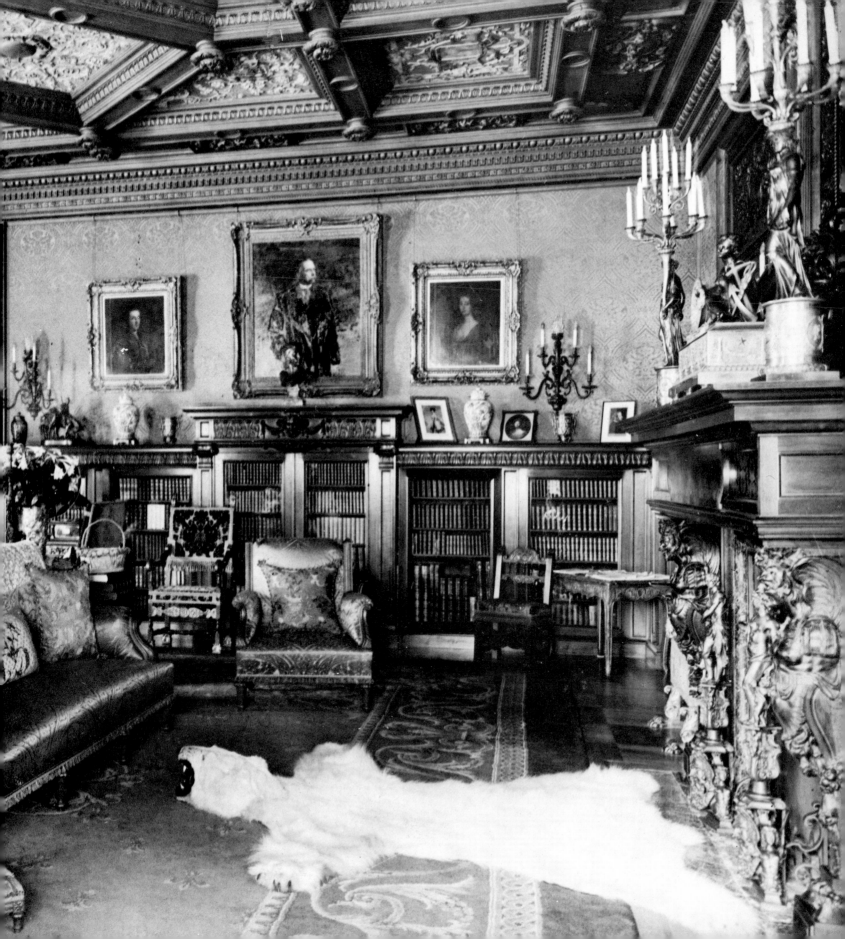

## 216, 217. Library, House of Mrs. O'Neill, New England, 1915

In the late 1890's, a particular type of Arts and Crafts furniture was called mission oak, or mission furniture, meaning that its design made its purpose so obvious that function became the object's mission in life. Later in the decade, and until well after World War I, mission oak was reinterpreted, in common parlance, to suggest a creative revival of the furnishings of the historic Southwest missions. Arts and Crafts furniture, on the other hand, was usually called Craftsman furniture, after the

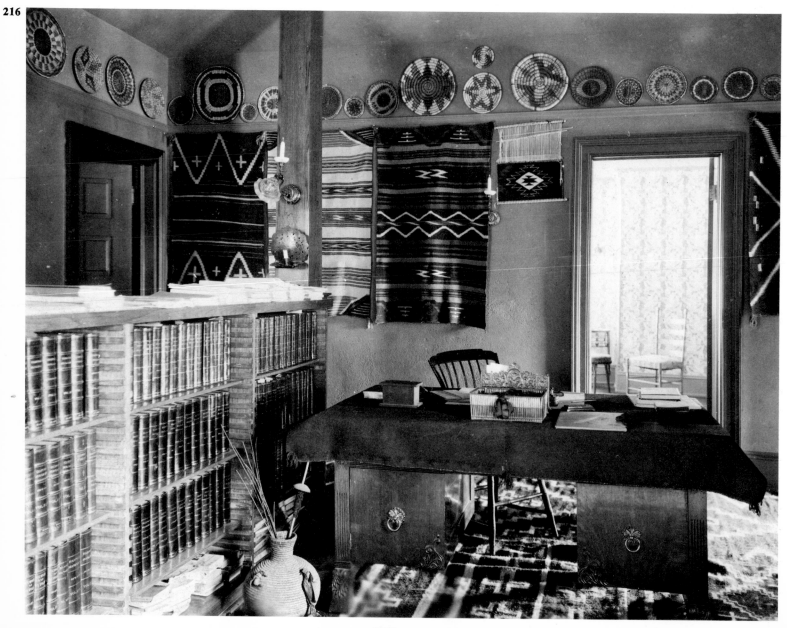

216

name of the Gustav Stickley Company in New York.

Here we see a room decorated very consciously in the popular version of the mission style. Mrs. O'Neill's library actually contains more that is colonial revival than mission oak. But the rough plaster walls, executed with adobe in mind, form a background for a collection of American Indian pots, baskets, and rugs, which thoroughly conveys the Southwestern mission idea. Replacing the deep wallpaper border still popular in American houses, Mrs. O'Neill has added a Free Classic plate rail at picture-molding height; there her baskets are turned up as plates, paralleling the low bank of bookcases, and giving it the kind of coziness its owner might well have admired in Santa Fe and Taos houses. This is the room of a scholar who has grouped her materials into units that flow into one another. The effect is architectural, and quite up to the Arts and Crafts ideas of the preceding fifteen years.

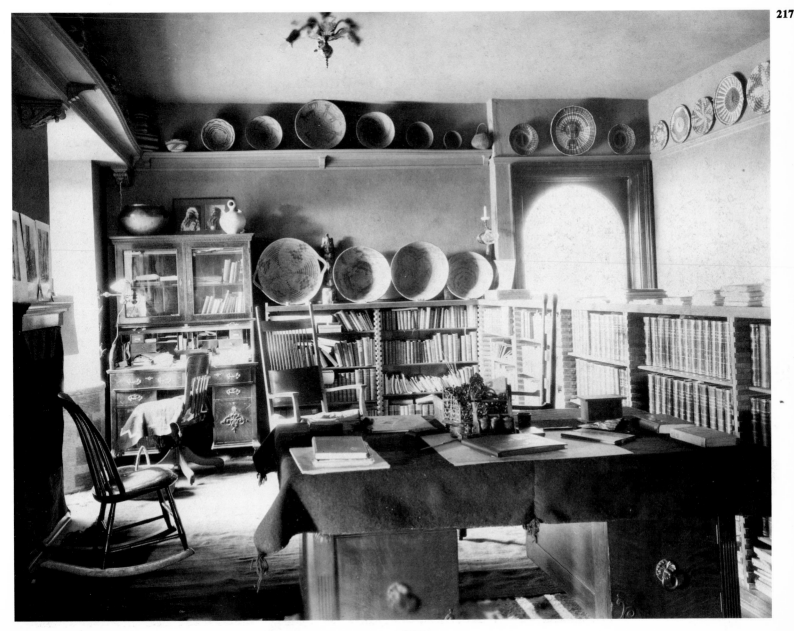

217

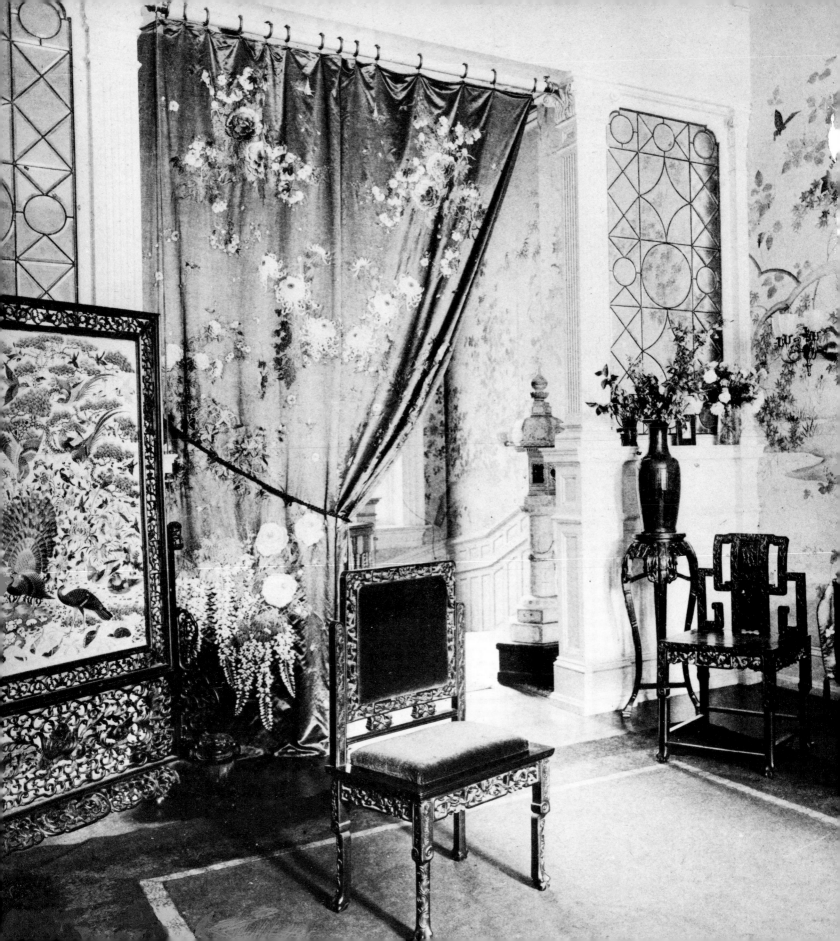

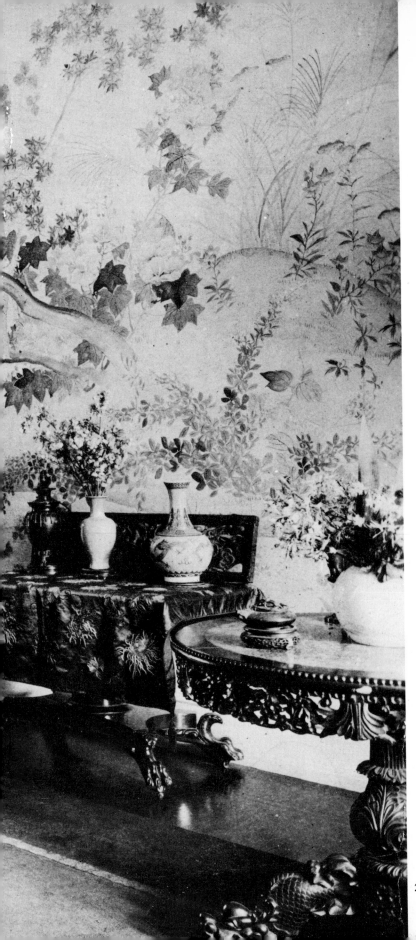

### 218. Upstairs Living Hall, House of Mrs. Charles A. Spalding, 17th Street and Rhode Island Avenue, Washington, D.C., 1915

This otherwise colonial revival hallway has been made into a Chinese corner, where one might sit and read, but probably not. From a manufactured curtain rod, a painted silk portiere hangs flat and is slightly pulled up with a cord. The way is prepared, for an ascending visitor, by a garden lantern at the top of the stairs. Chinese furniture, of the sort available now and then at Washington auctions and representing foreign service of one kind or another, is the predominant feature here. Against the wall, what appears to be an American Empire card table of about 1910 has been covered with an oriental cloth, to hide all but its claw feet, which seem to be friendly companions for those dolphin feet on the other table. Oriental wallpaper, hand-tinted and a favorite of interior decorators, flows from the hall down the walls of the stairwell, and is particularly luminous in the light from the stair windows. Silky wallpapers and grass cloth had prevailed in the oriental taste since the 1870's, whereas the Anglo-Japanese papers showing bamboo shoots, geometrics, and the like were largely abandoned by the late 1880's.

## House of James Campbell, 2 Westmoreland Place, St. Louis, Missouri, 1916

**219, 220.** The entrance hall and landing nook of this new St. Louis mansion were probably called Georgian. From the front door, the immediate view was of the grand staircase, which rose from a screen of columns up into a rotunda outlined by light bulbs. The lower hall's beams and woodwork are heavily varnished and are probably mahogany; this sort of woodwork could be purchased from catalogues and was usually intended for hotels and public buildings. Panels of stenciled canvas point up the architectural features, and the room is mirrored in its polished floors, which shine even more than the furniture. Cut-velvet portieres with tassels and cut-steel fringes break—with color, pattern, and texture—the austerity of the woodwork. The oriental rugs are imitations manufactured in the United States and were available to the Campbells in the best St. Louis furniture stores. Baronial chairs against the walls enhance the effect of this being a castle. Perhaps the center table is a product of the late 1890's; a creative revival based upon the Louis Quinze revival of the 1850's, it has the flowing

**219**

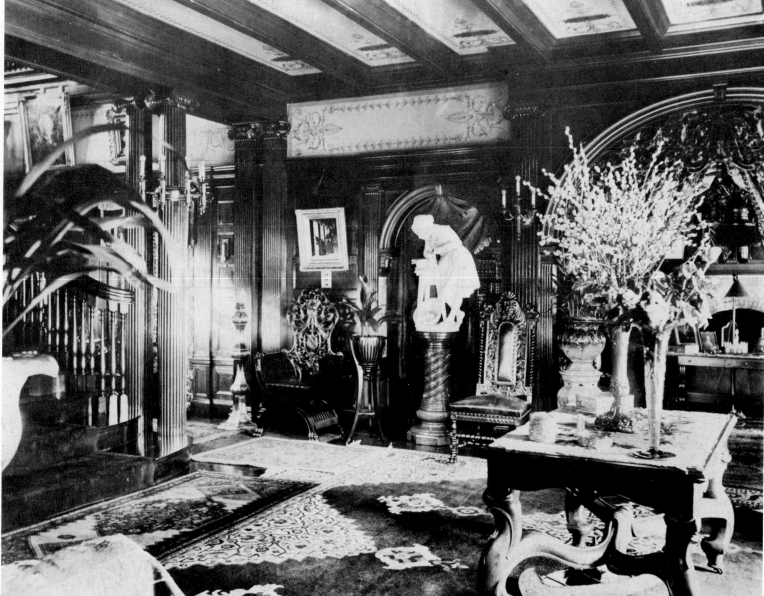

lines of the Art Nouveau, so seldom seen in American furniture. Plants, brasses, and European art punctuate the rich scene, and appear again two-thirds of the way to the second floor in the landing nook, a pleasant sitting room with leaded-glass windows. A grouping of manufactured furniture, creative revivals of sorts based on Jacobean and Chippendale, makes this an informal little spot but one elevated on a pedestal. There are electric sconces and also an emergency oil lamp with a fringed shade. The Edison record player, with albums of records nearby, suggests the purpose of this nook, and one can imagine the Campbells gathering here in the evening to listen to Caruso and Melba on the phonograph. Inserted in so grand and flashy an interior, this nook, which is like any ordinary bungalow parlor, is surprising and almost symbolic of the ultimately middle-class nature of the American rich.

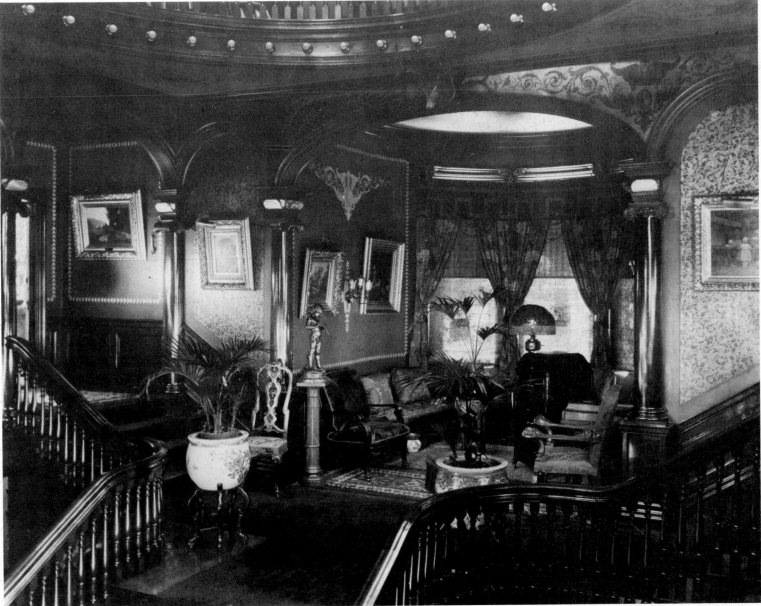

**220**

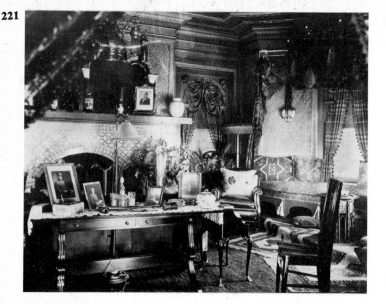

**221, 222.** In two places in the Campbell house the decorators and architects sought to create oriental moods. To the right of the entrance hall, the sitting room is in the Moorish style although that theme has been mostly overtaken by the comfortable furnishings and objects of daily life. If the library, or sofa, table—a Federal conceit—were taken away, the Moorish design of the room would be clear in the chairs and the sofa before the fireplace. Rich imitation morocco wallpaper in colors, a tiled chimney breast, Moorish cornices and curtains, and the ottoman, raised upon a dais, are the devices of an interior decorator. However, the Moorish room did not for long withstand the rigors of family activities. The little Queen Anne desk is perhaps the most insolent trespasser. On the other side of the hall, located off the parlor, was the Chinese tea cozy. Out of the stream of things —and rather out of style also—the cozy seems to have been a catchall for odds and ends. The decorator has insisted that every ray of light be filtered through, or sneak around, curtains. Festive swags in oriental prints tent the room, while Chinese chair, books, dolls, and cushions repeat the general theme. As it was completed by the decorator, this room was probably not so full of objects; but the owners were world travelers, and the souvenirs with the slightest oriental themes doubtless found their way here.

**223.** The dining room was done in the Jacobean revival mode of the day. Jacobean revival furniture was made in many classes and at many different price levels. There was even a bungalow version. These chairs would have been called Elizabethan a half century before; they are made better than those of the 1850's and 1860's, and their trimmings are richer. Companies in Philadelphia, Chicago, and New York produced, on order, embroidered velvet tapestries of the kind used here. Other decorating companies kept in stock quantities of Tudor, Louis Quatorze, and many other kinds of plaster molds from which such ceilings as this could be cast locally. Likewise, the "hand-carved" woodwork was available on order. Over the table hangs a very modern electrolier with glass panels and silk fringes. Everything about this Jacobean dining room has the look of a professional's work; yet very little about it seems custom-crafted. We feel that we have seen all this somewhere before. The scale of the objects is as it should be in relation to the

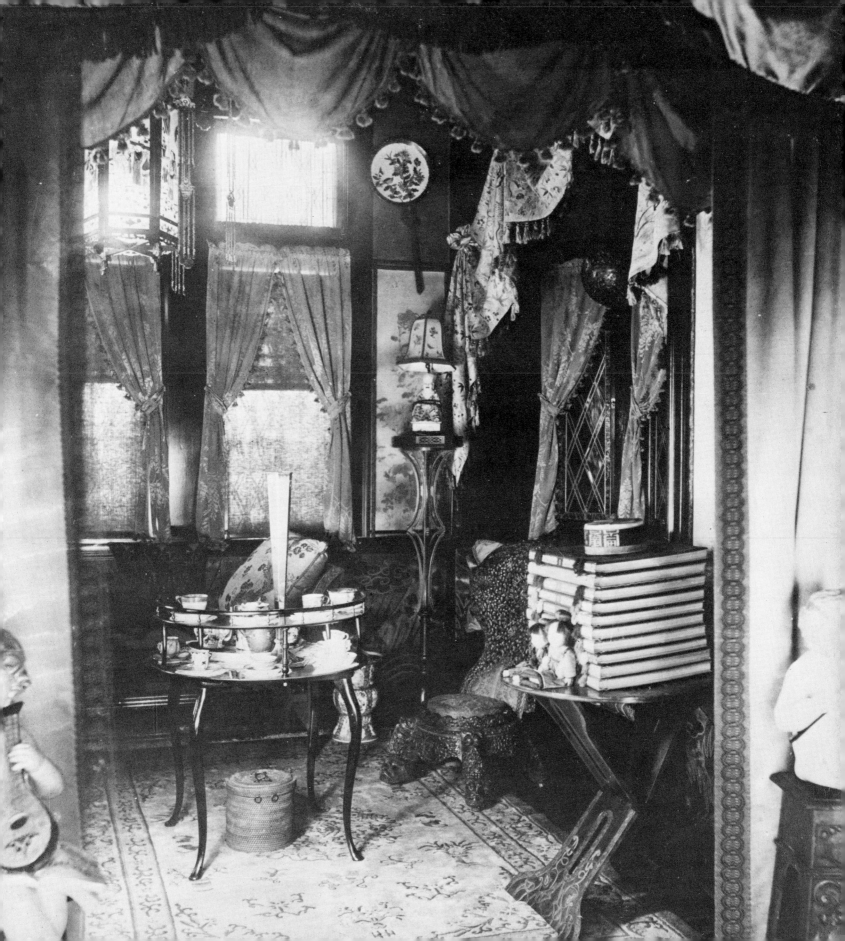

architecture of the room. Curtains, upholstery, wallcovering, lighting fixtures, and transient objects all blend with the room.

**224.** The parlor was decorated in the Empire, or Napoleon, style. There is not an antique to be seen. This was of course the Grecian and Roman furniture of a century before; now labeled as Empire, it carried greater dignity and reminded nobody of the horsehair camelback sofas, and jingling, china-filled sideboards of their grandmothers' houses. The walls are encrusted with gilded ornament applied to classical elements. At the windows are satin swags and panels, bordered and fringed. Empire electroliers hang from ceilings frescoed in the Pompeian style, and a grand Empire mantel in white marble frames the fireplace. Most of the furniture is gilded against a background of polished mahogany, and the upholstery is silk. A Chinese table, Sheraton chair, and Chinese Chippendale table are probably additions by the Campbells after the decorator departed. By banking objects here, the decorator attempts to capture the look of an old mansion and urbane Paris life; the highly architectural wall is a lacy backdrop for the ob-

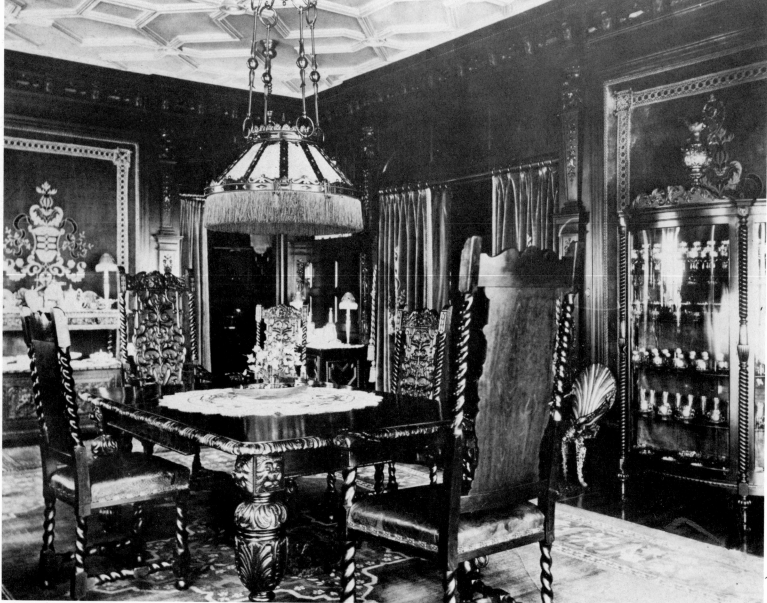

223

jects of comfortable and elegant living, and would have pleased, to a degree, the most sophisticated interior decorators in the United States at the time.

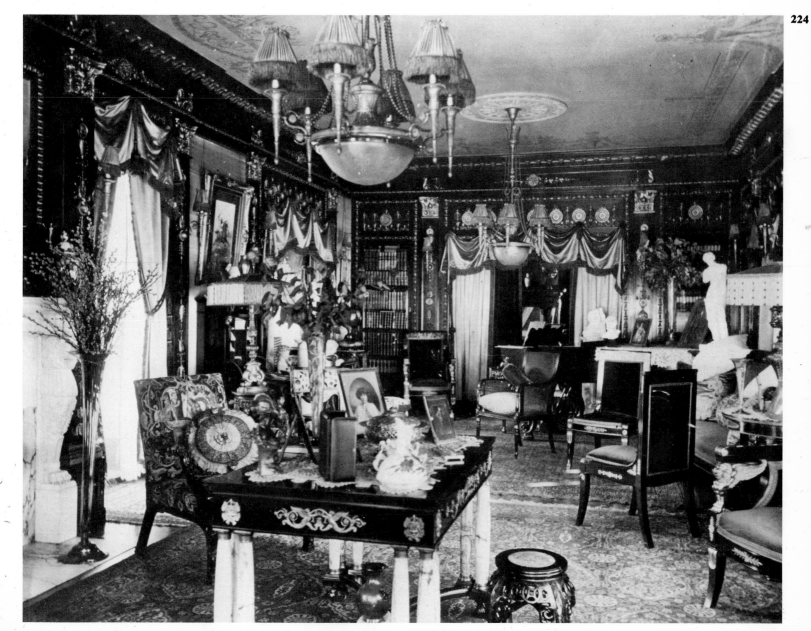

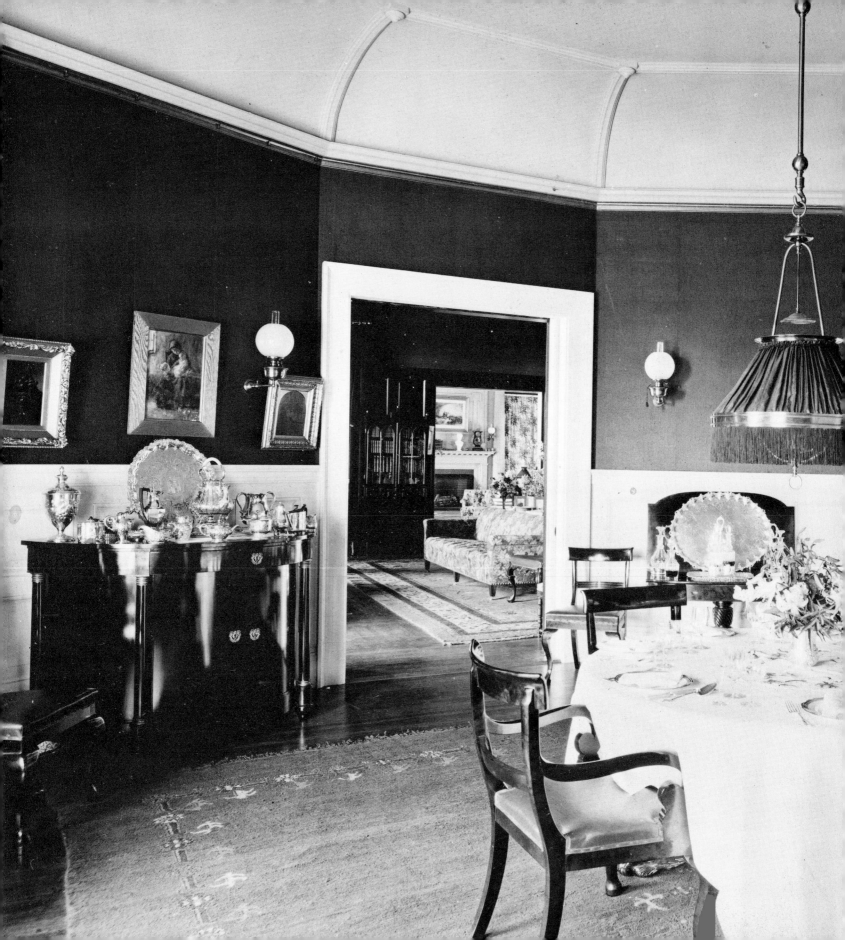

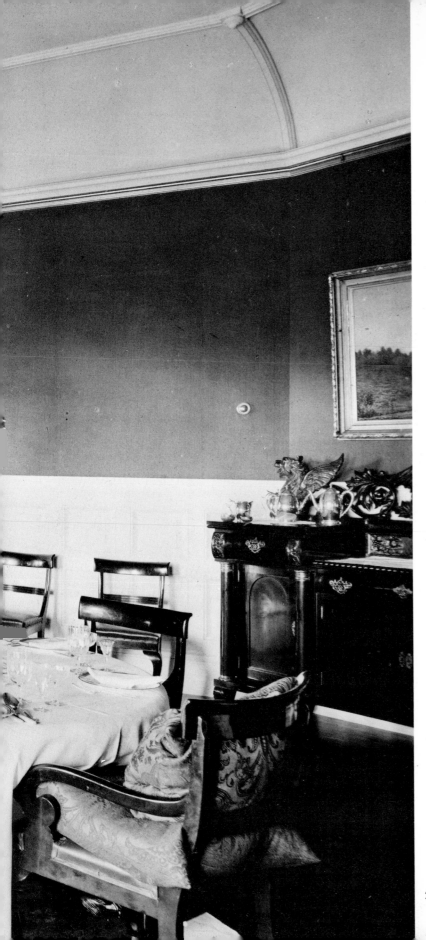

### 225. Dining Room, House of Mrs. William B. Walker, Boston, Massachusetts, 1915

This American Empire dining room contains no antiques but a very expensive set of the kind manufactured by Steul and Thuman of Buffalo, New York, and the William A. Berkey Furniture Company of Grand Rapids, Michigan. The curious chairs, properly Grecian of about 1830 from the seat up, and twentieth-century Queen Anne below that, would have been considered "adapted" in their day, and had they existed in the 1840's they might have been called Modern Grecian. In any case, they are typical of what seldom happened to the creative revivals in the twentieth century, for the buying public was by then more conscious of authentic detailing. Dark walls seemingly covered with fabric form a band which binds the otherwise cavernous white interior together. The floors are polished like the surfaces of furniture. Beyond the Empire chest, through the opening, the living room and living hall are apparently colonial revival, with chintz curtains and upholstery, library table brimming with books and flowers, and a sparse arrangement of furniture. Far in the distance the Georgian Colonial mantel holds a harp-shaped Grecian clock, attesting a further interest of Mrs. Walker's in that style. This dining room was probably not the work of a professional, although Mrs. Walker was clearly aware of what was going on in the world of interior decoration and may have been advised by her furniture dealer.

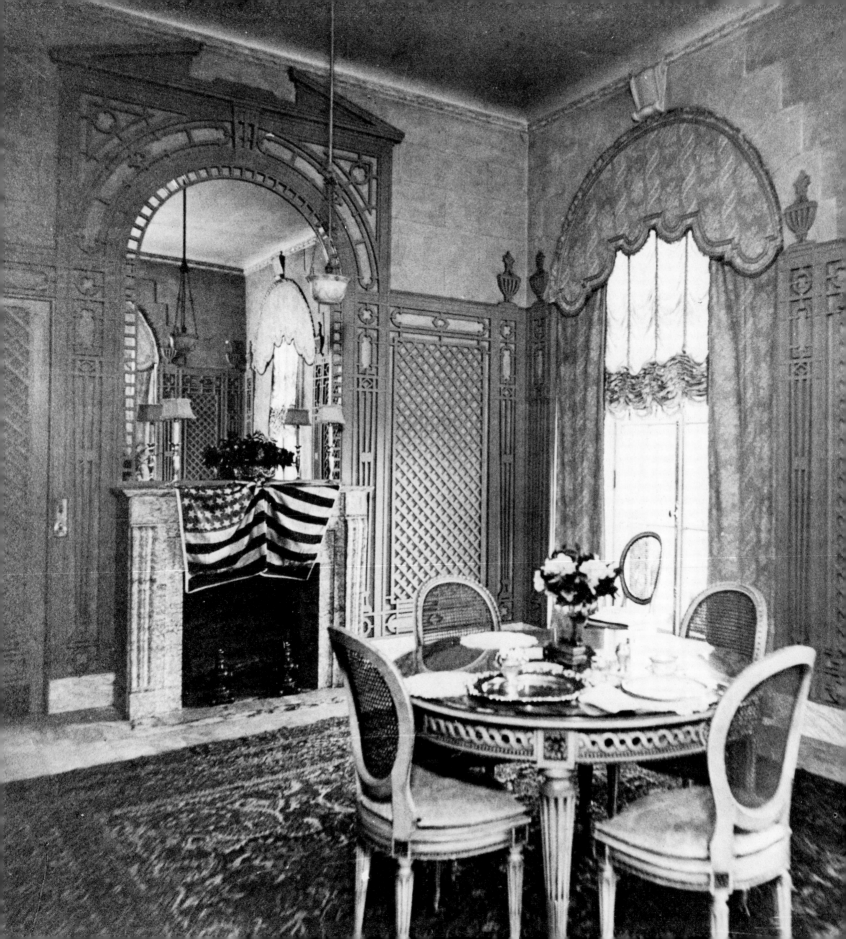

## 226. Breakfast Room, House of James Ross Todd, Louisville, Kentucky, 1917

For most Americans who could afford what they wanted, there were two desirable styles of interior decoration: colonial or one of the French Louis styles. Arts and Crafts, American Empire, Jacobean, and all the rest took second places to those two general types, which were produced on many economic levels. This barren breakfast room in James Ross Todd's house, the work of a New York interior decorator secured for the Todds by the architects Carrère and Hastings, contains the most expensive kind of Louis Seize furniture then on the market. It came almost certainly from John Helmsky's shop in New York, a very small and restricted manufactory producing reproductions of many kinds. Sturdy and only slightly inaccurate, it was considered highly appropriate for this large room, with its marble floors, marbleized and trellised walls, rich damask window hangings and sheer Austrian shades, and oriental carpet, which might have been intended originally to be imitation Aubusson. The whole room was created on the drawing boards of the decorator and Carrère and Hastings. There were doubtless water-color perspectives to show to the client in advance. In its slick, manufactured certainty alone, the Todd breakfast room ironically echoes middle-class American houses nearly everywhere in the United States by the time of World War I.

# Picture Credits

Page 1. Anonymous ladies at tea in a Turkish cozy. Library of Congress. Pages 2, 3. Library, House of Henry Charles Lea, 2000 Walnut Street, Philadelphia, January, 1910. By H. Parker Rolfe, Historical Society of Pennsylvania, Philadelphia. Pages 4, 5. Library, House of S. T. Hauser, Sr., Madison Avenue, Helena, Montana, 1898. Montana Historical Society, Helena. Page 9. Smithsonian Institution. Page 11. *Friends and Amateurs in Musik,* by Thomas Middleton, 1827. Carolina Art Association, Gibbes Art Gallery, Charleston. Page 12. From *Gleason's Pictorial,* November 11, 1854. Pages 14, 15. From Charles W. Elliot, *The Book of American Interiors,* 1876. Pages 19, 20. From Hudson Holly, *Modern Dwellings in Town and Country,* 1878. Page 21. From Albert Fuller, *Artistic Homes,* 1882. Page 22. From O. Judd, *Our Homes, How To Beautify Them,* 1888. Page 23. Cooperative Building Plan Association, *How To Build, Furnish, and Decorate,* 1883. Page 24. *The House Beautiful Magazine,* 1910. Page 25. The Athenaeum of Philadelphia. Page 27. Free Library of Philadelphia.

1. Courtesy of The Bostonian Society, Old State House. 2, 3. South Caroliniana Library, Columbia. 4. U.S. War Dept., General Staff photo no. 165-CN-10907. National Archives. 5. Collection of Ruth Molloy. 6. The Filson Club, Louisville, Kentucky. 7–11. Probably by Titian R. Peale. Curator, Smithsonian Institution Building. 12. Museum of Fort Monroe, Fort Monroe, Va. 13. By Josiah Hawes. From the Hawes Collection, Holman's Print Shop, Inc., Boston. 14. Museum of the City of New York. 15–18. Lockwood-Mathews Mansion Restoration, Norwalk, Conn. 19. By W. H. Jackson, Montana Historical Society, Helena. 20–26. California State Library, California Section Picture Collection, Sacramento. 27, 28. New Haven Colony Historical Society. 29. Courtesy of The New-York Historical Society, New York City. 30. Smithsonian Institution. 31. Courtesy of the New Hampshire Historical Scoiety, Concord. 32. Valentine Museum, Richmond. 33–36. The Society of California Pioneers, San Francisco. 37–38. Smithsonian Institution. 39. Collection of Denys Peter Myers. 40. Courtesy of The Bostonian Society, Old State House. 41. The State Historical Society of Colorado, Denver. 42. Courtesy of The Bostonian Society, Old State House. 43. U.S. War Dept., General Staff photo no. 165-CN-10911. National Archives. 44. From the collections of the Michigan History Division, Michigan State Archives, Lansing. 45. The Mariners Museum, Newport News, Va. 46. The Historical Society of Pennsylvania, Philadelphia. 47. Valentine Museum, Richmond. 48. Hawaii State Archives, Honolulu. 49. Courtesy of The Bostonian Society, Old State House. 50. Library of Congress. 51. Valentine Museum, Richmond. 52. Hawaii State Archives, Honolulu. 53. Library of Congress. 54. By S. J. Morrow. State Photographic Archives, Strozier Library, Florida State University, Tallahassee. 55–57. The State Historical Society of Colorado, Denver. 58. Boston Athenaeum. 59, 60. The Mariners Museum, Newport News, Va. 61. Montant Historical Society, Helena. 62, 63. The Boston Athenaeum. 64. Department of Manuscripts and University Archives, Cornell University, Ithaca, N.Y. 65. South Dakota State Historical Society, Pierre. 66–68. The Rhode Island Historical Society, Providence. 69, 70. Minnesota Historical Society, St. Paul. 71–73. Idaho State Historical Society, Boise. 74. The Boston

Athenaeum. 75. By A. D. Lytel. Louisiana State University Archives, Baton Rouge. 76. Courtesy of the Atlanta Historical Society. 77. Museum of the City of New York. 78, 79. Courtesy of The Bostonian Society, Old State House. 80. Library of Congress. 81. The Boston Athenaeum. 82. Missouri Historical Society, St. Louis. 83. Library of Congress. 84. Minnesota Historical Society, St. Paul. 85. The State Historical Society of Colorado, Denver. 86. Montana Historical Society, Helena. 87. The Historical Society of Pennsylvania, Philadelphia. 88. The State Historical Society of Colorado, Denver. 89. By A. S. Harper. State Photographic Archives, Strozier Library, Florida State University, Tallahassee. 90. Valentine Museum, Richmond. 91, 92. Idaho State Historical Society, Boise. 93. Montana Historical Society, Helena. 94. Smithsonian Institution. 95–97. Chicago Historical Society. 98–101. Probably by Eugene A. Fiske. Museum of New Mexico, Santa Fe. 102. Library of Congress. 103, 104. Department of Manuscripts and University Archives, Cornell University, Ithaca, N.Y. 105. Montana Historical Society, Helena. 106. The Boston Athenaeum. 107. Probably by Louis Melcher. Winedale Inn Properties, Round Top, Texas. 108–111. The Historical Society of Pennsylvania, Philadelphia. 112. Library of Congress. 113. Valentine Museum, Richmond. 114–121. The Rhode Island Historical Society, Providence. 122. By the Byron Family photographers. Byron Collection, Museum of the City of New York. 123, 124. The Historical Society of Pennsylvania, Philadelphia. 125. Library of Congress. 126. Minnesota Historical Society, St. Paul. 127, 128. By George François Mugnier. Courtesy of the Louisiana State Museum, New Orleans. 129. Department of Manuscripts and University Archives, Cornell University, Ithaca, N.Y. 130. Library of Congress. 131. From the collections of the Michigan State Archives, Lansing. 132–134. Merrimack Valley Textile Museum, North Andover, Mass. 135. By George Bain. Library of Congress. 136. By Frances Benjamin Johnston. Library of Congress. 137. Courtesy of The Bostonian Society, Old State House. 138. Wyoming State Archives and Historical Department, Cheyenne. 139–141. By the Byron Family photographers. Byron Collection, Museum of the City of New York. 142, 143. Museum of the City of New York. 144–146. By M. B. Paine. Museum of Charleston. 147, 148, By Frances Benjamin Johnston. Library of Congress. 149. By Charles Currier. Library of Congress. 150–151. Probably by May Flaherty. Montana Historical Society, Helena. 152. Courtesy of The Bostonian Society, Old State House. 153–155. The State Historical Society of Colorado, Denver. 156. By M. B. Paine. Museum of Charleston. 157, 158. Probably by Eugene A. Fiske. Museum of New Mexico, Santa Fe. 159–161. By Charles Currier. Library of Congress. 162. Courtesy of the Illinois State Historical Library, Springfield. 163. Courtesy of The Bostonian Society, Old State House. 164. Library of Congress. 165. Courtesy of the Illinois State Historical Library, Springfield. 166, 167. The Missouri Historical Society, St. Louis. 168. Valentine Museum, Richmond. 169, 170. Montana Historical Society, Helena. 171. The Historical Society of Pennsylvania, Philadelphia. 172–174. Montana Historical Society, Helena. 175, 176. Historic Mobile Preservation Society, Mobile, Ala. 177. Ashton Villa Restoration of Galveston, Galveston, Texas. 178, 179. Collection of William D. Hershey. 180, 181. Library of Congress. 182–184. By the Office of McKim, Mead & White. Courtesy of The New-York Historical Society, New York City. 185, 186. Alaska State Library, Juneau. 187. Nebraska State Historical Society, Lincoln. 188–190. Historic Denver, Inc. 191–194. The Rhode Island Historical Society, Providence. 195. Library of Congress. 196, 197. By Frances Benjamin Johnston. Library of Congress. 198–200. Collection of David Richardson. 201. Library of Congress. 202. Historic Mobile Preservation Society, Mobile, Ala. 203. Courtesy of the Illinois State Historical Library, Springfield. 204–208. Collection of Ruth and Florence Chambers. 209. The Mariners Museum, Newport News, Va. 210, 211. Collection of F. Clason Kyle. 212. Friends of Hyde Hall, Inc., East Springfield, N.Y. 213, 214. Library of Congress. 215. Probably by Frances Benjamin Johnston. Library of Congress. 216, 217. Library of Congress. 218. Probably by Frances Benjamin Johnston. Library of Congress. 219–224. The Missouri Historical Society, St. Louis. 225. Library of Congress. 226. Collection of Mrs. James Ross Todd. Louisville, Ky.

# Index